WINNER OF THE 2019 RESTLESS BOOKS PRIZE
FOR NEW IMMIGRANT WRITING

JUDGES' CITATION

In *Antiman*, Rajiv Mohabir sets forth on a journey with few parallels in the history of immigrant literature. While tracing his ancestors' peripatetic migrations from rural India to Guyana to Canada and the US, Mohabir examines both the bonds and disconnects between his American identity as a gay poet and the expectations and limitations of his diverse cultural inheritance.

Mohabir chronicles his global upbringing through a cross-pollination of literary genres—linear prose, various poetic forms, transcriptions of traditional myths, and simultaneous translations of family lore—that pays homage to the storytelling traditions of his family's homelands while breaking new ground all its own.

More than a memoir, this brave and beautiful book is a tale of the resilience of the human heart and of multiple family journeys across generations and four continents. With great intelligence and insight, Mohabir tackles questions of caste, ethnicity, and sexuality, spinning tales of tenderness, ignorance, love, and longing for that mysterious place called home.

—PRIZE JUDGES TERRY HONG, HÉCTOR TOBAR,
AND ILAN STAVANS

# ANTIMAN

## Also by Rajiv Mohabir

### Poetry

*Cutlish*
*The Cowherd's Son*
*The Taxidermist's Cut*

### Translation

*I Even Regret Night: Holi Songs of Demerara*
by Lalbihari Sharma

# ANTIMAN

## A Hybrid Memoir

## RAJIV MOHABIR

RESTLESS BOOKS
Brooklyn, New York

First Restless Books hardcover edition June 2021

Hardcover ISBN: 9781632062802
Library of Congress Control Number: 2021933540

Portions of this book have been previously published in different form in
*Arkansas International, Bamboo Ridge Journal, Cherry Tree Journal,* Drunken
Boat/Anomaly Press, *Go Home!,* Kweli Journal, Literary Hub, *na mash me bone,
North American Review, Thunder in the Courtyard* (Finishing Line Press).

This book is supported in part by an award from
the National Endowment for the Arts.

Cover design by Na Kim
Text design by Sarah Schneider

Printed in the United States of America

1  3  5  7  9  10  8  6  4  2

Restless Books, Inc.
232 3rd Street, Suite A101
Brooklyn, NY 11215

www.restlessbooks.org
publisher@restlessbooks.org

*For my Aji*
*For Antiman kind, everywhere*

# CONTENTS

# AUTHOR'S NOTE

IN THIS MEMOIR I have changed many names, places, and relationships in order to keep the spirits appeased—protecting kin is the work of the ancestors, but so is speaking truth.

I have represented the emotional truths that have led me up to the present—this crucible of years in which I discovered the poetry that also discovered me. I have chosen the title *Antiman*, consciously aware that it is upsetting—that the term is a violent one. I use it in order to shift its heaviness and release the trap of its letters—to embody it with a flourish despite those who would use it to condemn and damn. Those who are not familiar with the Caribbean slur may hear it as "anti-man": against man, which could be its own title. Another mishearing of the word, "ante-man": before man, is also apt. To my niblings I am very much an auntie-man, be I Chacha, Uncle, or Mamu. The word *antiman* represents and holds a history for me—one of migration and survival.

This is my own accounting of events as I remember them. I was entrusted with my Aji's only possessions: her melodies and words in her dying language of Guyanese Bhojpuri. They were seedlings from India, grown in the plantations of Berbice in Guyana, and pressed for their sweetness in Orlando, Toronto, and New York.

After her death in 2010, I was moved to collect what I could of her recordings and translate the songs she wanted me to learn. All her life in diaspora, far from Berbice, my Aji's songs were ignored. Her language and customs have died out with her, replaced in diasporic Guyanese spaces with Bollywood and other mass media. But in them I found the queerest magic.

She was born in 1921, was the grandchild of indentured laborers, and spoke as her first language a form of Bhojpuri blended with Awadhi called Guyanese Bhojpuri. This language, which falls under the larger category of what is called Caribbean Hindustani, is unique to her speech community and descends from North Indian languages with words borrowed from her colonizers. I was lucky enough to learn as much as I could before she passed. As I began to transcribe and translate her words, I puzzled over how to convey oral languages that change from generation to generation. Since so few people read and write in Guyanese Creole and Guyanese Bhojpuri, I developed my own orthography for them. Inevitably, such an orthography and the migration of these languages into Romanization depend on one's individual language philosophy.

When Aji sang I heard grief's bitterness. Bitter melon. Tears. The stem of a mango leaf given to the bride to bite before meeting her groom to remind her that separation from family spells despair. Did Aji know that she, too, would be exiled from her own house—like me—in diaspora in her own home?

She left me no guitar, no sitar, no flute. Just these two hands and my tongue. If we forget our ancestors, they disappear. We disappear.

I was born in an echo of forgotten songs. Anguish of the lost, the kidnapped, the absconded. I was born to be cast out, turned away into night.

I want to believe that her language—our language—is not dead. I began to write in it only after my dreams delivered themselves in this musical grammar. I do this clumsily and as a student, with reverence and overwhelming thanks for my Aji.

My Aja had a boat he named Jivan Jhoti: "The Light of Life." The real light, though, is a kind of ship. It is a life vessel my Aji passed to me, singing.

पोथी पढ़ि पढ़ि जग मुआ,
पंडित भया न कोय,

ढाई आखर प्रेम का,
पढ़े सो पंडित होय।

※

Reading countless books, the world died—
no one mastered anything.

A few words of love,
if you read them, will make you wise.

—**Kabir**

# ANTIMAN

# Open the Door

BEFORE SHE CUT her silver hair, it sat in an oiled bun, a Guyana full moon, atop her head, a Sunday hat for what the British called her: a Coolie Hindoo. Aji sat in the Florida room in my parents' house in Chuluota—just outside Orlando—and sang a story that came beating into this world as an uncaged bird from Indian soil, which was nurtured on whole grain in the paddy fields of Guyana and now was lilting here against the tiled floor in a second, new diaspora.

December. Even in Florida, the day bit the skin with a hint of ice. Her hands, well veined, wore two gold bangles and bore a tattoo of her husband's name, Sewdass, in India ink underneath a handwritten *om*. When she was newly wed, a fifteen-year-old leaving her father's cows, a barber came to mark her with this godna—a tattoo to keep her safe and the bad eye away. She never went to school but raised her four siblings, perfecting her magical spells: her phulauri and barah, her curry and roti, her first-aid massaging, her understanding of song—her poetry that would be my inheritance.

We sat in the Florida room, December blinking in color like Christmas lights about us. I was visiting home from the University of Florida in Gainesville for winter break. I put a cassette in the tape recorder. I wanted to be able to listen and listen again to our conversation—to savor Aji's Creole and Bhojpuri when she returned to Toronto and I to Gainesville.

Aji was the eldest of five children. Betiya was her call name, a name that means "precious daughter"—the "-ya" a suffix that personalizes and endears. She stood at the sangam of three linguistic rivers: English, Bhojpuri, and Creole. Born in 1921, she was the grandchild of indentured laborers and spoke these languages before the following generations drowned in the flow of English-medium schools, eschewing Creole and Bhojpuri. In our family and in our familial community, Aji was the last speaker of Guyanese Bhojpuri. Forged against the anvil of indenture on sugarcane plantations, her stories and songs were precarious—on the verge of being erased forever.

Gangadai, her other call name, was first named Bhagwati, after the goddess Saraswati—the goddess of language, reading, and music.

Aji was *anakshar*. Unlettered. Not *anpardh*. Not illiterate. In two languages. Each of her songs, a poem—a small devastation. Each of her stories, a fire to scorch my heart's forest: a door that, when opened, led to enchantment.

I wanted to know more. From childhood I was told that Aji was broken. She did not speak filmi Hindi—the kind that belonged to the "Indiaman"—but rather some other language that had been broken on the plantation. I was told that Aji's English was broken, too—an English of the damned, a Creolized version that would never count as literary or worthy of learning in school now that we were in the United States. My father's philosophy was to leave behind these backward ways and adopt those of the English and Americans.

Try as I might to ignore the brown of my hands, it betrayed me as Other constantly in the world of White celebration. I was different; I always knew. I was brown, but there was another difference that I did not share with my brother and sister. I sat at a crossroads: I did not understand myself but wanted to. I wanted to sit in the negative capability of my Aji's songs; to learn them to piece my own broken self together.

❀

# ANTIMAN

ultan sultan howe dono bhai ho
ultan sultan tare ho

pajire se kara kara bhaile dupahariya
kholo bahini baja rakhe ho

tohare dolar bahanoi janghiya par sowe ho
kaise ke kholo bhaiya, baja rakhe ho

lewo bahini lewo more sir ke pagri ho
bahini baja rakhe ho

> Dem been get one buddy an sistah,
> Come see who a come, sistah

> Da bright bright mahning a-tun black black night,
> sistah, keep a-doh hopem.

> a-you bahanoi de sleep pon me lap,
> tell me how me go hopem a-doh.

> Tek dis me sistah, tek dis, me head ke pagri,
> hopem a-doh na sistah.

Upturned, a brother and sister's bond.
Go and see who is at the door, sister.

*Early morning, midday, the sky blackens.*
*Open the door, sister.*

    *Your spoiled brother-in-law sleeps on my lap,*
    *how can I come open the door?*

*Take this, sister, take this turban from my head.*
*Open the door, sister. . . .*

# Home: Prolepsis

Home is the scrape of the trashcan against
   raked pine needle copper.
Shadows of Chuluota pine trees
   and palmetto and in the green tennis court paint on my jeans,
   the chalk white against beige stucco,
   the sprouting watermelon seeds in the pool from eating
   and swimming into being darker than all of my cousins.
Playing *The Little Mermaid*, my sister's hair in a chlorine braid.
The scent of pennies as the rain falls from the ground up,
   swallowing me in a pocket of mist
   and missed chances to run from that heavy hand
   of the father who pulled open my penis
   how glitter shakes the foreskin from the head
   and the blood,
   the apartment in New York where we came back from the doctor
   and Emile was crying and crying and bleeding.
     *You are nothing.*
     *No one will ever love you.*
     *You are fat and hairy.*
     *You are good for nothing.*
Home is the name Paul on paper how it sounds like the neighbor's kid
   when I wrote to Pap on a plastic Father's Day cup
     *Dear Dad, Happy Father's Day, Love Paul.*
He laughs, his belly shaking in Niagara Falls,
I have never been his son. A shut door.

# ANTIMAN

He says, *Don't call me Pap.*
Aunties who hate the fact of you—

this disavowal of the son is a home
   is the reason for the Diaspora
     every little boy grows into poetry and feathers and how.

# Aji Recording: Bibah Kare

BEFORE MY BROTHER Emile's wedding, Aji sat at the dinner table wrapped in my childhood comforter—a blue-and-white floral print over her pink dress. My tape recorder hummed and beat out a cassette-tape pulse. Emile was not the first of Aji's forty-two grandchildren to marry, but he was special to her. He was her second son's eldest son. If they had been *back home*, it would have been time for community. I was twenty and could feel the ghosts that haunted our new rituals—some ghosted magic haunted our family. I was eager to write down and learn what I could of poetry from this woman with coarse white hair, a tattooed forearm, and a developing aneurysm swelling with love.

"Tiday is de hardi," she said. "Tiday de dulha ke mummah go rub he wid haldi."

"Rub him with haldi? Why?" I asked, taking notes.

"Fe mek he skin shine so he go deh handsome an' de dulhin, de woman na go tek one nex' man." She laughed a deep croak. Aji loved her jokes, especially when it came to teasing me, my sister, and my brother. She grew up in New Amsterdam, Guyana, the daughter of Jangbahadur and Anupiya Singh. Jangbahadur was known all over for his mithai and pera; he owned several cows and made his sweets from their milk. Aji spoke often of her love for him. Her mother, Anupiya, however, was not the same gentle soul. She insisted that Aji be raised in a proper fashion, learning to chownke daal and bele round-round roti—not to climb mango trees and run and skip in the black water trenches that lined the streets before the stilted houses.

Aji sat at the table recalling the Amazon jungle, how her husband married her at fifteen—and how her mother protested.

"He been big fe me six years." She fingered her engagement ring. "He been put dis ring on me fingah and tell me papa he go married me." It was a rose-colored Guyanese insignia ring with the initials SM printed on it. SM—Sewdass Mohabir, her husband was named as a servant of Shiva. The ring was one of her most cherished possessions, though it was not the actual ring that Aja had put on her finger, but something remade perhaps in Toronto by a Guyanese jeweler. The ring itself was filled with Aja and Aji's love story—with all the wedding-time songs and rituals that made her life a life. Every recounting of their connection imbued the ring with more history.

"What did your father do?" I was incredulous at my Aja's bold and rash behavior. I had never known my Aja. He died when my father was seventeen—many years before I was born.

"He seh na mattah, Betiya, you wan' married he? An' so come so done."

Emile was marrying his pregnant girlfriend, whom he met working at Pizza Hut in Gainesville. He had moved up to live with me briefly, while I attended the University of Florida. Though he was older and more attractive, Emile was slimmer and shorter than I, and my long curly hair and round features made me look older.

Emile proposed to his girlfriend and put a different ring of gold bought in the United States on her finger, and now our preparations involved making curry and roti—but not lawa to offer to the fire god, Agni. Instead of Hindu rites, a wedding ceremony would be performed by a Lutheran pastor in a flower garden. My family had converted sixteen years before when we were new immigrants to the United States, and Aji had to adapt to the whims of her children. But now she sat at the table recalling the "proper" ways that things should be done in order for her son's eldest son to marry.

"What kinds of songs should we sing today, Aji?" I asked, writing furiously. I wanted to keep her voice forever.

"Abi mus' sing de lawa song. Me go sing one—hear." Aji began to sing. From her throat the aging voice of a once good singer poured forth. It was said that when the Ganga River acquiesced to the prayers of Raja Bhagirath and descended from the mountain to the earth to rescue his ancestors from being forgotten in Patal, she made a deal with Lord Shiva. Instead of crushing the earth with the force of her descent, she would fall upon his head and flow from his dreadlocks, gently, removing generations of sins. Gangadai, my Aji, had such force behind her song. It was mediated by her aging body: a dam—a dreadlock that betrayed its profundity just below the surface. Aji sang with power and might in the voice of a trickling stream.

*Dulha ki mayi re bhuje lage lawa*

She looked at me through her round glasses. She was named after the river Ganga, and my Aja was named for Lord Shiva, creating together this sacred story once more. Behind her gray eyes were songs that could crush the earth with their impact. I knew that she had stories she could sing with the voice of the sea. She said that here, every ocean is the holiest river, because that is precisely where it flows. The stream starts in the Himalayas as glacial melt and trickles through the land, through Lord Shiva's matted locks and deltas in the Sundarbans, and loosens her own tresses into the Bay of Bengal. Ganga was a journeyer like Aji. It made sense that she would call the sea Ganga Ghat—or the steps to the Ganga—every time we took her to swim at the beach.

Behind Aji's eyes, the Himalayas pushed up into cataract crags, river dolphins traded their eyesight for echolocation, and I understood the reason for prayer. It was to connect me to this woman, this living ancestor.

"But sing me the oldest song you can remember, Aji," I asked, the cassette recorder meting out its pulse. It was a drum by which Aji could remember.

"Me na hable, beta. Me boice na good," she closed her eyes. She opened her mouth and out streamed the Ganga's crash:

*kekahi chaho to mango*
*rani tu hamar jaan bachaiyal*
*ajodhya tohar hoijai*
*je mango to mango rani*

*je mango to mango rani*
*ham mange ram banbas jaye*
*aur bharat raja chalaye ho*
*je mango to mango rani*

"Da song mean dat Kekahi been mek one trick. Kekahi tell 'em me na want none t'ing now—me go ask later. 'E want Ram must go in de forest and 'e son Bharat must rule the t'rone," Aji explained.

"*Kaikeyi?* You mean King Dasharath's wife?" I asked, correcting her pronunciation of *Kekahi*. I didn't realize then how I was enforcing Hindi pronunciations on my Aji.

"Yes, when she been young she been save Dasarath an' take out a pimpla from he fingah. He been so overjoy dat he give she two bardaan dat whatsoevah she wan' he go give she. She can wish fe what she want. She wait until Ram been ready fe mek king an' den she ask Dasarath. And Ram been go. 'E left 'e mummah an' puppah an' go a banbas in de forest fe live fourteen year."

"But Aji, Kaikeyi saved Dasharath's life on the battlefield. What do you mean that she pulled out a splinter from his hand?" I asked.

"Beta, the splinter bore he hand an' he get sick an' dat is how."

"But Ramanand Sagar's TV show says something completely different." I thought she must be mistaken—she even referred to Kaikeyi as Kekahi: a clear corruption of the names and story arc that I had learned in books written in English by white scholars.

I scribbled in my notebook. I knew the story of the *Ramayana*—of Ram and Sita and how they were exiled into the forest because the evil queen wanted her own son to be king. King Dasharath had three wives and his four princes were born under magical circumstances. I felt a connection with this story beyond its magic, because it was about exile and return, the defeat of evil. In my mind this was a mythological metaphor for the suffering of colonization, indenture, and sugar servitude to the British. I could see how these colonial damages played out in my ancestors' stories and in my family. I translated Aji's song to mean:

Kekahi, wish what you will
Rani, you saved my life that day—
Ayodhya is yours,
What you wish is yours.

Whatever you want, ask.
I want Ram in exile,
For Bharat to rule the throne.
Whatever I want is mine.

# My Eyes Are Clouds

WE SAT IN Auntie Sonia's Brampton living room, some of my cousins sipping tea and others brandy. It was winter and the snowbanks were taller than the car. Aji had recently cut her hair; her arms could no longer reach to comb it. It was so white, it sparkled blue and gold. She oiled her white tresses before twisting them into a bun that she piled on her head. Aji never wore it down; it was a wild Guyanese bird.

Auntie Sonia's house was filled with laughter in English. My father, mother, sister, brother, and I loaded up the rental car and drove from Orlando to Toronto in a nonstop haze of coffee and calypso music blaring from the radio. I had just turned twenty-two and would be leaving for India in six months. Emile, three years older, came along; it had been ages since he'd seen our father's family. Emily, three years younger, was a new undergraduate at the University of Central Florida. I was the middle child, restless and ready to cross the ocean.

It was Auntie Sonia's birthday and she was having a simple celebration, inviting only her siblings—which worked out to be four of the twelve families, plus Aji.

✣

Aji's leaving Guyana was not of her own volition—she went where her children went. I remember in my young adulthood my father telling me the story of their arrival in North America. According to him, in 1975 she had been widowed for ten years by the time her youngest made the motion to go to school in Toronto. Her other children had already left Guyana in pursuit of fortune in London and New York. The four—Aji, Sonia, Rani, and Pua—went to visit Toronto on tourist visas and overstayed, like my father, whose visa was for students. Pua married to stay in Canada and then sponsored Aji to move herself. Because Sonia and Rani were minors, they were allowed to stay, too.

When we visited Aji in Scarborough, a Toronto borough, we mostly spent time with Pua and Pupha and two of my cousins, Jake and Clarice. Jake was one year older than I and knew everything about computers. We wrote frequent letters to each other and later, after Pua and Pupha moved to New York, we communicated via email, with a hand-written letter sent at least once a month.

Jake was one of the few people in my extended family I could talk to in a serious way. He was shorter than I, skinnier, and he had straight black hair. Mine was curly, which caused my father's side a lot of anxiety.

My Aji was Jake's Nani—my paternal grandmother, his maternal grandmother. As children we would sit with Aji and ask her to tell us stories. Our favorite was "The King and the Koyal." Like me, Jake was interested in her stories and learning about where we were from, but he stopped shy of trying to learn her languages.

Jake knew me. I told him over the phone, in my early twenties, that I was into guys.

"Like, sexually?" Jake asked from Queens.

"Yeah, I've been with girls, too, but I just know I like guys," I said. I could trust Jake. He knew what it would mean if our family found out.

"There is no word for it in Hindustani, I don't think," I remember saying to him.

"Well, there is *antiman*." Our conversation stalled.

"Antiman," I repeated. I had heard my aunts and uncles laugh around the table enough to know antiman meant pariah. To be an antiman was to be laughable, it was a secret that could cost me my family if they found out.

"If I were gay and ever told my mother, she'd disown me and kick me out of the house," Jake confided in me.

"Me, too," I said. "I mean, if I told my father, he'd never really accept it." I feared worse. It would mean fire and brimstone. I was certain that he would disown me fully, given his rants about homosexuality being a perversion of God's order. I could lose my brother, sister, and mother, too. Pap's word was law, the bricks that were the structure of our patriarchal home.

Though I knew no way to say it in Hindustani, Aji might have known the scorpion's sting of the word antiman. Or she could have had other ways of understanding it. In any case, I didn't need to worry about it yet.

❋

Aji acquiesced to the wishes of her children and left her mango and coconut trees, the hourie and gilbaka sea, the parrots and twa-twa birds in the sky, the black trenches filled with hassa fish, to grow bora and tomatoes on a concrete balcony in a Scarborough tenement. Aji left the Mahrajin, the pandit's wife, the milkman, brothers and sisters, neighbors, the colorful village gossip. She was caged in an endless winter, friendless except for the Jamaican woman down the hall. No one in the market was able to speak to Aji; she knew no "proper" English and called her Hindustani "broken." And that's how people treated her, like she was broken. That's how the missionaries treated my family, like they were broken. When she arrived in Toronto her children told her not to speak her broken languages in public. Jake told me once that our uncle told Aji, "You must say CAAAAAAR, not CYAAAR." It was better if she didn't do anything to embarrass them. I feared that I had done the same thing to her by correcting her pronunciation of Kekahi to the more bookish Kaikeyi. I could understand wanting to recognize myself in the world around me. Was this anxiety also an ancestral inheritance?

Now she sat on the floor in Auntie Sonia's living room, not entirely following her children's and her grandchildren's fast English. She hunched over her plate of daal, rice, and bhaji, and ate with her fingers. I sat next to her, chatting while she gnawed whole wiri wiri peppers like candy.

This woman who has come so far lives like a bird with clipped wings, I thought. How can she cope when no one speaks her languages? Being so isolated in this hostile and racist place must be difficult for her—those stares from people in her building, the sideways glances from white Canadians upset that she is benefiting from the welfare system, her children who ignore her during their get-togethers. She must feel like Sita, exiled from her own home, again. What does it mean to be completely dependent on a system that thinks you're an idiot?

"But Aji, *Ram bura rahe, Sita ke ban mein chhordawe khatir, na?* Wasn't Ram bad for what he did to Sita?" I asked her. I was glad to hear her talk about the *Ramayana* again. It was her protest: a sparkling ruby of dissent against the conservative patriarchal thinking of her homelife, resistance to the forced colonial education of her children. She used the story to lament her plight but also to dream a possible future for herself.

Ram abandoned Sita in the forest after she faithfully followed him into exile for fourteen years instead of living like a princess. Ram abandoned Sita when she was pregnant. It's kind of like Aji being widowed at the age of forty-four, I thought—to fend for herself and her thirteen children alone in Berbice.

"Yes, he was, beta. What men do in this world is awful. But what can a woman do?" she asked.

"Well, Sita eventually told Ram that when he abandoned her in the forest, she was pregnant with Luv and Kush, then asked Mother Earth to swallow her whole," I piped up.

"True-true t'ing, beta, what Ram do no one else go do. He exile he pregnant wife." She looked out the window at the snow, which had begun to fall again. The flakes scraped the windowpane with their crystalline bodies. Some in clumps of twenty. Some solitary yet ornate.

Silence. My mouth burned.

We sat looking outside at the snowfall for several minutes. *"Ek go gaana sikhao, na, Ajiya?"* I asked, "Teach me one song, na, Aji?"

Aji unfolded a song of separation and the loneliness of betrayal.

*akhiya hamar badal rukhi*
*kahi naahi sukhi sukhi*
*tinhu lok me hamesa*
*tohar birha se hi bhigal*

*sare duniya me ghumat hai*
*pavan aur nadi ke pani se*
*ekgo hi nisan paye ke*
*baras me kehar aram karab*
*hamar saiya baahar bhejaile*

"What does that mean?" Pap walked into the sitting room. He put his cane down as he lowered himself onto the couch. In 1984, the year Emily was born, he was diagnosed with multiple sclerosis and filed for disability, which, even back then, was not a livable amount of money. He narrowed his eyes as he looked at Aji and then at me. I could see that he was fuming.

❁

I started to learn Modern Standard Hindi from books and from speaking with friends in my teens. Pap had insisted that I learn some *useful* language like Classical Hebrew or Greek—that way I could translate the Bible instead of gyaffing with my elders.

I wanted Hindi and Bhojpuri instead: these old Guyanese and Indian traditions sparkled on the horizon, catching my eye from their past lives. Through them I could learn the deep ocean of stories of where we came from and breathe into them new life. At these family gatherings and whenever I saw her, I would spend hours sitting, recording, and later transcribing and translating my Aji's Bhojpuri songs. Pap hadn't wanted to hold on to these things. He and his siblings all started taking communion and going by Christian names for the sake of assimilation or genuine faith. It must be genuine faith when the only way to get an education was to go to the Lutheran school. It must be genuine faith when the only way to get scholarships was to mimic the British. To survive they had to create social distance between their Coolie home culture and the English world through mimicking the latter. In certain conditions when my father addressed white people, daal became split pea soup, aloo, potatoes, and he called himself *Glenn* when his name was Surjnarine. Split pea soup and potatoes for Glenn—the phrase itself a code for survival.

Pap did not want any of his children, especially his sons, to learn about the *Ramayana*. The year I was accepted to the University of Florida, a friend gave me a book filled with art from the Hindu epic.

"I'm worried that you're going to turn Hindu if you leave home and go to Gainesville," Pap said. "I will forbid you from going if you don't remove that book from the house this instant." As he decried the paintings of a feminized Ram shaded in blue, draped in gold and pearls, it felt like he was trying to communicate something else to me. That in living beyond his watch, I might *experiment* with who knew what.

"Get rid of it," he repeated.

He called my mother over, and she appeared in the dark dining room. "Bring your *Ramayan*," he commanded. My mother kept the R. K. Narayan translation of the epic in her section of the bookshelf. It was hers from long ago—a vestige of her natal family before she left them forever in England.

When she handed it to him as he reemerged from the study, he opened it up and ripped it into the smallest pieces as he could. "Now bring the incense," he commanded.

My mother went to the cabinet drawer and withdrew a single packet of sandalwood incense marked with an image of Ganesh, the elephant-headed god said to have been the transcriber of the *Mahabharata*.

Grabbing it out of her shaking hands, he threw it in the fireplace and burned it up. I remember him later that evening cleaning the ashes into a gray plastic bin—a kind of cremation ceremony for his previous life.

Mom's eyes darkened, but she said nothing. I searched her face. She gave me a faint smile and sighed. She had kept these things as a last connection to her family.

From that day, everything that reminded him of his childhood, the religion of his parents and community, was banished from the house. No Indian clothes. No incense. But he couldn't banish his mother's songs, the same ones she sang as he formed in her womb.

✵

I spent many days like this, sitting and listening to Aji's songs. Now I translated the best I could. I looked at Pap and said:

*My eyes are clouds,*
*nowhere is dry.*
*The three worlds are forever*
*soaked in grief.*

*I roam the earth*
*for signs in wind and river.*
*When rain falls, will I stay dry—*
*my love has exiled me.*

"So Sita is in the forest?" he heckled and laughed. I looked at Aji. She looked at the floor, avoiding my eyes. "Ma, what are you teaching Raimie? The *Ramayan* is for Hindus—not us."

"Not for *us*?" I said. "This is your own mother singing a song that her own mother taught her. How is this not *us*?"

He broke into Creole as his face reddened. "You wan' go a pandit an' ask 'am to open de book an' give you answer?" The next room, where his sisters and their families sat, went quiet.

"Nothing—me na know what kine madness dis one a talk," Aji replied before I could answer. She didn't want to upset her son. Aji's survival strategy: Make as many people happy as you can. She turned to me and said, "Beta, you mus' mine you daddy."

A different kind of instruction: Listen to and respect your parents.

"You mean, 'I don't know why he's asking these sorts of questions,'" Pap said, correcting his mother's English. He glowered at me and considered the subject closed.

It was time to cut the cake. Pua called us all into the kitchen, where she lit the ten candles. The cake was white. White as refined sugar. White as snow. White as English. Auntie Sonia blew out the small yellow flames that flickered and died, releasing their last breaths of smoke: white and curly. Outside winter kept brushing its feathers against the doors and windows.

Everyone: my cousins, aunts, uncles, mother, father, brother, sister, and I took the white cake deep into our intestines. We were warm inside, drinking tea and sugaring ourselves. We ate cake and licked the frosting from plates and forks. We laughed and painted our lips in white frosting. We curled our tongues around the frills, the letters on the cake that read "Happy Birthday Edith." Edith was Auntie Sonia's Christian name. We spoke fast English with correct grammar, my Canadian cousins with the proper *eh*'s and us Floridians with the requisite *y'all*'s. It was a blizzard of ascendancy. We no longer lived in the village and only dreamed of eating cake. This was all ours.

Aji was eating her daughter's Christian name in the next room when I came in and sat next to her. She ate with her hands.

"Raimie! Come!" I could hear Auntie Sonia calling for me from the couch. It was time for us all to sing. Usually during these events, Uncle Willie brought his guitar and everyone assembled would sing old calypso songs. "You can't leave until you sing us all a Hindi song," Auntie Sonia said, half testing me to see if I actually knew any.

I had just been accepted to a program that would send me for an academic year to India, where I would study Hindi language, Bhojpuri language, folk singing, and astrology—all things that make a descendant of indenture giddy. The family would tease me, saying things like, "Oh, you wan' tun pandit?" or as Pua said, pointing to her temple, "People who go to India come back real simple." For her, going to India was a reversion to an uncouth past. To return from a trip to India, would mean that I would come back less intelligent, having regressed. How was it that these people who I came from hated themselves so much that they would rather kiss a white person's ass than call themselves Indians?

❋

There was one place where Aji could talk to the shopkeeper: PD Market, though she called it Piri's after the proprietor. He would greet her with "Ram Ram, Nani" when she walked in.

"Tohar jiew achcha hai?" she would respond. As a child I loved this dance between them. It was the only time when I felt Aji was joyful, when she was reminded of home.

They conversed entirely in Hindi: the shop owner speaking Modern Standard Hindi and Aji speaking Guyanese Bhojpuri. After greeting the dukan-wallah we walked to the back of the store where Piri's parrot perched. She would say "Ram Ram," and the bird would call out "Ram Ram" in reply. It was a blue and gold macaw, the same kind that she had had when she was a little girl living in New Amsterdam.

Rabaht, Aji's mother's macaw, was completely wild and would visit their house for leftover rice and daal in the morning. Her mother would call, "Rabaht, Rabaht, Aao, bhojan karo," and Rabaht's blue and gold feathers would appear. Aji held the rice and peanuts in her hand while Rabaht perched on the fence in front of the house and ate from her open hands.

They kept feeding him. He followed Aji to the market where she bought more peanuts. He even knew a couple words like *Sita-Ram* and *Betiya*. They were friends, about the same age. Rabaht had just shown up one day and Aji's mother had fed him. When he came back the next day, Aji's mother fed him again. On the third day that Rabaht ate from her hands, the family adopted him. There was no need to cage Rabaht or to clip his wings. He lived outside, wild, and came and went as he pleased.

One day Aji's mother went outside with her plate as usual and called for Rabaht. She called for hours, but Rabaht never came. She left the plate outside until the rice dried up, uneaten by the parrot but scavenged by ants. Rabaht never returned. She suspected that the bird had been caught and sold to the United States as an exotic pet or killed for its feathers.

Piri's was the only parrot in Aji's Toronto, amid the familiar smells of the Indian market, but askew, not quite her own: Indian but not Guyanese. "Indiaman different kine people," she used to say. Their language, their Hinduism, their songs.

❉

I sat on the crushed velvet couch and wiped the sweat off of my palms on my jeans. The afternoon sun was now looking into the window, as my aunts and uncles encircled me. There was silence. What song should I play? Everyone wanted to hear something that they knew. Maybe I should play "Mere Sapno Ki Rani" or "Suhani Raat," I thought. These were crowd-pleasers. All of my aunts leaned forward in their chairs. I thought of Aji and how she was listening sitting on the floor of the next room. What song would she want to hear? I started to pick the chords, A minor, G, A minor, G, I was hardly a guitar player. I caught the rhythm and began:

*akhiya hamar badal rukhi*
*kahi naahi sukhi sukhi*
*tinhu lok me hamesa*
*tohar birha se hi bhigal*

Aji unfolded her legs and rose. She walked in her empire-waisted flo-ralprint frock and shuffled into the room where we were awash in her music. She sat on the couch next to me and joined in:

*sare duniya me ghumat hai*
*pavan aur nadi ka pani se*
*ekgo hi nisan paye ke*
*baras me kehar aram karab*
*hamar saiya baahar bhejaile*

Tears glinted like Sita's golden deer in my aunts' eyes. They sat with mouths agape. Auntie Sonia asked, "How does Ma know this song?" She shook her head in disbelief. Ma only knows broken Hindi, I'd heard her and her siblings repeat countless times before. She shook her head in disbelief.

"This is Aji's song, not mine." I answered, gesturing with my head at Aji next to me.

"Me mummah been sing dis song come time fe plant rice," Aji said. It was a work song. A song that women sang in the rice fields, that Aji and I sang now in a middle-class living room in Brampton, Ontario. I thought of all the women who once sang this song—how it was important for both doing the work and expressing the sadness of leaving their father's homes, of leaving their India to come away to Guyana—and now, Aji sang this song of bitter separation having left her home for the snow.

Auntie Sonia said, "Wow, you're a real Indian Cat Stevens." Her own children didn't know Aji the way that I did. It didn't matter what Auntie Sonia meant by her remark. I would soon be leaving for Varanasi, firmly in the Bhojpuri belt, where I would learn about the rainbows of rivers and epics that Aji regaled me with, finally seeing them firsthand. I wanted to plant our language back in my mouth—the language that had been stripped from us through indenture. I wanted to live in a world of Aji's music. I wanted to be colorful, too. Aji was perched on the couch next to me, growing back her tropical plume.

# South Asian Language Summer

I SAT IN the ice cream parlor on State Street on my first afternoon exploring downtown Madison. I was there to participate in a six-week Hindi language intensive hosted by the South Asian Summer Language Institute at the University of Wisconsin. My cayenne-flavored chocolate cone stung my lips with its own summer heat. Across from me was a guy about my age. He wore a Grateful Dead T-shirt and had dreadlocks.

"You here for SASLI?" he asked me.

"Yeah, for Hindi—you?"

"Tibetan. Dude. Madison is awesome. I'm from Eugene and here it's crazy. I heard that Madison was built on a bed of rose quartz and that the Dalai Lama said that this city *glistens with psychic energy.*" His blue eyes were high beams.

I looked at his feet. Hemp anklets and hairy toes. I realized that no one knew me here and I could be something new entirely—I could reforge wholeness from the brokenness I believed defined me.

"It's trippy," he continued. "Because we're here now and did you know that Tibetan doesn't have tense markers on its verbs." I had stopped listening. Outside, a man in shorts with large thighs and a tight T-shirt strode by. I could feel my ears redden. This was going to be a great summer.

I lived in the International Co-op with about thirteen other students from the University of Wisconsin. Pot-smoking, acid-dropping hippies became my quick friends, delighted by the prospect of being pals with a "real" Indian.

One woman who lived there put a copy of Ram Dass's *Be Here Now* in my hands. I opened it to a page with a sketch of Hanuman, the monkey god, and looked up at her.

"Before you came, I had a dream of Lord Hanuman. He promised me that I would meet the love of my life." She looked in my eyes. I looked to the other side of the room.

"Is that a fire door?" I asked. I started singing the song by Ani DiFranco.

"Come see this silk I have," she said, her brown curls falling down past her well-glossed lips.

I obliged and asked her, "What's the deal with Ken?" Ken was an international student from Indonesia who was staying in the co-op as well. He lived on the first floor and I had seen him a couple times. When I would smile at him, he would smile and look down, blushing. He was short but sturdy-framed with a muscled back and handsome. I wanted to see more of him.

"He's new here, he came like a week before you did," she replied.

"He's super-hot. Do you know if he's queer?" I asked. She got the message and with a huff threw the bolt of silk on her bed.

❊

I walked downtown from the co-op, past all the shops and cafés bursting with collegiate imagery: croissants, espressos, dread-headed white boys studying the Tibetan language, skaters, smokers. I felt free and wore my hair down and wild with its curliness. I rushed in to meet Virendra Singh, who had been teaching Hindi in this program for about twenty years.

He sat nursing a cup of chai while looking over some disheveled papers on his desk. His white hair was neatly trimmed and even though it was summer, he wore a green sweater-vest that contoured the curve of his paunch.

"Namaste, sir-ji," I greeted him.

"Namaste ji, baithiye—" he motioned for me to sit down on the leather armchair facing his desk. He continued, "I've asked you here because I know that you already speak some Hindi and I want to gauge just where I should put you in our class and for when we are in India."

Virendra-ji, as I was to call him, began with the test, asking me questions in Hindi. Where are you from? What do you like to do for fun? Where were you born? I was used to stumbling through my answers to these questions in Modern Standard Hindi.

"What language does your parents speak?" he asked.

"They speak English and Creolese. We've been outside India for so long. They've never really known or spoken Hindi."

"Oh, so you're not a real Indian."

Silence.

"My Aji speaks Bhojpuri though," I added.

"Arrey, your Aji speaks Bhojpuri?!" his surprise lifted the wrinkles off of his face. He switched to Bhojpuri, "Achcha tu Bhojpuri gaana gaa sakela?"

"Yes," I replied in English, stunned. "I can sing some Bhojpuri songs. In fact, that's why I'm here—to learn enough Hindi so that I can understand the language that my family has lost."

Virendra-ji rubbed his chin and nodded his head. He turned to his desk and gave me a paper. "Okay, please write in Devanagari, *aapse milkar bahut khushi hui.*"

I wrote down what I thought it should look like. The vowels in short and long form mixed up. Aspirated consonants for retroflexed letters. After a moment's pause, Virendra-ji said, "I think it's good for you to be in beginner Hindi. You already speak some, but your writing would benefit from starting over. It will get rid of your bad habits in speaking Hindi." His smiling face was like sunshine. "I've seen this a lot with NRI kids—they know a lot but need to iron out all the issues."

✸

I called home that day and my mother picked up after several rings.

"Hi Mom. How are you?" I asked.

"Hi! Finally, a call. Are you okay?" She replied. She stopped whatever she was doing to give our conversation her full attention.

"Yes, everything here is okay. I'm having fun. The co-op is interesting with a lot of people here from all over." I looked up and down the hallway. No one was there.

"That's good. How are classes going?"

"Classes are okay. The teacher thinks that I speak Hindi okay already! And get this—he also speaks Bhojpuri!" I tripped over my words with excitement.

Silence.

"Mom, did you hear me?"

"He speaks Bhojpuri?" she said, drawing out her vowels.

"Yeah. You know, Aji's language, and also the kind of Hindustani that Nana must have spoken. Your father spoke Hindi, right?"

"Yes, he spoke it. That's amazing. Are you going to try to learn Bhojpuri too?"

"As much as I can while I'm there I guess." This was a major reason why I wanted to go to Benares in particular.

"I can't believe it. It's like God is watching over you," Mom said. God. She was talking about Christ Jesus, whom my family had tightly embraced upon arriving in the United States.

"I guess so, if your God spoke Hindustani," I said. "And it's so cool that I can learn Aji and Aja's language there, too—like all of Pap's older relatives will be able to talk to me."

Silence.

"It would be so great to learn their songs from Crabwood Creek—" I continued.

After another pause my mother spoke. "You only care about your father's family. My family is nothing to you," she cut into me.

"Well, I don't really know anything about your family except that they're Hindus and hate Pap. They come to Florida but don't even visit us," I cut back.

"Well, you have two parents who had parents who spoke Hindi—or Bhojpuri as you called it," she reminded me.

"Wait, Nani spoke Bhojpuri, too?" I asked.

"She learned some because my father made her."

"And what about all my mausis and mamus? Do they speak?"

"No—my father would try to teach them, but when they couldn't get past the alphabet he would beat them for their mistakes. It was Mummy who asked your Nana, 'Would you rather have dead sons who speak Hindi or living sons who don't?'" She laughed.

"Why did he start with having them read it? Why not just speak it to them?"

"I don't know. Are the other people who are going on the trip with you nice?" she asked, changing the subject.

"There's a guy here who I like in the co-op," I said, avoiding her question. I had told her that I was gay almost two years prior, as I folded laundry and talked about the white bisexual man I had been on two dates with. The date didn't go anywhere, but we did do ecstasy together and learned a lot about each other's childhoods. She cried and asked me to stitch my lips with silence. She didn't want anyone in the extended family to know.

"Oh, that's nice—what about your teacher, you like him?"

"The guy's name is Ken and he's very nice." I had not yet had many interactions with Ken, just the occasional "hello" and "how are you." I wanted my mother to acknowledge the fact of him.

Silence.

"Well, the weather here is nice, too," I said, trying to pick the conversation back up. "How's Pap?"

"That's good. You know you can never tell your father. It would kill him to know."

This time I was quiet.

"Are you sure, Raimie? You just haven't met the right girl as yet," she said.

"Mom, we've been through this. You know I've slept with women. It just doesn't work for me in the same way." I looked over my shoulder. I was glad there was no one in the co-op that day.

"I just don't understand what two men can do together. It's just not anything that I would ever want for you." She was crying on the other end.

"I am not explaining it to you right now, but I will sometime if you want me to. I just can't keep having this conversation again and again."

Ever since I told her, our conversations have ended with her crying. She cried on the phone every time we spoke for two years. She wanted to bear this secret alone, not trusting that my father would ever fully support or see me as someone who was not straight: their worst fear in the world made manifest.

❀

Lake Mendota was everywhere, surrounding the UW isthmus and beckoning students in the hot summer months to be free of our garments and dip our bare skins in its cool waters. After class and before the nightly hang with the other students, I hopped in as often as I could. Being from Florida, I was used to relaxing at beaches, in pools, in rivers, and, when I was willing to risk being attacked by alligators, in lakes.

I spent this particular day with a well-shaped white boy from Boston University. His brown hair and green eyes made me blush as I stripped off my underwear and followed him into the water, hurling myself from the dock. I had also invited Ken.

Just as I was about to get out of the water and warm myself in the sun, Ken appeared and took his clothes off while keeping his eyes on mine.

His body shone like gold in the sun. He jumped in and splashed near to me. By this time, we were alone.

"Do you swim a lot?" he asked.

"I do love to be in the water." I felt his leg brush mine as he lunged away from me.

"Catch me then!" he said. I swam after him, but he was quicker than I was. He jumped onto the dock and bent over to pick up his towel. "See you later," he said as he dried off.

&#10042;

At Der Rathskeller, the bar on campus that opened out to Lake Mendota, I met Mae for the first time. Der Rathskeller's deck had twenty round tables, and we sat with several other classmates from around the country. Also among us was Jegga from Richmond Hill: the Indo-Caribbean neighborhood in Queens, New York, that was in my extended family's orbit. Jegga had been conscripted to teach ESL in Varanasi through a fellowship from Oberlin College.

Mae was advanced in Hindi and had come to study Urdu more fully before going to India. A student from North Carolina, she originally came from Colorado. She had curly hair, too; it was light brown and fell to her hips. Mae had spent a summer in Nepal and was bewitched by the songs that she heard there, and we were drawn to each other right away.

"Let's walk down to the water," Mae said. We moved away from the crowds and the lights. The stars were gleaming on the lake surface. I looked over the wooden boards of the dock. Elodea waterweeds swayed in the subtle surf below our feet.

"Nangi Village had some really neat people. I met one woman who really was something special," Mae said. "I want to return to South Asia because I'm so in love with how the culture speaks to me." She was a Hindi/Urdu major who was passionate about South Asian Muslim issues as they related to labor. Mae continued, "You love your Aji's songs. Do you know any?"

"I do," I replied. "But I want to hear the song you learned in Nangi Village. Would you sing it?"

"Oh, sure." We sat down and put our feet in the water. Even though it was summer, the cold waves bit our toes. Mae looked at the moon and then looked at me and smiled. As she began, the words curled out of her mouth like smoke. I was captive to the lilting and bending of the words, which in Nepali sounded similar to words in Bhojpuri and Hindi but were completely beyond my understanding.

The gentle lake skin kept irregular time on the shore and licked the dock's wooden legs. "It's about a girl who doesn't want to leave her home but has to," Mae said. "What about you? Why do you want to go to India and learn Hindi?"

I had rehearsed the answer to this question many times. In my application letter I wrote something about wanting to learn my familial language—but this was a lie. Hindi was the closest thing to Aji's Bhojpuri, which she called *Hindustani*, that I could find taught in study abroad programs. But there was more.

I confided in Mae, "I want to connect with my Indianness. I want the things that my Aji taught me, the things that everyone said were worthless, to be remembered. That's all. I want to tell her stories and sing with her voice, adding my own. Like how folk songs are passed down. Instead of planting rice and singing, I would sing from where I am." I looked into the sky. Venus was close to the moon. The planets and stars looked down. It devastated me to think that these songs and stories would be lost for good.

"Sing one," Mae insisted.

With my back against the wooden boards I sang:

*akhiya hamar badal rukhi*
*kahi naahi sukhi sukhi*
*tinhu lok me hamesa*
*tohar birha se hi bhigal*

*My eyes are clouds,*
*nowhere is dry.*
*The three worlds are forever*
*soaked in grief.*

✳

That night, after I sobered up and walked back to the co-op, I opened my email and saw that Jake had written to me. It said something like this:

I dreamt of you last night. We were on a ship en route to Florida. I was dropping you back home but in the middle of the ocean I wanted to turn back. But we were far out to sea. You wanted to stay on course, so I jumped out and swam to the beach back to New York. You stayed on the vessel and I guess you made it. I'm not really sure.

I have this dream a lot but typically I'm alone and make it to wherever it is that I'm going. But this one was strange. You were there. I feel like we are similar and are doing similar things in life.

I think you should tell your dad about your—you know. It's only a matter of time. What are you going to do about it in India?

As I left the computer lab, I saw movement in the dark hallway. The bathroom light flipped on and Ken's door was open. He was awake. I waited for him and when he came out of the bathroom and smiled at me. He wore a purple and brown lungi cloth around his waist.

"You're home already?" he asked. He raised one eyebrow in a delicate arc.

"Oh yeah, I met a friend and we sang songs," I said rubbing my head.

"I want to come next time," he smiled, looking directly into my eyes. My stomach lurched.

"That can be arranged," I said.

"Well, I don't really get to be myself at home. You know, things are different where I'm from." Ken looked down and rubbed his upper arm.

"I was going to get some food I left in the fridge downstairs. Want to come with me?" I asked. Downstairs I took out yogurt and mixed it into the daal that I had made earlier that day. We sat at a table lit only by the light from the kitchen. Shadows painted his face half dark, half lit.

"Want some?" I asked.

Ken grabbed my hand. "Only if you feed it to me," he said.

I placed a spoon of yogurt in his mouth and he licked it clean. I put the spoon in my mouth and placed it on the table. I got up from the table and kissed him. Ken opened his mouth and I picked him up as he wrapped his legs around my waist.

"Let's go upstairs," I said, pulling away after a minute.

"My room," he replied.

In Ken's room I traced his abs. I pulled loose his lungi. It fell to the floor. He reached for me in the dark. In the morning I left while he was still sleeping to get ready for the day's Hindi class.

※

The summer language intensive programs culminated in an annual student talent show. Mae and Jegga both insisted that I sing one of my Aji's songs for the evening's performances. They were also excited to meet Emily, who would be arriving soon—she had agreed to come up and drive back down to Florida with me at the end of the program, with a stop in Toronto. I wanted to sing a song that felt important, one that

Emily would recognize. I thought of Auntie Sonia's house just a few months earlier. I remembered the dock with Mae and how held I felt by the songs that she and I had sung. I put my name on the list.

I took out my journal, wrote down the words, and translated them, as people would inevitably ask me for the chords and the meaning. Emily would want to know exactly what the song meant. I wrote down the words for her.

*kekahi chaho to mango*
*rani tu hamar jaan bachaiyal*
*ajodhya tohar hoijai*
*je mango to mango rani*

*je mango to mango rani*
*ham mange ram banbas jaye*
*aur bharat raja chalaye ho*
*je mango to mango rani*

*Kekahi, wish what you will*
*Rani, you saved my life that day—*
*Ayodhya is yours,*
*What you wish is yours.*

*Whatever you want, ask.*
*I want Ram in exile,*
*For Bharat to rule the throne.*
*Whatever I want is mine.*

I wondered how I would explain this to Aji—that people in a university where white people go to learn Hindi would be interested in her songs, when her own children didn't think them worth learning. The grandchildren of the same white people who told her generation that they were backward and broken now wanted to claim her knowledge systems as artifacts for study. These people would take our songs and stories and make careers out of interpreting them for other white people. I had seen it before: white scholars who tried to out-Indian me by adopting the study of India as their entire personality. My own interest was deeper than academia. Wading into the sea of this music and trying to understand it was like struggling to see myself.

When Emily arrived, she stayed with me in my room at International Co-op. This meant that she would see my interactions with Ken. Emily saw me living my queer life.

"Ken's real cute, isn't he?" she ribbed. "He's everywhere you are—he's like totally following you around."

I laughed. "Yeah, he's sweet."

"Are you going to keep in touch?" she asked.

"Nah," I said.

I had told her about my queerness two years prior underneath a pecan tree outside of my apartment in Gainesville. She was not surprised. "The constant Broadway duets and your obsession with black-and-white Hindi movies kind of gave it away," she said.

Emily and I got ready. I wore red corduroy pants and a gingham button-down. She wore a cotton summer dress with an Indian pattern.

At the auditorium we sat in the back and watched the SASLI students show off their newly acquired language skills. Mae and Jegga sat next to us. People performed skits in Tamil, sang songs in Malayalam, and recited poems in Urdu. When it was time for me to go up, I borrowed someone's guitar and started to strum Aji's song. As I sang, I could feel someone else's voice come up through my throat.

After I was done, I went back to sit down with Emily. A white graduate student at Wisconsin, about five years older than me, approached.

"Hey, Raimie. That was great. I was wondering, could you write down the words to the song you sang. It looked like it was really easy to play the chords." He looked at my sister and me with a crooked smile.

"Oh, sure," I said. "I will give it to you tomorrow." I smiled. Emily, Jegga, Mae, and I walked out of the hall. The International Co-op was having a party that night.

As Emily and I walked down State Street, she asked, "Are you really going to give that guy Aji's song so that he can sing it to people?"

"I would if he were Coolie," I laughed. "I just said that to get rid of him. I'm going to forget to give it to him tomorrow." We smiled in the dark as we headed back.

"I have this for you." I pulled out the translation that I had written down in my journal and gave it to Emily. "You're the one who should have it."

The next morning it was time to leave the rose quartz of Madison behind. My heart chakra felt purified. Ken came out to my car and gave me a long hug. He was leaving the US soon to return home to Indonesia and would most likely never be back. He'd be long gone by the time I returned from India.

"It was good to get to know you," I said.

"I will think of you," he said.

"I won't forget you or the day by the lake," I said as Ken kissed my cheek. He handed me the purple and brown lungi he'd worn all summer.

❋

The road to Toronto through Ohio and Niagara Falls was easy driving. The forests skirting the highways and through roads were deep in their summer green. Wildflowers beckoned all manner of flying insects to their petals, many of them interrupted by my windshield, now streaked in guts. The early morning fog made this journey feel like a pilgrimage, a return to the source, to Aji, after I had studied a year's worth of Hindi in six weeks.

"It was so good to see you living your life without worrying about anyone seeing you and telling Pap," Emily said, looking at me.

"It's freeing to be in a place where no one knows you—like I can be anything I want to be," I said, wishing the same for her.

Once we arrived at Aji's Brampton flat we fell at her feet, placing our foreheads firmly on her toes.

"You come?" she asked. "Me lovin' son, a come." After bringing our bags in we sat on her sofa and Emily went to put the kettle on for tea.

"You mus' go to India now? Who go mine yuh papa?" Aji asked me, blinking through her cataract lenses.

"Yes, Aji, me go gan. Me been a 'Skansin fe study Hindi an' me wan' go til a India jus' now." I said. Then I slipped into Hindi with Bhojpuri words and phrases—our own new lingua franca. "India mein jaike hamke kya kya dekhna hai?"

Aji looked at me. "Me na know wha' you mus' see. You mus' go til a Ganga-Mata and adar kare 'am."

She wanted me to bathe in the Ganga river. "Aji, you know meh Ganga ke kinare ke shaher—pavitra Varanasi ja raha hun?" *You know I am going to the city of the Ganga—the holy city of Varanasi?*

Aji clapped her hands together. "Well, yes! You go see sadhu an' pujari an' pandit an' cow an' all kine ting!"

"How do you know? You ever been?" I asked, laughing.

"Me see 'am on TV," she replied. "Dem get one real nice station wha' play all de t'ing."

I got up and opened Aji's entertainment system decorated with pictures of her children and grandchildren. Underneath were some records that I used to like to play. Aji loved them, too. I pulled out the LP with a picture of a monkey in flight. Against a rainbowed background the monkey wore a crown and carried a golden club. In his left hand he held what looked like a mountain. *Hanuman Chalisa* was printed on the front.

"Aji, you does pray dis?" I asked, knowing full well the Hanuman Chalisa prayer—forty verses to Lord Hanuman.

"Yes, de Hanuman Chalisa is very good. You seh 'am an' wha' you wan' go come true." Aji began to sing the prayer and took her tea from

Emily, who came with a tray. She placed a cup by me on a coaster on the entertainment system and sat down next to Aji.

"You see how he does carry de mountain deh? He a bring de medicine fe help Lachman who fall doung pan de ground. India get all kine t'ing like a dah." Aji's story was ready to unfurl. This time I didn't have my tape recorder. She told us of how when Hanuman came back with the medicine, Ram was so happy that he hugged Hanuman and that Hanuman's other name was Mahabir—like our name.

"But we spell it with an *O* and not an *A*," I said.

"Na mattah—monkey is a monkey," she joked. We all laughed as I continued to look through the albums, pulling out records like *Let's Dance with the Champ* and old Bollywood records like *Sangam* and *Humraaz*.

"Play some Babla and Kanchan," Emily asked. I put on "Raat Ke Sapna" and Emily and I danced in Aji's living room while she clapped along. I tried to pull her up and she danced for a few beats and then sat back down, exhausted.

The next morning Aji got up to pound some mango and ball-of-fiyah peppers into chutney for us to take back home to our father and mother. She also packed some frozen hassa, saltfish and bake, barah, and phulauri for us to eat on our drive. When we left Aji stood in the road crying. She didn't know when we would see each other again.

❉

The night before I left for India, Emily came into my room.

"I have a gift for you," she said and handed me a spiral-bound journal. There was an inscription that read *I figured a sketch pad might work for you. I love you!*

"Thanks, Em," I said and gave her a big hug. Her eyes shone through tears. I looked through the blank pages. I lit some incense and Emily hopped on the bed.

"It's going to be like you're in Gainesville and you won't come home for a year." I hadn't lived in Chuluota since I was eighteen, five years earlier.

There was a knock on the door and Mom walked in. Her wavy hair was down to her shoulders. She'd just dyed it jet-black and it curled around her face. She stood up to my shoulders and was as dark as I. Emily and I got our shoulders from Mom and our round faces from Pap. Mom held something in her hands.

"Is that sandalwood you're burning? It's my favorite." She held out a black-and-white photo of a family of eight in the water. "That's my father and mother—your Nana and Nani—when they moved to Allahabad. They're bathing in the Ganges here. Your uncle sent it to me from London."

I took the photo from her. I could recognize some of her siblings. Auntie Chandra looked just like my mother did when she was younger. "Where are you?" I asked.

"I was conceived on the boat when they came back from India," she said.

"So you're like the essence of a Jahaji!" I laughed. I gazed into the picture. My Nana was old-looking. His children looked sweet. My Nani's eyes looked tired.

"There's another thing," Mom said. She handed me a book with a black-and-white photo on the cover. It was a man delivering a speech from what looked like a pulpit. The title read *Lil Lil Dutty Build Dam (Little Pieces of Earth Build a Dam): An Autobiography by Hari Prashad*.

"Your father's book?" My voice crescendoed. I had a copy when I was young but had misplaced it a long time ago.

"Yes, your Mamu sent me some copies and I thought you should have one."

My Nana wrote this autobiography about his travails in life and how he came to terms with his own Indian identity in Guyana, India, and eventually England. He left Guyana in the 1960s before independence and was a British citizen for his entire life, though second-class.

"It's funny how you and Pap come from such different places—Aji is unlettered, Aja may have had a second-grade education. And your mom didn't have much schooling, but Nana knew enough to write an entire book."

"Yes, he was also a pandit—people would come to listen to him give *Ramayan* katha," she said almost proudly.

"Was he happy that you married someone named Mohabir? With both of your names in the Hanuman Chalisa?" I laughed.

Mom sang a couplet from the prayer:

*Ramdut atulit bal dhama*
*Anjani putra pavansut nama*

*Mahabir bikram bajarangi*
*kumati nivar sumati ke sangi*

Emily and I looked at each other. "Does Pap know that you know this?" I asked.

"Yes—it's where I'm from. It's where he's from, too, though he doesn't like to admit it. Somewhere inside him he is proud of you for who you are, though you can't see it." Mom was signaling something to me. *Don't tell Pap.* My secret was okay as long as it stayed stuffed in my throat.

"You know that Anjani is the mother of Hanuman?" I said.

"That must make you a monkey," she laughed.

"Well, I am about to leap across the Kalapani." We were all silent for a moment.

"Don't go off by yourself, wandering all about. Walk good, and come back home," Mom said as we all erupted into tears.

# Aji Recording: Dunce

HINDUSTANI BHASHA BARDI accha hai sikhe ke. But jab sikhe tab bidya bhi pardh le. Den you go know. You go learn to read de book.

Dem seh:

*Utho bahino pardho bidya*
*yahi sikhsha tumhari hai*
*bina bidya ke pardhne se*
*burdi halat tumhari hai*

So if you na know fe read, you punish an' knack from da pillah to da pos'. But if you know fe read you go stan' up right hiyan an' all wha' knack about go come back ti you.

Da one sang de mek. Get up sistah, sistah a sleep an' all bady gan a school. 'E brudah com an' seh, "Git up, wake up. Go an' tek you education. Go an' read."

An' if you know fe read people go hana you. If you na know fe read people go kick you. Me brudah been tell me "Git up an' read dis a you one." If you na know fe read you go punish.

*Utho bahino pardho bidya*
*yahi sikhsha tumhari hai*
*bina bidya ke pardhne se*
*burdi halat tumhari hai*

Git up. Na sleep. An' go read. An' when you read you get education an' you brain go function. You can talk anyt'ing an' deh between anybady. An' people go hana you. But if you continue sleep people go call you lazy kordhin. Who go do wha' fe you? Tell me? All bady go scahn you an' walk out. You a no good, man. You is no good.

Bidya mean fe read. 'E sistah so lazy. People go hana you if you git up an' read. An' da true. Me see am wid me own eye from now. If you na read you na good. How me deh now—me na know fe read. All bady siddung an' dem talk deh story an' me got a siddung in de cana cuz me na know wha' dem a do an' wha' dem a talk an' wha' dem a read. Me na know nut'in'.

Beta, dis t'ing a mek me shame da t'ing a fail me. Me na wan' go anywhere like party an' t'ing deh me na wan' go—me go shame. Dem a get book, dem a get t'ing fe read an' me go siddung like a statue an' watch. Me can tell you wha' dem sing, but me jus' watch. Wha' me go do? Me na dunce? Me dunce. Da is me own.

Well me faddah na been give me education. Me faddah seh gyal pickni na should git none. Da why me married young. Langtime, India people seh when you get twelve-t'irteen year you gah fe marry. Me time, me stan fifteen year. Me muddah been get five year. Five year! An' me papa been get ten when de married. An' me mama an' papa live til dead togedah. De live out dem life.

Me mama sistah—you na go know 'am—Sarupiya Mausi been get four year. 'E been small da you gah fe carry am 'roung de marro. Me nani go 'roung wid de pickni. 'E been cyan't walk, 'e been too little. Da been a India rule. You pickni tuhn ole you cyan't married am. You got to marry you pickni when 'e young. When dem do kanyadan dem put de pickni in you lap, an' when 'e tuhn big you cyan put a pickni in you lap.

Me papa put me pan 'e lap when 'e gi' kanyadan. Me been got fifteen year but 'e put me pan 'e jangh an' siddung me he' an' gi' de kanyadan.

# Evolution of a Song

VARANASI, THE OLDEST continuously inhabited city in the world, stirred with prayer. The cobblestone streets were littered with wet buffalo shit and little shrines to Shiva streaked in bright vermillion. Flower garlands piled up. Burnt-out clay lamps and leaves along the alleyways lent their color to the city's dazzle. To die in this city, they said, would bring liberation from incarnation. The devoted chanted *Victory to Ram, Victory to Ram.*

I sat on the cement floor in my rented room on Assi Ghat. It overlooked the Ganga River, flowing with glacial melt and silt made of minerals and waste from the devout. Moisture tie-dyed the blue-washed walls in mildew, and I sat cross-legged, all my weight on my ankles, looking for faces in the black crusty patterns. It was the night before Holi—the festival of colors—and tonight, supposedly, all social laws of caste and gender would be turned on their head. I had been living in India for eight months. Through the monsoon. Through winter. And now, the beginning of summer.

In Madison, Virendra-ji, upper-casted and unaware of my complicated relationship to caste, had told me that Holi is not complete until you embrace a Dalit. I wondered what it would be like to roam the streets at night with all the naked men. But here I was at home instead. Shira, a student from Smith College, and I had invited all the women from our study-abroad program over for chai and namkeen. From the window the city glowed as a flickering flame.

I smelled the charring effigies of Holika, Prahlad's mythological sister, who sat her younger brother in her lap while they were both ignited in the fire. Their father, Raja Hiranyakashyap, commanded his son to worship him as a deva—mightier than Vishnu. When Prahlad refused, the raja tried to burn him but was unsuccessful. Prahlad chanted *Narayana, Narayana, Narayana,* and Vishnu, incarnated as Narasimha-dev—half man, half lion—saved him from the flames and disemboweled the evil raja. The beast-god wore the raja's intestines as a pink flower garland.

I was learning so many stories in Varanasi. The mustard fields and burning trash coupled with cow feces and potent spices were a smell that made sense. It smelled like life, like the life that I could have had, had my ancestors remained here and not, as Aji had said, "left to live in Foreign. Dem arkotiya been tell abi leh abi go dat side abi go tuhn rich rich. But when de jahaji reach now, dey punish. All India people what been come dis side been a poor. Ham India chhordke bides rahe lagi hai. Uu arkotiya suar rahi. We left India to live in Foreign. The recruiters were swine."

Sitting on the floor, she had one leg before her the other folded in a half crisscross. Her hair wild like a gray cloud. Underneath, a storm of music and epics brewed, preparing for deluge. I knew that Aji's tongue was different—a form of Bhojpuri that was forged in the Guyanese plantations—and inscrutable to the majority of South Asian immigrants' children who I knew and went to college with. I wished desis would recognize me as South Asian, that I would fit in to the community that was a swirl of rainbowed silk—a garish gallery of multicolored gods and food that yellowed my fingers. I no longer wanted to feel like a forgery—a fake South Asian.

Varanasi, also known as Kashi—City of Light—and as Benares, is the holy city of the River Ganga, known to Americans as the Ganges. Aji's call name, Gangadai, meant "that which the Ganga gave." Part of me was from this holiest of places. My father's family was originally from the Gangetic Plain, and the Ganga River featured heavily in pujas and stories. But that was so long ago that Aji's accent was Caribbean.

Abroad, as I sat in the holy city of Shiva, the Lord of Ghosts, I drank enough bhang to tell the truth. It was night, the time for nakedness. Ghosts and spirits swirled around me. Four of us sat listening to music and laughing at the gossip from the program house. The directors told us not to befriend any Indians in order to protect ourselves. We all knew this was bullshit.

Mae sat behind me to oil my scalp, her long brown hair curling like the clouds over her beloved mountains in Colorado. I sat cross-legged in front of her, facing the room's only window. Outside, fireworks and laughter streaked the night like fire. She started to massage my head. High from the bhang, I began to remember stories from Orlando. I remembered an Indian girl I went to high school with who began to teach me Hindi and who pointed out just how broken my family was. She came over to my home and opened my fridge.

"Teri fridge thordi hi desi lagti hai," she accused. I gave her a blank look. "Your fridge is not very Indian," she laughed, translating. Her Hindi seared like a half lion, half man's claws. By opening my fridge, she opened my guts and saw just how pretend I was. I wanted so much for her to see herself in me, to validate my Indianness.

"Would you ever think about going to your Nana's village, Rajiw?" Mae asked, using her own nickname for me.

"I want to," I said. "I brought my Nana's autobiography that he self-published in London. I want to go and see the earth that made my ancestors' bodies, though I'm not sure that the people there, if there are any, would recognize me."

"What do you mean, Raju?" Jegga asked. Jegga, the tall Italian-descended woman I'd met in Madison, waited her turn for her own scalp massage. She lived in Richmond Hill, close to Pua and Pupha. The summer before, she'd been my tour guide to all things West Indian in Queens and New York City. Her eyes were the blue of Lord Shiva's throat.

"I just mean that my family has been outside of India for so long, we're not exactly India-Brahmins, and I would have to pretend to be something that I'm not to even enter the home of anyone I find. If I do find anyone," I said. Temple bells rang out, shaking the still air. "Going there would mean confronting who I am not."

Jegga knew that I wasn't an NRI, Non-Resident Indian. She knew what I meant when I said I was Indian: I was an aluminum karahi, frying aloo pie and phulauri, I was floral print and plastic on the couch, I was gold teeth and Creole. I looked at Jegga and then back up at Mae. My cheeks were wet and my nose was running.

"What's the matter, yaar?" Mae asked, raising her eyebrows. Her touch was gentle, and I didn't think I deserved gentle. I lit a cigarette.

"Nothing." I pulled myself away from her and blew smoke out of the window. It curled through the screen and mixed with the burning Holikas outside.

"I hate being Guyanese. I wish I were a *real* Indian." There, I said it. Something that had haunted me since landing in New Delhi. I could see only my difference. My darker complexion meant that I was not "desirable" in any way.

"Raimie, are you okay?" asked Jegga.

Even my call name wasn't Indian. I hated my name, Raimie, the one my parents called me, because it was so European and damningly feminine.

Being Guyanese was too complicated. Every time someone asked where I was from, I had to tell some kind of shortcut or lie. If I were to tell the truth, it would usually go something like:

*Where are you from?*
*I am from Chuluota, outside of Orlando.*
*No, really.*
*Well, I was born in England.*

*Where were you from before that?*

*Before I was born? My parents are from South America.*

*But you look Indian or Middle Eastern.*

*My parents are from a community of Indians that migrated to the Caribbean to work British sugar plantations in the late 1800s. We are from there.*

The British did all they could to erase the Coolie in the Coolie and made it impossible for Indians in remote parts of Guyana to attend school unless they converted to Christianity. In doing so, the British had carved their nation into the very bones of my parents. McCauley's infamous essay "Minute on Education," written in 1835, proved that the British wanted to make us brown on the outside and white on the inside—always lesser than white but "better" than brown.

My parents had given me an Indian name, too. *Rajiv.* I started to use it when I lived in India because it was more easily recognized—*Raimie* sounded weak, an astrologer told me as he looked at my palm and asked me about my caste and clan. Another lie. I come from a place where caste is mixed and not remembered in the same way as in India. Aji would insist that she was "Brahmin and Kshatri—all two" and that Aja, her husband, "been one Ahiri." A cowherd and a warrior. My mother's castes were Brahmin and unknown—most likely Dalit and Musalman. Would the pandit drop my palm in horror of my being unclean and fettered with the caste-mixing of diaspora? I longed for a simple story.

In my mind, if I were Indian without South America, the Caribbean, or the system of indenture, then I would speak Hindi fluently. I would have a single-caste identity. My name would not be Raimie. I would be marriageable to Punjabis or proud Tamilians. Savarna, upper-caste people, would not look down on me as though I were a Bhojpuri/Tamil mixture of castes and histories—a South Asian mongrel. White people couldn't understand my frustration.

"Why would you ever say that?" Mae asked. She was shocked by my candor. My embarrassment wafted like secondhand smoke. I snuffed my cigarette's cherry in a stainless-steel tumbler.

"We are not a real people," I said, turning to face her. "My family doesn't even speak Hindi and people don't acknowledge us as Indians. We speak 'broken Hindi' and 'broken English.'"

"What do you mean you're not Indian?" But Jegga spoke up. "Raimie, I know Richmond Hill. It's Little Guyana in Queens. You guys have soca chutney music and know how to wine. And besides, your food is awesome. You telling me that you'd give up daal puri and buss up shut for what—chapati?" She was a light. I could recognize her olive branch but was convinced that I knew better. I had inherited too much suffering.

"When people go to Indian restaurants, they don't order phulowri, barah, daal puri. In fact, they don't even exist unless it's a Coolie store. They order samosas, chicken tikka masala, and naan. We don't have those things. Our foods are different, and we are not treated like we are real anythings," I said.

"Yeah," Mae said. "What about your Aji, too? If you were from Delhi she would be your Dadi."

Dadi. That word was all wrong for my Aji. Dadi was Shah Rukh Khan's mother and the young Anjali's grandmother in the film *Kuch Kuch Hota Hai*. Aji was personal—someone who sat in my family home in Florida, who narrated long stories of rajas, ranis, and rajkumars. She knew about exile. She knew its songs. Aji spoke Hindustani.

※

In Varanasi, I had been studying folk singing with Pintu Rai, but he did not speak English, nor could he assist in translations, so the program coordinator appointed Kumar to lead me into places of music. Kumar was in his late thirties, wore a cleanly pressed dress shirt about his meek frame and tucked it into his khakis. His shoes were spit-shined, and I looked at my face's reflection in them.

In order to fulfill the requirements of the program, each student had to write a thesis on some aspect of Indian life. Mae wrote about the

Muslim weaving community and focused her efforts on Urdu and her friend Saleem—the old uncle who was missing many teeth but knew of the best fabrics around Sonarpura. My housemate Shira wrote about Coca Cola's exploitation of Mehandi Ganj village's water and how the people there resisted the imperialist efforts of the multinational corporation. Remembering Aji and how broken I felt, I decided to write about the Bhojpuri folk singing culture as it related to the *Ramayana* to make sense of our connection, or lack thereof, to this place.

Kumar met me at my house on Assi Ghat at seven in the morning. "Today we will go to this Ram Mandir," Kumar said, looking over our list of names and places. The old women lined their platforms with neem branches to sell as makeshift toothbrushes, children carried baskets filled with chrysanthemum blooms and small clay lamps in leaf bowls to sell to pilgrims to float downstream. The sun began its climb, red as a vermillion forehead smear, as people young and aged came to bathe in their dhotis and saris. Brass temple bells, *Shri Ram Jai Ram Jai Jai Ram*, and incense wafted above the city at dawn.

We walked to his motorbike and I climbed on behind him, clutching his waist for support. We zoomed down the gullies, past the vegetable vendors crouched down next to their sheets lined with eggplant, okra, tomatoes, and onions sweating into their *Alua, Baingan, Bhindi, Tamatar*. We zipped past the chai stands with old and young alike chatting about politics as macaque monkeys marched in troops in the bel and ficus trees. A pig in the ditch on the side of the road fed on a dog carcass. Cows, pigs, stores, and rickshaws were a blur of lows, oinks, *ka ho gurus* from our perch on Kumar's bike.

We stopped for chai at Kumar's favorite place. The blue wash on the wall was powdery with trails of gecko footprints. The fluorescent light hummed above us as though it were getting ready to sing.

"Doh chai," Kumar asked, "Chai piyenge? Will you have tea?" The milky, sweet chai was poured in a cup made of local clay fired in dried cow shit.

Outside four men carried a stretcher with a body wrapped in a cotton cloth. They proclaimed *Ram Naam Satya Hai.* "The name of Ram is truth." They were taking the body to Manikarnika Ghat to burn on a pyre. Above the chai shop the smoke billowed. I didn't know if I was breathing in exhaust or the smoke from the body of the latest liberated soul. In this city, life was death was life. The living and the dead lived together in one house. The lord of this house was Shiva, the god of ghosts and ghouls—easy to anger, easy to please. I sipped the sweet, milky chai and wondered if in this place I would encounter any ghosts of my kin, of the people we once were before we left for Guyana. I burned my tongue.

"It's very close, only, this ashram that we are going to." Kumar turned to me. I could feel my body relaxing and tightening from the caffeine. Kumar's role as interpreter had been invaluable. We went to see a famous birha singer, Hiralal Yadav, who was convinced that I was from the government and there to steal his songs. Kumar explained that I was just a student who was interested in his art. *Which would be easier to think?* I wondered into my chai.

We smashed our cups on the road and mounted the bike. We wound into a gully. I could sense the moisture in the air, hanging about like a song. Shopkeepers threw water in front of their stores in the morning in a ritual to keep the dust from flying up and into their faces. We entered a square compound. In the center was another square space surrounded by grass. As we walked farther in to the ashram the outside chaos fell away. Along the perimeter were rooms with wooden doors painted teal. In the middle stood what looked to be the shrine, yet there was no deity enshrined—rather an old man in a kurta and dhoti sitting, waiting for his guests. His hair was pure white. His beard hid the inward sloping of his cheeks. His bones were as old as the city he lived in.

"Come, child," he smiled at me and patted the space next to him. His Hindi was broad and rustic—a peepal tree in the village square. Something about his voice and demeanor reminded me of Aji. It wasn't just the white hair, his smile felt like home—warm and bright. He was a sannyasi, someone who renounced his earthly connections as a youth and was living a life of religious supplication.

"Tell me, would you like some chai?" the baba asked.

"No, ji, thank you, we just had tea before we came," I admitted.

"What is your name?" he asked me.

"Rajiv."

"Rajiv what?"

"Rajiv Mohabir."

"That's a strong name, beta. Rajivalochan, he with eyes like a blue lotus—steady in stormy weather. And Mohabir—*maha* and *vira* meaning 'great warrior.' What is your caste?" The baba tilted his head and narrowed his eyes.

The question stung. "Gwalbans Ahir." It was a familiar lie.

"What does your father do?" He relaxed his eyebrows.

"He is disabled but he was an accountant. My mother works as an assistant principal of an elementary school." His questions were not rude or overly inquisitive but polite things to ask. "Baba-ji. What is your name?"

"There is only one name, beta, and that is the name of god. People call me baba."

His hands were soft, the lines dark and numerous. A century of life hung from his bones, the collagen giving way to time. His fair skin and the Bhojpuri lilt in his Hindi conjured a field in rural Bihar. He relaxed when I said my family were cowherd people. Was he a farmer before he renounced his life to pursue religious and spiritual *moksha*? What could my caste matter to him, a sannyasi? There is no name but god, which was Truth—*Ram Naam Satya Hai*. He was close to death. I was close to his death. I could see from the deep creases on his face that I had come in time to ask him to sing for me.

"We have come to ask you about songs you know about the *Ramayan*." Kumar's interjection was down to business. I didn't mind—after all, this was a job for him, not an experience to relish. For him such babas were common and students like me, work. For me, it was the realization of a dream: India was a place of people and songs like this baba and his repertoire.

The air was thick, not with exhaust fumes, but with my hope. It descended like the fruit bats that returned daily to their dawn perches having eaten their nightly fill in the trees in Madanpura. The baba reached back into his childhood in Bihar. He closed his eyes.

"This first one is a thumri," he said and began to sing.

His voice was fluid. Clear. Strong like bricks that make a dam. I didn't write down the words, but I recorded his voice on my tape recorder. He sang about the monsoons and about how King Dasharath was injured on a hunting trip. The king killed a deer that was really a boy and was then cursed by his parents. But stumbling through the forest the king pricked his finger. The splinter made him deathly ill, so he called for his beloved queen Kaikeyi. She came and removed the splinter and restored the king's health. He gave her two promises to be fulfilled later.

I was astonished. I shifted in my seat and thought about Aji and the way her own version of the *Ramayana* echoed this baba's.

"But that's not how Kaikeyi received her two boons," Kumar interjected. "She drove the king's chariot into battle and saved his life on the battlefield."

The baba looked at him for a while and then at me.

"This is an old version that we tell in Ghazipur." Ghazipur was the district in Bihar where the baba was born. He had admitted some truth about his former self—this self that belonged to the world of living and dying, samsara.

"I know this version," I chimed in. "My Aji sings a song about this, how Kaikeyi actually saved Dasharath by pulling out a splinter from his finger." This was a broken part of our diasporic identity, an alternative version that Valmiki's *Ramayana*, the Goswami Tulsidas *Sri Ramacharitamanasa*, and the television serial *Ramayan* all worked to erase. Maybe all stories became fixed when we tried to stretch them to fit everyone and everything. Maybe there was no one singular *Ramayana*, no one way to tell the story. If Kumar didn't recognize it as the *Ramayana*, maybe my Indianness was fluid, too.

"You know, there are so many differences in the way that people tell the *Ramayan* story here from how they do in Ghazipur. The real *Ramayan* is in the heart," the baba said. A flock of doves had been released in my stomach and I sprouted wings: I could feel the sensation of flying—perfect weightlessness. But there were still several major problems: The *Ramayana*'s Ram upholds caste, the name of truth betrays his wife.

"But baba, how do you justify the cruelty of Ram? If he really were Vishnu incarnated into the world, why would he have tortured his wife by leaving her in the forest to die and constantly questioning her fidelity?"

"We cannot understand the entirety of the lila, the play of the gods," the baba said.

I stood up. The blood flowed hot into my thighs and legs. My feet could feel their thirst. I wanted to believe but could see only metaphor. I sat back down. Though my learning here was deeply spiritual, it was not for my own religious edification. I was trying to understand my Aji's music and the ballads I came from. My father's ancestors were mostly unlettered; our stories were invaluable—our literature bloomed as lotuses from our throats.

"Aur gaaiye ji, please sing some more," I asked. With a clap on my back the baba smiled and laughed. The sudden slap knocked the frustration out of me.

"One day your questions will change, beta."

The baba closed his eyes and out of his mouth streamed Bihari rice fields, mustard flowers, ancient kings, the gods, the monsoon clouds gathered in the courtyard above us and there was darkness. The baba lit a flame with his words and the sun shone through the rain and there was the earth under our feet.

We sat with the baba. The sun shone its brightest gold. Kumar looked at his watch and made a motion to leave. But I wasn't done. I touched the baba's foot and then my head. He blessed me in music.

"It looks like we have to go soon, but baba-ji, before we go, can you sing the oldest song you can remember? Like one of the songs that your mother or grandmother used to sing before you took brahmacharya and became a sannyasi." Only after I uttered these words did I realize what I had done. My heart pounded. My ears grew warm. I couldn't believe what I had just asked the baba. Was that thunder in the background or the sound of my pulse?

Becoming a mendicant meant that the baba would never marry— these ancestral songs that passed from grandparent to grandchild would meet a dead end. At least in linear Western thinking. For him, I suppose there was no difference between blood relations and strangers. As a sannyasi, he renounced his worldly attachments and familial bonds, staging a pretend cremation to sever all ties with where he came from before making the decision to live in an ashram as a mendicant, worshiping the Divine day and night. My mind was a small one, incapable of thinking beyond descent, trapped in the world of samsara. I was asking a holy person to reach back into their life of birth and death and to bring it forth. That past was dead to the sannyasi. What would he care about a stupid song sung by mortals?

The baba looked at me with stormy eyes. I was a koyal bird perched on a branch before the July deluge. I knew that I had crossed a line. I shifted my weight from one leg to the other as I sat. The breeze started to blow and dry the sweat creeping down my back. It was as if cold fingers traced my spine. A small sparrow eating rice flew away.

I smiled like an idiot at the baba and said in my Aji's Bhojpuri, "Bahut dur batiya hai, na baba? Such a distant thing, no baba? It's no matter."

He shook his head and said, "Of course I will sing. I was remembering back to the village where my mother gave birth."

Kumar and I exchanged glances. I exhaled a cloud and my shoulders fell.

"Ramayan ke upar this song is a purbik, an Eastern song. It's so old and I don't know exactly where it came from but it was sung in my village," the baba told us.

The afternoon sun began its burn, but we were shaded in the middle of the courtyard. The baba sang.

*avadh nagariya se nikale do kumar*
*dhanus leke chale gailan*

*kekahi mange bheje khatir*
*raja ke jaan bachaiyal manchwa par*
*ajodhya tohar hoijai*
*je mango to mango rani*

*ham mange, raja, tohar batiya*
*ham mange ram banbas jaye*
*aur bharat raja chalaye ho*
*je mango to mango rani*

I was a frozen stone. I couldn't believe that this baba at Ram Mandir ashram was singing my Aji's song almost word for word. Aji had been separated from India for over a century, but this song that I was hearing now was intact.

Two princes leave the town
carrying bows

Kaikeyi wished to exile them
having saved the king's life once.
Ayodhya is yours,
Whatever you wish for, ask.

I wish, King, for your boons.
I wish Ram exiled
and Bharat to rule the throne.
Whatever I wish for I ask.

I gulped. I looked around. The birds in the courtyard were listening, too. I was pecking at the grains of my connection to this place. The grass in the direct light began its daily wilt. I glanced at Kumar. He checked his watch again. My time with this baba was coming to an end.

"What else can you tell me about this song?" My mouth was dry. I surprised myself with the desperation in my voice.

"It's old is all I know. I know that women used to sing this kind of song about the *Ramayan*. I call it a purbik because it comes from east of here." The sun started to paint shadows of canyons on the baba's face. His skin sagged and folded too heavily for the muscle that once held it in place. I remembered Aji's own frame when she first sang her version of this song to me. The song itself showed that even queens are servants in their own homes; the feminist critique of this song would show the scars of patriarchy marring all the members of my family. My Nani, Aji, my mother, my sister, my queer kin, and my own body had been indelibly carved and scarred by this story. Sita was eventually swallowed by the earth as final proof that she was chaste, devoted to her husband when Ravan kidnapped her.

As an undergraduate I read about the Ramlila of Southall, that once in England in the 1970s, Caribbean women and Indian women came together to protest Enoch Powell's National Front. They told the story of empire and how it kidnapped others. My sister used to say the rhyme, "Ram and Sita been a ban / Ram fall down and bruk he han' / Sita cry *Maiya!*"

I thought of Aji and how I imagined her memory, her language, her Hindi as broken, and now sitting here in front of a man her age in Varanasi, I realized that Aji was whole. That I was whole.

"Baba-ji, I know this song. My Aji used to sing it to me and taught me the stories that you are telling me," I said with wide eyes.

"Sing for me the version you know," he smiled and looked at Kumar. I began.

*ham mange, raja, tohar batiya*
*ham mange ram banbas jaye*
*aur bharat raja chalaye ho*
*je mango to mango rani*

Everything around me stopped. The sparrows froze. The grass stopped wilting. The wind calmed. The clouds stood still. Even Kumar's watch stopped. For a moment I felt that I had made a real connection with this baba—that, singing his song back to him with a Guyanese accent, I had come from a tradition that had survived and changed in constant motion. I sang through my tears. A river raged behind my eyes. My lips quivered.

"Tohar Bhojpuri bahut sahi ba babua. Your Bhojpuri is very good," the baba exclaimed, nodding at Kumar who raised his eyebrows and nodded in agreement. "You keep saying the word Aji. Most people use the word *Dadi* instead. How come you know that word, too?"

"Aji is what I call her because that's what she said I should call her. Sometimes I call her Ajiya, or when I tease her, I call her Gangadai." The truth was that Aji felt like Aji not Dadi. Aji was Bhojpuri. Aji was Guyanese.

He laughed. "Ajiya—how sweet. And Gangadai? That name is very powerful, it means that you are definitely from this place and that her songs are gifts from the river, too."

I held my head high. Aji and the baba's family had come from the same song lineage. I was discovering the truths about my history—that being Guyanese did not mean that I was less Indian, it meant that I was a descendant of survivors. It meant I was strong.

"Achcha baba-ji," Kumar got up and folded his hands in namaste. It was time to go. Kumar had to get back to his other work and the ride home would be long.

I touched the baba's feet. "Thank you for the blessing of your music. It means so much to me that I heard you sing my Aji's song," I said.

"Jug jug jiye, beta. May you live long," he said with a smile.

As Kumar and I sped down the narrow gullies cluttered with women wrapped in saris, men with hennaed beards, children chasing puppies, there was only music. Music in the streets. Music in the cows. Music in the pigs. Music in the shop fronts. Music filling my ears. Music flooding my heart. The baba's words mixed with Aji's. *May you live long. May you live long. Jug jug jiye, beta.*

# Bhabhua Village

GOLLU, MY HINDI teacher's son, took me to Bhabhua Village, just outside of Varanasi, to the home of his friends—twins named Adish and Vagish. He sat me at the back of his motorcycle and we sped past the city and into the paddy fields that fringe the City of Light. The lane was lined in tall trees that offered shade and cooled the air. The balm of the paddy fields was a relief after the dust and dry heat of the city. Women wore saris and covered their heads and faces as they walked down the lane, water jugs atop their heads, paan in their mouths. Schoolgirls looked at us and giggled behind their fingers. A line of black buffaloes lumbered. In the gutter a pig muddied itself.

We reached the village house, which was more like a mansion made of fine brick and mortar. Adish and Vagish's family made a feast—cooking lamb especially for me, even though they didn't eat it themselves.

"Come, Rajiv, the food is ready. We have made lamb for Gollu and Adish, you should have some, too, if you want," said Auntie, Adish and Vagish's mother.

"Thank you, Auntie, but I can't eat any meat today."

"Why not?" she narrowed her eyes.

"This month is Maha Shivratri. . . ." I said. It was a time sacred to Lord Shiva, the god of Varanasi. My Aja's name was Sewdass—or Servant of Lord Shiva. To be in Benares and eat meat for me, as an outsider, would have been an insult even though I grew up eating everything. I could hear my Aji complain to me.

Auntie let out a laugh that shook the room. "Ai, hai, Rajiv has made you all into chutiyas, into assholes! He is not from here, but he observes his fast better than any of you do!" It was novel to hear a woman curse so loudly. Bhabhua Village was a fertile place.

After eating we climbed to the roof to watch the stars. Adish and Vagish's Aja was lying there on a cot and welcomed us. It was time to be formal. I'd heard that he was a severe old man.

"Come. Come. Sit next to me. You have come from far away, beta."

"Oh, yes, Aja, Benares to Bhabhua takes a while."

"No, you bahin-chod, I am talking about Amrika."

Everyone burst into laughter. He just called me a "sister-fucker." I'd never felt more lovingly insulted.

"I hear from Gollu that you like Bhojpuri music. Do you know any songs?"

"I know a couple that my Aji taught me—you know we've lived outside of India for over a century."

"So sing one in Bhojpuri, majaa jarur aiba, it will make all of us happy."

✿

I loved Bhojpuri. It was musical when spoken and had always been like a puzzle for me, a knotted skein of wool to untangle in my mouth. The language Guyanese Bhojpuri developed from an amalgamation of several North Indian languages such as Awadhi, Maithili, Oriya, Bengali, and Bhojpuri grammar (with loan words from Dutch, English, Creole, and Portuguese as well) into plantation-specific versions that émigrés could use to communicate with one another. Most people called this language Hindustani, as that's what the British planters and colonists called it. After one generation, the language regularized and developed a unique system of grammar and meaning: a Guyanese Indian language of its own, filled with history and power.

It was a language that upset the colonial hegemony of English domination, and as a matter of language evolution, it bore testament to the survival of the laborers, who despite being labeled as *Coolie* in all the colonial ledgers maintained a sense of their humanity. My Aja and Aji, second- and third-generation speakers for whom Guyanese Bhojpuri was a first language, did not pass their unique tongue to their children. In Guyana in the Westernizing decade of the 1950s, my Aja insisted that his children speak English and go to the Christian school. My Aja believed that reading was the key to his children's success: his sons and his daughters must learn, which ultimately meant that they must forget.

My Aji used to play these games where she would singsong phrases and ask me if I could understand. Once in Toronto I looked at her and asked her why she no longer made phulauri and she laughed and said, "Hai beta, jawani ke rail chala gail. You h'undahstan wha' me talk?"

*Jawani ke rail chala gail. Youth's train has departed.* Aji was so clever. She spoke in Bhojpuri metaphors. Mostly she talked about not being understood by her children's generation, who had all converted to Lutheranism—first for the opportunity to be educated and then to assimilate into white North American neighborhoods. I did not fault anyone for their acts of survival—what they must betray to continue.

One of her favorite songs was "Raat ke Sapna," originally recorded by Ramdew Chaitoe, then by Sundar Popo, and most famously by Babla & Kanchan. My cousin Jake referred to it as a *chune*, or a tune that needed to be played loudly. He sent me a remix that he recorded in his parents' basement and that now, in an Indian village, would come in handy. I couldn't wait to write to him and tell him about this.

❋

I looked at my palm. I imagined each line was a road that led me here. I was from this place, but from nowhere. I took a breath and thought of what village I must have come from. I began.

*Na more angane mein nimiya ke perwa*
*kekar chaaiya bithaiya hamko*

*In my courtyard, not a single neem tree—*
*In what shadow will he sit me?*

What courtyard did I belong to? Aja insisted that this was my new home. The stars shone down as Aja lay on his back and looked up. Adish admitted later that drops like pearls fell from his eyes.

# Neech

IN THE SPRING semester, I decided to take a trip by myself: half a test of my Hindi skills and half a test of my blood. I slid open the doors between railcars and lit a Capstan cigarette. The police usually pretended not to notice me if I offered them one. Fields and fields of mustard in bloom raced by me, a whir of green and yellow flowers. I wondered what it would be like if Bollywood film stars actually danced in these desi fields of mustard instead of in the flowered fields of Switzerland.

I went back to sit on my berth. An old man, likely in his late-sixties, looked at me curiously and asked how far I was going.

"Rudauli. You?" I replied.

"You're not from here, are you? You must be from Delhi? Mumbai?" The train bounced on its tracks.

I had been advised by my Hindi teachers to tell people that I was from the city as a way to excuse my lack of Bhojpuri and have my difference recognized. The hope was that I would get the same treatment as an Indian in university.

"Well, uncle, my family hasn't been here for a very long time. It's been over a century."

"Oh, you mean NRI."

Non-Resident Indian. I balked at the label. What did this even mean in my case? The India that I am from is not the India with the monstrous political borders that shut people out, but rather a different, older demon, that of colonial India—a British invention. In the Caribbean, *Indian* actually just meant people from East India. We didn't need to specify where exactly our families were from, although I did make the distinction that my mother's mother's family was from Madras—now Chennai. We were exploited for our labor, and India was erased from under our feet. Bhojpuri and Tamil were the rural languages of backdam, of road-end, of the Hindu, Muslim, and Christian diasporas from India.

I carried my Nana's autobiography with me. In 1885 his father left Kolkata aboard the SS *Bern* for Lusignan. In his early twenties he placed his hand on the Indian dirt and touched his heart before he boarded the ship, indentured by the British East India Company to work the Guyanese sugar plantations. He had come from the village Rudauli zila, Barabanki, Patgana, then in the United Provinces—firmly in the *Ramayana* belt. He stayed in Guyana and was allotted a land parcel as a settler, displacing indigenous people there. In this new space his children changed with the land. Their language standardized into Caribbean Hindi and then Guyanese Creole. Like our language, my family's caste identities transformed into a sleeping memory: unimportant and distant—a difference I would soon discover.

"Yes," I answered. I had learned to speak of myself in shortcuts. "We are NRIs who live now in Florida." A simplifying lie. I looked through the bars of the three-tiered sleeper car. Outside, villages and fields whirred past. Eastern Uttar Pradesh smelled like salt, toil, mustard, incense, and prayer. Somewhere a temple bell rang. Somewhere adhan broke out across the dawn.

"Good. We are almost to Allahabad. You will have to get down there and take another train to Barabanki," said the questioning passenger. He looked at the other men in the train car and said, "Desi murghi videsi chaal." Eastern Uttar Pradesh smeared its mustard and green in the background. *Indian chicken, foreign gait.* It was true. Even I laughed. I may have looked the same as everyone else in the train car but there was something about my gait, about my affect, that betrayed my upbringing.

At twenty-three I had my grandfather's frame and my mother's curls. Most people read me as belonging to Delhi or Kolkata—recognizably Indian, but with a marked difference. Perhaps it was my affect—being queer, having grown up Guyanese in Florida, having learned Hindi only from the age of fifteen, being driven to decode the mystery of my Aji's songs. I stuffed an invisible *gamcha* into my mouth to keep my secrets inside. If I revealed too much about my origins I would be shunned.

"Shukriya, thank you, uncle. I have never been there."

"May Ram bless you on your travels, beta."

As the train car pulled to a halt, outside India watched me back: goats and houses built on piles of brick, each marked with the name *Ram*, cows wandering unwatched; black buffalo driven by cowherds; butchers with skinned goats—the eyes still in—hanging from hooks in the window; sleeping dogs with severely damaged spines; old men streaking the streets with their streams of expectorated betel nut; the walls with their piss; boys riding two and three at a time on motorbikes.

I got down from the train in Allahabad and waited to transfer to one that went locally to Barabanki. Three women in niqab passed by me on the platform, followed by a child, maybe eleven, maybe ten, in a topi, hanging on to a red-and-green kite. I squatted down to wait for the next train, and it arrived within the hour. There was only one class of travel from Allahabad to Barabanki: general. I had only ever traveled in sleeper. The windows were open, barred with horizontal stainless steel rods to keep people from falling out. This train was orderly, unlike the previous one. It was sparsely populated. I could smell the man next to me: sandalwood and cumin. No one hung from the roof or the opened doors as in American fantasies. No one was interested in me, my Western jeans, my curious North and South Indian traits: round face, broad shoulders, dark color, my strange way of speaking.

※

At Barabanki I got down from the train and headed toward the closest paan stand that I could find. I had after all come "khaike paan Benares wala"—developing the habit of chewing betel nut.

"Ek tho do, bhaiya, give me one," I had become familiar with asking. The paan-wallah folded the betel nut into a paan leaf sprinkled with tobacco, black and brown goo, fennel, and elemental lime. I took the triangle and put it in my mouth. The supari was hard, like chewing someone else's teeth. Benares had spoiled me with its soft betel nut.

"Is there any place to stay here?" I asked. It was getting late and this place did not exist in guidebooks.

"Sorry, no hotels around," he replied, "but there is an ashram just there that you will most likely be able to sleep at tonight." He pointed down the street. "Take the left by the tree and walk until you see the building on the right. They will be starting arti in just a bit so you will be able to hear the evening prayers as well." As I walked down the street, my body knew where it was going. I heard the bells start to chime. Hands clapped out a rhythm. *Om jai jagdish hare. Victory to the god of the universe.* I took off my shoes and rang the temple bell as I entered. Everyone stood facing the shrine.

After the prayers had been offered everyone sat together and began talking: old and young men together. I wondered where the women were. One old man with missing teeth turned to me, "Where are you from?" he asked.

"I'm from here." My Hindi shook on my tongue.

"I mean where in India are you from?" He must have thought I was an idiot.

"Uncle, I mean I am actually from here—this very place."

Wide-eyed, he pointed down to the ground and said, "Aap hiyan ke hain?" He was so surprised that he had to repeat this phrase several times. Then he asked, "What's your caste?"

In Guyana there was a breakdown of caste identity. Brahmins, Shudras, and Dalits all did the same work and lived in the same logies. Caste was less damning there than the caste practices still thriving in South Asia. The truth is that my father's father was a Gwalbans Ahir, a cow-herd like Krishna, and we descended from King Yayati's son, Yadu; my mother was a Brahmin, the priestly caste on her father's side. My Nani, my mother's mother, was Tamilian and came from parents who were Christian converts. My Nani's mother was orphaned on the boat that reached Guyana on June 18, 1894. She may have had a Muslim mother and was adopted by a Black family in Annandale.

But according to legend, my father's ancestors were stripped of their titles and became Shudras, the lowest of the castes that were not Dalit. In fact, according to the Laws of Manu, if a Shudra man should marry a Brahmin woman, their offspring would be a special kind of Dalit called *Chandala*. Aji used to call us that when we frustrated her. "You a real Chandaal," she would say. There is not much of an accounting of the women's castes past my grandmothers. Even this is a too-convenient recounting, as we have been of mixed caste since 1864.

It was explained to me like this: since we had a Brahmin's "high blood" we were still able to do some inauspicious religious work—performing the funerary rights—despite being outside the caste system. According to the Vedas, I would have been a body-burner by caste, though I had lived a life of relative privilege in the United States without the direct oppression of caste inflicted on me.

If I admitted my caste story openly I would not be allowed inside the ashram. I would not have any access to my ancestral home. I would be shunned and considered dead. Of course, in Guyana I could claim to be an Ahir, following my father's father's caste. But I would do so knowing it was a lie, one that everyone in my family overlooked.

"I am a Brahmin. I descend from someone from this zila who was taken to South America in the year of 1885. His name was Sant Ram Mahraj and he lived in Patgana," I lied through my paan stains. Mahraj—not *Maharaja* as most people in the United States hear it—is a title given to a Brahmin as a sign of respect.

All the uncles looked at me and then at one another, stunned as though they had turned to bronze like the statue of Krishna in the background. He was my ancestor and relative on my father's side. Maybe it was my good luck or karma that led me to his temple in time for prayers.

The uncle with missing teeth was the first to respond. "Accha?" He scrambled to his feet and went into a back room. Three minutes later he emerged with a scrap of paper with something written on it in Hindi and placed it in my hands. "Don't open this as yet," he said. "Take this note and get on the train to Patranga—it's a twenty-minute ride into the village. When you get off the train walk to the end of the only road in the area. You will see a sari shop on your left. Go inside and give the shopkeeper this letter." His eyes sparkled with secrets.

This was all so mysterious. The pujari spoke up, "Beta, welcome, you can stay here tonight. There is some extra room available in the back. There are two boys about your age who are here from their villages learning the Vedas, so you can sleep with them."

I took my gym bag by the handles, shoved the paper scrap into my pocket, and followed the pujari into the dark room where I shed my clothes and climbed onto a cot that I shared with a man called Govinda. In our whispering at night he told me that he lived far from his village and that he left his wife pregnant three months prior. He liked my mother's name, Anjani, and promised to name his daughter after my mother so that his daughter, too, would be inspired by my ancestors' great adventure across the sea.

That night I felt through his chaddis for his hard penis. I closed my eyes and imagined the stars that my ancestors must have seen when they crossed the ocean. Those nights must have been dark and the stars so colorful. I entered into dreams.

✿

I woke up before dawn and took the first train to Patranga. Govinda led me to the platform and insisted that I ride it until I saw the sign—if I had questions, ask the older men. He also insisted that I ask for clarification when I didn't understand the Hindi or Awadhi spoken in this area so I wouldn't get lost. The problem was that the village that I was supposed to go to was called Patgana in my Nana's autobiography, *Lil Lil Dutty Build Dam*. In it he chronicled his rise to prominence in Georgetown, Guyana, as a politico and as a pandit, a learned man, someone who knows religious texts. My Nana had studied Tulsidas's *Shri Ramcharitmanas* all his life and would give mini sermons from it.

It was from this autobiography that I learned the name of the village that his father came from. It was called Patgana in 1885. In 2004 there was no Patgana on any map. None of the villages in Rudauli zila were called this—the closest village name was "Patranga"—the name the uncle had written down for me. I thought this an excusable mistake given our distance from this part of the world. Like my last name, Mohabir—pronounced "Maha-beer," the "O" miswritten by a British agent of the indenture machine. I decided to follow the uncle's directions and leave off being skeptical as an offering to Krishna.

I got down from the train and headed for the only street I could see. It was dusty and uncrowded by bicycles, motorbikes, rickshaws, or pedestrians. The more I walked the more doubt flowered in my stomach. Wildflowers with large fleshy petals that turned into wings—not wings like butterflies, but wings liked flying foxes—thrashing about, webbed and black.

The sari shop stood at the end of the row of shops, its doors gaping open like a mouth. Inside two men sat on the cushioned floor drinking chai and waiting for their first customers of the day. Outside they had already splashed water to calm the dust and keep it outside.

"Welcome, come in, come in. What can I do for you? Are you looking for a sari for your wife—or your mother?"

Wife. Another frequently asked question. *Are you married, bhai-sahib?* My *no* was always cause for concern. I usually replied with something like *I'll marry after my studies are finished.* It made good desi sense. Better to get my affairs in order before I got married and had children. But this was another lie that I had habituated into a queer truth. I would never marry a woman.

"Actually, you know, bhaiya, I'm not looking for a sari. I've come to speak with you." My voice quivered. "I was told to give this letter to you." I handed him the note scrawled on the paper scrap. I didn't know what to expect. Maybe the floor would melt, or my arms would fall off. Maybe he would grow wings and a vulture's beak and tear the flesh from my ribs. Maybe he would laugh. Maybe he would send me away, telling me to get the fuck out of this place.

He took the long strip of paper from me and uncurled it. He read it a couple of times and then showed it to the other man sitting on the cushion. He was taller, leaner, had broad shoulders and a face that made my knees weak. He leapt to his feet. I could see tears running down his cheeks. He threw himself onto me in a tight embrace.

"You've come back!" he exclaimed.

"I–er . . . are you my bhaiya?" I asked him if he was my older brother or kinsman.

"No. I'm Prem—I am your neighbor. My house in the village is the house right next to your ancestral home."

I was dumbfounded. I felt a singing in my ears and the flying fox flapped out of my throat as I gave a deep laugh. I laughed from the anguish of traveling. I laughed from the deepest pit of the Unknown that I feared would swallow me whole. I laughed until tears crawled their itch down my face and neck. I had come home.

He quickly mounted his motorbike and motioned for me to sit behind him and to hold onto his waist. If we were related, the connection wasn't too close for me to take joy in having him ride in front and holding him from behind. We wound the dusty avenue until we came upon a lane fringed with trees. He slowed his bike down so that all the people passing could see. They were carrying baskets, earthen pots, bags filled with sabzi, schoolbooks, puppies.

A group of about five boys and girls trailed us asked, "Bhaiya, who is this?" to which he replied, "Mera parosi, my neighbor has returned from abroad!" All of the children giggled at his outcry. I reached into my bag and withdrew a Dairy Milk chocolate bar and gave it to the eldest girl I saw. I knew this would come in handy. We rounded a corner and there was a large courtyard behind a kuaan, a well that connected this village temple to Durga.

"Before I take you to your home, you must come and eat with me. My mother will be so happy to see you," said Prem. We parked the bike at the side of the brick-and-stone house. The floor was a cool, polished linoleum, beautiful by any standard. Prem called out, "Ma. Come. Look who has come into our house." An old woman with her white hair tied back in a bun emerged in a tan-and-white sari.

"Who has come, beta?" she asked.

"It's our neighbor. He has come back from Guiana." He said it wrong. He said the colonial name, not *Guyana*—"Guy-anna"—but "Guee-anna." Land of tea and sugar. Land of gold.

"It can't be." She approached and came up close and looked me head to toe. I folded my hands.

"Sada pranam," I said as I reached down to touch her feet. She caught my hands on the way down and smiled.

"You must never touch the feet of someone whose caste is lower than yours," she said. "We are Kshatriyas, warriors and princes. You are Brahmin." I looked down at my feet, embarrassed by my faux pas. If she only knew. She laughed and commanded her daughter-in-law to bring in three plastic chairs for us to sit in. In she walked, her face covered by her pink sari. She placed the chairs in a triangle and went back to scrubbing the corridor floor on her hands and knees. I was shocked to see how this woman, my bhauji, worked while we all sat and talked.

"We are like the devas," Auntie broke the silence. "Two Kshatriyas and one Brahmin. How far have you come, beta?"

"I am now living in Florida, America, but I have been in Varanasi for the last year studying folk singing."

"What about your wife?" Again this question. I wanted to stop hiding. I wanted to tell them that I was queer. Queer sexually, queer religiously, queer by caste, and queer countried. I wanted to scream but I had to play this shadow game of hiding myself to learn anything about where I come from. I had to pretend to be a high-casted straight man.

"After I am done studying, then I will marry."

"That makes good sense," chirped Prem, looking over his shoulder at his wife. "Shilpa, bring the food. Can't you see that Rajiv is hungry?"

Auntie, too, chimed in. "Ohe bahu, bring the food. Rajiv has come from so far away and you have not even offered him water. Come." Shilpa approached, head and face still obscured by her sari, and offered me a glass of water. I hesitated and glanced from Prem to his mother. Prem looked at me. "Don't worry, it's filtered."

Unlike most anxieties, this one was well worth the worry. I had recently been diagnosed as having three intestinal parasites from drinking contaminated water. The worm *Ascaris lumbricoides* and giardia coiled about my intestines—hungry to be fed. The pain was crippling. Being bedridden for at least three days every two weeks was common. I felt like my insides were being stabbed and I would shit and vomit at the same time—sometimes unable even to stand up to make it to the squat toilets.

Shilpa brought out the stainless steel thalis with katoris of daal and fresh rotis. Before Prem took a bite he circled his thali with his water three times and poured a little out. Then he took a piece of roti and scooped some of the vegetables in it and muttered the bhojan mantra. I only caught the piece that I know:

*om sahnavavatu*
*sahnau bhunaktu*

*sahviryam karvavahe*
*tejasvina vadhitamastu*
*ma vidvisavahe*

*Together, may we be protected—*
*nourished together.*
*Let us join together to benefit humanity—*
*our learning be of joy.*
*Let us never be possessed by hate.*

With that blessing we ate the fruit of Shilpa's sweat.

❁

The time had come for Prem to take me to the village in Patranga. We had eaten and digested. It was now well into the afternoon, and I was anxious about continuing this journey. Again Prem tapped the back part of his motorcycle but this time he gave me a wink. I mounted and we sped from the side of his bungalow, around the kuaan, passed the temple to Durga, around the bend that led to the paddy fields. We kicked up dirt as we gained speed, dodging large stones in the road. Faces of people walking by raised their eyebrows in surprise. Brave dogs, excited by the commotion, raced behind trying to keep up with the bike. Tears streamed from my eyes. My heart leapt as we sped through the rice growing heavy on their stalks. I was finally going home, to the place I always referred to when explaining where I was "from." I thought, *My body is made of this earth, my blood of this very water.*

Above us the sky clouded. The nimbus were purple, swollen with rain. I was full, too. From all directions women sang kajari songs, songs pleading for their lovers to return to them, to save them from wasting away in anguish during the monsoons.

*barsan lage*
*saiya gaile bides*
*bole lautbe saawan mein*
*kali badariya*
*dardwa na jagao*

*Rain begins to fall,*
*my love is gone abroad,*
*said he'd return come Sawan.*
*Black cloud,*
*do not wake this pain.*

Aji used to sing these same kinds of songs. I wondered how many monsoons it had been since my family had returned to this balm, this cradle of song and peacock calls. Come the month of Sawan, the koyal bird begins her mourning. How those left behind must have called out for those who left. And when they didn't return, how they must have smashed their empty clay vessels on the ground.

˙Did these very fields, flooded with rain, collect her songs and nourish the rice in her anguish?

We reached the village in Patranga. The walls of the house were low, made of dried mud and straw. The roof was thatched.

Prem called out into the house. "Gita-bhabhi! Aa jao, come see who has returned." He grabbed for my shoulder and pushed me in front of him. A woman came out in a pink ghagra choli.

"Eh, Prem," she greeted him without a smile. "Who has come?" Her eyes narrowed as they looked me up and down. She tightened her eyebrows and tilted her head.

"This is your son, come home after all of these years," Prem beamed in Awadhi. "His name is Rajiv." Gita-bhabhi looked me over again. The lines in her face looked like some strange language. I looked to see if her eyes were like mine. Her skin was fairer than I imagined it would be from living in this house and working outside—which I assumed she did. Her eyes betrayed nothing. We stood watching each other.

Prem continued in Awadhi, "American to see if you . . . from a long time ago with the British to Guiana . . . Brahmin . . ." Gita-bhabhi grunted in understanding every time Prem asked, "Samjhe? Get it? This Awadhi that they were speaking was too deep, too different for me to follow. As far as I knew, my grandparents all spoke Bhojpuri; this was an alarming twist to my story.

Prem looked at me. "I am going to go back to my shop, you stay here and Ashok-bhaiya is coming back just now." He snapped his bike into gear off of its kickstand. Ashok-bhaiya was Gita-bhabhi's husband. He was able to speak English, Hindi, Awadhi, and Bhojpuri. He was coming home from work to speak with me.

Prem drove off in a cloud of dust; Gita-bhabhi and I stared at each other wide-eyed. She motioned, "Come inside. Have some water . . . must . . . exhausted," she spoke through her veil. We walked into the mud house and into the outdoor courtyard. It was a large square with a well pump in the middle. There were trees with wispy leaves in the center, a pile of stainless steel dishes piled up by the pipes, and a clothesline from one side to the other. Along the perimeter of the courtyard were rooms, four altogether, which opened out to this central hub of activity. The roof hung over the sides and provided shade in front of each room. The ground was cool. We sat down in the shade, I on a cot and she on the ground. Gita-bhabhi placed the glass in my hand and raised her palm and gestured for me to wait.

A man about my age ran into the courtyard. He wore a lungi and a polo shirt. Sweat dripped from his forehead. He looked at Gita-bhabhi. "Eh, Ma, is it true? Has he come back?" he asked, looking around until our eyes met. He ran up to me. I stood up. He threw his arms around my neck and kissed both of my cheeks. We introduced ourselves. No wife. Him neither. His name was Prashant and he had rushed back from a chai stand where he was hanging out with his friends.

"Do you know how we are related, Prashant?" I asked.

"We have to wait for papa to come to tell us exactly how we are connected." His Hindi was like liquid. He sat next to me on the cot looking at my face and curling his lips into a smile. His facial hair had just started coming in and he kept a moustache—typical of young men in their early twenties. He placed his hand on my knee. I didn't know exactly how to feel—my heart lurched as he continued to look at me. His mother watched us and smiled.

"You have another brother," she said to her son. I didn't ask how long we'd have to wait for Ashok-bhaiya to return from wherever he was. I wanted to sit in the shade of this home and to hear the wind against the thatched roof. The sound of footsteps and laughter. This mud, this courtyard must have heard so many songs. There was a knock at the door. Prashant rose to answer it.

"Yadav-sahib, you've come. Did you bring the wire?" Prashant's friend had been asked to work out some issues he was having with his CD player. I was struck by the name Yadav. It was the name that came from Yadu—my mythological ancestor. An Ahir like my father.

Gita-bhabhi didn't let him in. "He's an Ahir?" I asked Prashant. To which Prashant answered, "Neech hai voh. He's a low caste, a neech— he can't come inside." His Hindi was a dagger. *Neech*. It could also mean "lowlife" or "scum." If they had known just exactly who I was, I doubt I even would have been allowed in the village. I had come so far to be here. I had lied. Any gain was ill-begotten. I was a mixed-caste bastard.

Into the village house walked a middle-aged man dressed in slacks and a dress shirt. His appearance was neat, his clothes looked well colored, unlike the clothes that hung from the line. He rushed up to me. "I've come quickly from work because I heard that you had come." His English was flawless. "When did you arrive?"

I looked at my watch. It had been about an hour. "I just came, only," I replied, approximating Indian English. I looked at my feet and picked at the skin on my thumb.

"Welcome!" He rushed to embrace me. I reached down to touch his feet—I was home, after all. He let me touch his foot and then my heart. It was a gesture of putting someone above myself. It was my submitting to his accounting of a familial history.

Ashok-bhaiya grabbed my shoulder, squeezed it and motioned for me to sit on the cot. Gita-bhabhi and Prashant looked on at us. Prashant's teeth were straight and white. Gita's nose ring looked like a little flower adorning her face in gold. The earth of the courtyard was gold. The sun sneaking through the paddy fields and into this mehfil, this gathering, was gold.

Ashok worked as a teacher in a school in Patranga, teaching English and math.

"So you've come here to learn about your family, no?" he asked, wiping the dust from his glasses.

"Yes. I am living in Varanasi for the year."

"Ahh—Varanasi is a very good place. Your mother-father know you have come here?" he asked, crossing his legs and leaning in.

"Well—" I stammered. I hadn't told my mother and father that I was going to search North Indian villages to find our kin. They had heard so many things about India—some good, most terrible. Their memories had been colonized into believing India was the backward cradle of plague.

"This is your nanihal, the place of your mother's father. I am so glad that you have returned. We have waited a long time to hear from you."

I was shocked that they even knew anything about me—that we existed in the United States.

He continued, "Your nana came here in the nineteen-forties, yes? He bought a house in Allahabad and lived there with his family."

I nodded, dumbstruck. My Nana had indeed returned to live in Allahabad in the late 1940s—or was it the early 1950s? He sold all his things in Guyana and moved his then nine children to India. My Mausi had stories in which monkeys stole the roti from their rooftops when they were in the kitchen. But my grandfather was second generation: the first to be born in Guyana—what did he really know of living in India?

"He was a pandit, a learned man who studied the *Ramayan* and knew Bhojpuri, Awadhi, Sanskrit, and English," Ashok continued. I nodded excitedly.

"He also played the sitar and was an excellent musician."

These words echoed. This wasn't in any family stories. Maybe my Nana had played the hand cymbals, the manjira, during puja, but he certainly didn't play the sitar. I replied, "Actually, he didn't play the sitar."

Ashok-bhaiya furrowed his eyebrows. "Yes, he did. He gave great concerts in Allahabad and Varanasi."

My stomach sank. I had just eaten a stone. What did he mean? This was no longer my story. Up until this point the stories had aligned to create harmony. Now, this dissonance. I had come all this way—no, I thought, there is a mistake. I chimed up, "Are you sure?"

"Yes, your Nana moved here from Georgetown. Hang on, I have a picture of him I will show you." He got up and disappeared into the bedroom's shadows. When he emerged moments later, he clutched a picture that faded into sepia tones. He placed it in my hands. I looked at the image and then at my face reflected in the glass. The picture was a man sitting cross-legged holding a sitar. He wore a pagri, a turban. This was not my Nana. He had neither my Nana's dashing face with his chiseled jaw and almond eyes, nor his broad shoulders. What a waste. I had come so far, and for what?

"This is not my Nana," I choked. Tears began to cloud my eyes. I couldn't see nor could I think. Now what? Whose house was I in?

"Yes, it is," Ashok-bhaiya insisted. "We are your family. Your mother is from Georgetown, so was your Nana from here. This is your home."

I looked around. This meant that there was someone else whose family had crossed the Kalapani, bound by a contract of indentured servitude from the same zila that my Parnana had come. They lived in Georgetown. "Do you keep in touch with them today?" I asked.

"Yes, let me show you." He returned to his bedroom and came back with an envelope with a name written on the front with an address. The name was Hema Mahraj. I didn't know anyone by this name. I hung my head.

"This is not my rishtedaar—not anyone I am related to or know." My voice trailed off.

"Yes it is. We are your family," Ashok-bhaiya insisted, looking at me and curling his lips in a smile. "You should come and spend some time with us. Maybe even work the fields that you belong to. We have a rice crop to harvest. How long are you in Varanasi for?"

"I am here for at least another two months."

"Come back and spend at least two months with us. We will do your janeo, your sacred thread, and you can begin learning the Vedas—I know someone who can teach you." He looked over at Prashant. "Prashant would love it, too, to have a brother in the home."

I looked at Prashant and then at Gita-bhabhi. Their eyes reflected sunlight. I could see my silhouette in Prashant's eyes.

"Yes," I replied. "I will come back soon, but probably not for another year and a half. I have to return and finish my studies before I can afford to come back this far."

"That's a good idea," Ashok-bhaiya said. His face looked nothing like my Mamu's.

"That makes excellent sense. You will stay at least for a couple nights, now, though," he insisted.

"Well, I have to catch the last train to Barabanki this afternoon at five o'clock so I can be back in Varanasi before it's too late. I have to be back to school tomorrow. It's Monday and I am writing my thesis." The truth was I could have stayed a couple of days if I had wanted to. My professors would have understood.

Prashant looked at me with wide eyes. Ashok-bhaiya looked at him and then at me. "Actually, there's a bus that goes directly from here to Allahabad that you can catch. It's better than taking the train because if one arrives late to the station you will miss your connection. Better to take less of a risk." He was being helpful. I couldn't tell if he was hurt that I wasn't going to stay at least one night. I promised I would return, though. "Prashant will take you on his bike."

We passed another hour talking about my mother and father. He sent gifts with me: a silk dupatta for my mother and a cotton gamcha for my father.

I touched Ashok-bhaiya's feet and said *namaste* to Gita-bhabhi. She asked me to bring gold from America when I returned. I climbed on the back of Prashant's motorcycle and held his waist. We zipped past acres and acres of rice fields where women worked with their mothers and daughters, draped in colorful cloth. I could hear a woman's voice clearly as we stopped at an intersection. She was singing a song that begged her lover not to leave. I wondered about my great grandfather. Had anyone begged him not to leave? Did he meet this man, whose descendants I had just met, from Patranga in the shipyard at Kolkata or in Guyana? Surely they must have known of each other, coming from the same fields. Somewhere in all of this green was a village once called Patgana where I was from. Somewhere in time it slept, its women sang songs that welcomed men back from afar. Its courtyards witnessed the greatest of joys.

When the bus came, I boarded. I gave Prashant a hug. I would never see him again. He begged me to come back. He didn't even really know who I was. Would he have begged me if he knew that I was a neech, lower than the Yadav who wasn't allowed in his house? I turned to look at him. Prashant fell to my feet and touched them. From the bus window I watched him slowly disappear as we moved along, the bus creaking rhythm as it bounced over potholes and stones.

# Ganga Water

MY TIME IN India was ending and I still had so many questions. There were stories that I wanted to learn, more songs I wanted to record and sing. I had spent the rest of my time since returning from Patranga collecting as many Bhojpuri songs as I could about the *Ramayana*.

I went to Assi Ghat's pilgrims, to the local folk singers like Pintu Rai and Hiralal Yadav. I sat at the feet of the Dalit cook Shamma-Mayi who prepared food for the students and teachers at the University of Wisconsin program house. Everywhere I went there was song. Anytime I heard music I withdrew a blank cassette and the recorder I kept in my bag. I wanted to recount the ballads in the ways in which folks retold them. These unlettered people were keepers of vast poetic knowledge. Their morning prayers streaked the sky red as the sun rose daily over the Ganga ghat.

The story of Ram and Sita, of Lakshman and Hanuman, of Dasharatha and Ravan, had so many iterations. There were specific parts of the story that my Aji told and sang about that only exist in Bhojpuri songs by women. I wanted to somehow connect the songs my Aji sang in my own living room in Florida to those in Varanasi.

As the story goes, the evil queen Kaikeyi asks King Dasharath for two boons that he had promised her. I was interested in this Kaikeyi and whether or not she was really evil. Wasn't she just fulfilling her duty? If she hadn't asked for the boons, would the *Ramayana* ever have been written? In the folk songs, King Dasharath is ill—his finger is infected from a splinter. He sends for his favorite queen, who comes and tends to his wound. The king is so pleased in his fever that he promises to fulfill two wishes for the queen. Kaikeyi is more interested in her husband's health and says that she will make them later. It is later that she asks for Ram, the king's first son, to be exiled.

On one of the last mornings, I turned in a 179-page thesis with an appendix of songs I'd collected. I titled it *Bhojpuriya Lok-Git Mein Ramayan—The* Ramayan *in Bhojpuri Folksong: The Colloquial Interpretation of the* Ramayan *Narrative in Varanasi.* The title in academese was suggested to me by the program director. I wanted to title it something more exciting like *Exile / Banbas.*

Assi Ghat was a hum of activity. Vendors selling marigolds, neem sticks, gutka, and chai pleased their pilgrim customers. Mae, Jegga, and I met here for the best chai on the ghats.

"I'm drawn to the *Ramayan* story because it speaks to how my family has been separated from our stories and culture because of colonization. Sometimes I think of the demon as being all the bad things that face me," I said to Mae and Jegga. "Like if Ravan were homophobia or racism—demons to be defeated by the brave. Sometimes I imagine the story is about standing up to fear—like a David and Goliath story about empowering people."

"Yes, Rajiw, it's interesting, but also it's too bad how the *Ramayan* is used against Dalits and Muslims as though Ram's return to Ayodhya brought joy." Mae took a sip of her chai as we sat on the steps of Assi Ghat looking at the river. It was true—the *Ramayana* was used by religious conservatives to justify caste-based dharma: that the rightness of a person's actions was dependent on caste identity. In this way people were trapped in their statuses, which they could never really change, despite the Indian constitution's provisions for Dalit people. The *Ramayana* traded in caste identity: it could never be unproblematically liberating.

"Not to mention the Babri Masjid," Jegga said.

"Yes—true. Ram janambhumi—the whole idea is just ridiculous," I said. "These RSS-BJP assholes want to say that the Babri Masjid was on the birth-ground of Ram. Give me a break." The Babri Masjid was believed to be built in 1528 by Mir Baqi to honor the Mughal emperor Babur. This Ayodhya dispute was the cause of the 1992 riots across the country in a right-wing nationalist fever that threatened to burn India to the ground. Mobs of Hindus hunted and hacked Muslims to death.

The geopolitics of India could not be neatly separated from the contemporary practice of Hinduism. For me, the practice of Hinduism in the Caribbean—particularly in my family—felt anti-colonial and radical. It meant not venerating a white, British, blond-haired blue-eyed murti of Jesus. It meant honoring my name, Mohabir, as complicated as it was.

I laughed. "I mean look at the Ganga. It's filthy with human waste and dead animals. Also the ashes of everyone being cremated on Manikarnika Ghat and also Harishchandra Ghat. No wonder the dolphins are blind."

"Damn, that's harsh. Isn't your Aji named after the river?" Jegga asked. She was right. I couldn't explain my cognitive dissonance. I loved the river as I reviled it.

Mae, Jegga, and I finished our chai and smashed the red clay cups on the stone steps. The river was low today as it bore the ashes of countless people off into the sea and into the next world.

Around the corner the Tiwari brothers had installed a high-speed, cost-efficient telephone system that anyone could use without spending thousands of rupees per call to the United States. I went in, touched my hand to my heart in greeting, and stepped into the glass booth to dial my home phone number.

"Hello?" It was Emily.

"Em! It's Raim. What's up?" I asked.

"Raim! How are you? What are you doing?"

"I just had chai with Mae and Jegga—they send their regards," I said. "I am so excited to come home! I can't believe I leave India in a matter of days." I was leaving to go to Delhi in two days. The flight from Delhi would put me in transit for at least twenty-nine hours with a layover in Amsterdam.

Silence.

"Is everything okay?" I asked.

"Well, there's something that I need to tell you." She hesitated. "We were talking about you coming back home and Pap sat the family down on the couch. 'I think Raimie is gay,' he said. Mom looked at me and I looked at Emile who got up from the living room and went into the kitchen." Emile was never good at lying. "I asked Pap, 'What makes you say that?'" Emily continued. "'It's just a feeling I get. Raimie said that he used to believe that prayer worked, and I think that he prayed not to be gay and when that didn't work, he decided not to believe in God.'

"'And if he is?' Mom asked.

"And then he said, 'We'll cross that bridge when we get there.'"

Silence. I watched the red numbers counting my time on the phone flicker.

"Well, at least no one admitted knowing, even though you all did. Pap can just go on pretending like he doesn't know." We both laughed.

"Oh, rass," I ended our phone call. At least now I knew that Pap knew. I walked around the corner and up the steps into the house where I rented a room. It was time for me to rejoin my family. There was something that I needed to do for them, to connect me fully to the people I came from. I showered and changed my clothes.

❁

The next morning I put on a white kurta and dhoti, both newly bought. I walked down from the third floor of the Yadav's house and into the gully where the neighbors kept their water buffalo. I passed the temple on my left and climbed down the stairs. I turned onto the walk and headed toward Tulsi Ghat—the peaceful ghat where the poet Tulsidas was said to have written the Awadhi version of the *Sri Ramcharitmanas* that my Nana and Aji both cherished. I had collected a different version of this story through songs, and this felt right to me, too.

I waded in the water. The mud was hot on the river floor and it grabbed my feet as I walked into the brown water up to my chest. I took three handfuls of the Ganga and prayed over it and offered it to the sun.

I offered water for all of the ancestors that I knew, calling them each by name. I offered water for the ancestors whose names my family had forgotten. I offered water for my family, for Mom, Pap, Emily, Emile, and Emile's first child. I offered water for all those my brother and sister would bring into the world and for their offspring, too.

They say that bathing in the Ganga washes your sins away. I had many. Maybe it also helped to lessen the damage of our destitution through colonization, too, on some otherworldly level.

Varanasi was the home of the poets Tulsidas, Kabir, and Ravidas, among others. People were warned never to go and live in Varanasi because the city would infect you with poetry and God-fever.

Now I was ready to leave.

❖

# Prayer

The water winds pink with grit
where the Varuna stream
meets the Assi, the City of Light,
the city of Vishwanath and Ganga,
of silks, weavers, and paan,
on the ghats flower garlands,
clay chai cups, women in saris sing
with a dholak, at dawn the adhan calls
the city to prayer while downriver,
a man bathes his buffaloes' black skin
while bodies smolder on pyres,
pilgrims gather here to disappear
into eternity, a boatman says,

*Live here long enough*
   *and you will lose your mind*
*to God, look at Ravidas*
   *and Tulsidas—look at Kabir,*

bathing here removes sin;
once King Bhagirath performed
tapasya the waters crashed down
from heaven, through Shiva's dreads
to free his ancestors, but he performed a yagna
and I do not know any mantras—

as the first of my family to wade into the silt
for one hundred twenty-five years,
I hold each name
I remember as a prayer,
I cup my palms to the sun.

I offer water for Taylor, for Emile, for Emily,
for Surjnarine, Anjani Devi,
for Bhagwati Gangadai, Sewdass, Mahabir,
for Lachman, Phulkumari, Janghbahadur, Anupiya,
for Lakpat Singh, Tukrayan, Jakti Singh, Rampur-Nani Nandrani,
for Hari Prashad, Emma Louisa Vera,
for Sant Ram Mahraj, Etwariya, Arthur Vera, Maude Janaki Watson,
for Kisnasamy.

# Pap

WHEN I RETURNED to the United States, thirty pounds lighter than when I left from being infected with three parasites—*ascaris lumbricoides*, paratyphoid, and giardia—I was greeted by my family and friends holding signs that said, *Welcome Home Raimie*. India had changed me. But not in the spiritual sense that I had been expecting. Yes, I wore the kurta pajamas, the dhotis, the prayer beads made from amethyst to help my third eye open. And open it did. I saw that the ways that I used to think of India had been Orientalist. India was not any more spiritually advanced than the West—it was marketed to be so by The Beatles. It was a place of beauty, yes, and also dire poverty. I couldn't wait to tell Aji in person what I had done when I was there.

Old calypso blared from the tape deck. It was like I was eight years old again, taking a road trip from Orlando to Toronto to see Aji. Pap and I drove the 190 to the Queen Elizabeth Highway from Buffalo to Brampton. I couldn't understand all of the words—it was as though they were submerged in water and tinny. He sang the lyrics with relish, savoring their brine, a salt wind that once held the promise of crossing the sea to London where he would study with his older brother and wine the women with his faux British accent and penchant for American country music.

Pap sang:

*Dove and Pigeon were two good companions*
*I say, Dove and Pigeon were two good companions*

*But because of jealousy they both start to disagree*
*So Pigeon call a contest to prove to Dove that he is best.*

His singing Lord Nelson betrayed this mask made of tinned fish cans—everything foreign was somehow better than what was in the jungle. As a youth he must have turned up the radio every chance he got. Somehow the music would make him more American. Maybe I would do the same with Bollywood music? He wanted us to call him Papa but with British accents. Paa-pa for poppa—like the *A* in apple. The white flesh so alluring, he surely wanted it as his own.

Eventually as his beard grayed and he filled out from medium to large to extra-large, we shortened it to Pap. Pappy. Southern. Emily, Emile, and I grew into our skins in Florida after all. And now, the radio played his childhood in Guyana from its ribbons and magnetism.

He smiled as though there was a life we could never know, just beyond the strip of highway where we were headed, someplace where his kin waited for him with rum and his mother's pepper sauce. The tar of the road was Kalapani, black water, leading him home. Or maybe home was a moving target. He would whisper on the phone to his sisters and change his tone when I walked into the room. He'd smile, thinking he was holding a secret. I looked at him, back down to a medium, his skin blowing like white hair in the wind of the opened window. I had never known this man, this Pap.

Pap hated himself. Where he was from. The gods that sang him into life. After we came to the United States, he did his best to keep us from knowing our Indianness.

He would rather have silence than Sanskrit, hell than Hindi. To him everything Coolie was backwardness in motion. Our food. Our language. Our customs. Even our names. He started going by Glenn instead of his Surjnarine. These were the unspoken rules in the house until, at fifteen, I read the *Ramayana* for myself—a gift from a friend's mother.

Pap was furious about this self-acculturation and my interest in Hindi language—at least until he was with friends from "back home," and my hard-won knowledge was something he could leverage for social cachet. Like the lyrics to the songs from his childhood films.

"What does *mera jivan kora kagaz* mean?" Auntie Sonia asked to test me once. "My life is a blank page."

I turned up the volume and looked out of the window as upstate New York parted its green hills.

*I didn't have to figure; I knew Dove was smarter*
*Pigeon sure he had Dove covered*
*So he decide they would eat some pepper*
*He say, "One thing you must remember.*
*Eat all you want, don't ask for water."*
*Dove smile and said, "Agree."*
*And they both flew on the pepper tree.*

I asked, "Do you think that Aji will be buried like a Christian or cremated like a Hindu?"

Pap looked over from the steering wheel. "What do you mean? She's a Christian."

"No, she certainly is not." I did not make eye contact, just stared out of the window at the gray sky. This would be my first time seeing Aji since coming back from India. We were on our way to Toronto to celebrate the nikkah of one of Pap's friend's daughters but would stay with Aji. The bride's father and Pap were friends in Guyana. Though it would be a dry wedding, as both the bride and groom were Muslim, it was to be a big affair.

"You think you know my own mother better than I do—than the rest of her children do?" He puffed up his chest. Pap pointed a finger at my face. "She's *my* mother."

I wanted to break his hand. Instead I sang:

*Coo coo coo-coo bansimande*
*Necky yecky bansimande, wayo wayo bansimande*
*You mustn't say, suuuu-haaa, you mustn't say, suuuu-haaa*
*And nobody shouldn't say, suu-haa, suu-haa, suu-haa.*

I knew this song pretty well. When Pap was happy, he was all grace notes and melodies. When he was angry, he was a storm of fists and riding crops against child legs and arms. I sang along under my breath. These songs were different from Aji's, the songs I studied in India, but still they were home, Creole and ballad-like.

We drove a little farther. I knew that when my aunts would see me they would say, "Oh, look how dark you've become," or "My, Raimie, you've really put on some weight," even though I was parasite-thin. The road was a hum of asphalt and rubber that father and son knew well. Silence between us grew. I had secrets, too—like how I wished then that I could have a father as a friend.

What did he see when he looked at me? I said out of nowhere, "Do you know the story of Ardhnarishwar?"

"No. Who's da?" He thought he was being funny, speaking in Creole—it was his language of joking.

"It's a deity that's half Shiva and half Parvati. Part male and part female."

"Na na na na na na na. I don't want to hear about anything like that," he snapped.

"But it's interesting and important," I insisted. He was committed to ignoring me and my faggotry until one of us died.

"Why don't you ever want to talk about the weather or cars?" he asked. I looked at him. The car's interior was a dull gray plush. The lining of the windows, gray. The dashboard, gray. The carpets, gray. Colorless and bland—like my relationship with my father. He didn't actually want to know anything about me. It was easy for him—he wanted an uncomplicated relationship that required minimal effort. He wanted me

95

to worship him as the paragon of masculinity. I wondered if he knew the story about Raja Hiranyakashipu.

Pap pulled up at the nearest rest area and slammed the door as he got out of the car. I went to the field on the side of the rest area and picked a few wildflowers. When I got back to the car, I put the dandelion and Queen Anne's lace in the air conditioning vents. As soon as Pap returned, he pulled the flowers out and threw them out the window.

Coming with Pap was the only way that I could afford to visit Aji. She said that she had been dreaming of Aja. I never knew Aja except by stories. He was a strapping man with a barrel chest. Aji said that I resembled him, though she also said that to my other cousins. Aja was a merchant, studied in school, and was capable in rudimentary reading—so the stories go—but I was left wondering what was true and what was familial exaggeration. If I believed everything my father said about his father, then my Aja was a giant with the power of ten oxen, multilingual, and American before being American was cool.

Aja was born in Berbice and lived in Crabwood Creek—I heard from Auntie Pini, my father's cousin, that he was an alcoholic, drunk and swinging in his hammock in the bottom house by eight in the morning. Aja wanted a different life for his children and forced them to attend the Lutheran missionary school that set up shop on the north part of his property—a deal struck for land: your children could be educated for free.

The pastors required their parishioners to forget the perfume of sandalwood, the sohar songs that the aunties and mothers sang during the first nine days of a baby's birth.

They had to turn away from Phagwa's explosion of spring colors, to the clay, ghee, and warmth of Diwali flame. They had to change their names from Hindu ones to Christian names.

The pastor came from Canada. To him, Christian meant anything legible in North America. Many people in Crabwood Creek did this nominally, so I was told by Uncle Naresh. Pap didn't. Pap changed his name from Surjnarine to Glenn and performed his holiness as a Christian man.

I smirked to myself as we drove. *Whatever, Glenn.* The song played its saccharine hum.

*This time Dove eating and singing,*
*Bouncing, flapping his wing*
*Pigeon sure how he winning,*
*Eating like a champ, won't say a thing*
*Then all the birds gather 'round to see what was going on*
*Still Pigeon kept up the pace,*
*Confident he go win the race.*

Pap drove on, enjoying his brief foray into the Caribbean. I knew why this kind of calypso was big—it hid the trauma of being the son of an alcoholic. It allowed some kind of respite from feeling poverty. It let listeners imagine themselves as clever and as victors. What was life in Guyana like for him? I had been to Crabwood Creek once and it was very much how I imagined a developing nation would be: there was a road surrounded by black water trenches. Houses were built on stilts. People were poor, but they seemed to respect each other. Then why did Pap have so many stories about people who were idiots, people that he fooled?

Like the story of how he, Ghost, and Madan took a white sheet and hid in the trench one night. As the dhoti-clad pandit rode his bike down the lane, Milky Way in full view, they jumped out and frightened him. The pandit lost control of his bike and landed in the mud chanting the Hanuman Chalisa as protection against the evil spirit. He should have prayed for protection against evil-spirited children.

But to Pap this was more than just a prank. It somehow showed just how stupid people in Crabwood Creek were to him and his family. Especially Hindus. Even though he was born a Hindu—to two Hindus. He must have learned in Christian school how to hate where he came from. One way for him to distance himself from his neighbors was to believe that his new American affect made him better than his neighbors. He showed up to school one day in blue jeans and an Elvis pompadour. Everyone else wore their school costumes and Coolie hair.

Did Pap have to believe that he was superior to everyone in order to survive—in order to make a life that his father would be proud of? A life far from the rain forest and hassa? Is this why he preferred calypso to chutney songs—because with Harry Belafonte, calypso had more purchase in the Western world than Sundar Popo? For me, music was a vehicle into the deepest folds of memory. Pap had never been very forthcoming with his motivations. I looked at him. I could smell nostalgia and regret. He held countless secrets.

Pap moved to London when he was twenty-one. He admitted that he may have another son somewhere in the world, much to the shock of my mother, brother, sister, and me. His sisters sat together and said things like *It's so sad that Surj gave up his first child and now his family doesn't even want him around.*

I could imagine what life was like for him in London—he always said that he had to send money back to his mother, to Aji, for her to take care of the rest of the children. Pap was one of thirteen. Well—Aja had thirteen children and Aji had eleven. The other two, the firstborn, were the children of Multajin, a Muslim woman whom Aja "married" by common law and then hid in a chicken coop from his parents. Pap had followed Aja's lead. Did my secret brother have Pap's sharp nose? His rounded face and broad shoulders? Did he stand five-eleven and drink his tea with tinned milk? Did my brother smoke cigarettes and drink El Dorado? Did my brother ever beat his children until they were black-and-blue with a riding crop that he hid in his bed's headboard? Did he call his sons fat? Had my brother ever told his faggot son never to call him *father*?

*Friends, I know you won't believe me*
*But Sparrow was there, if I lie just ask he*
*When the pepper start to burn Pigeon*
*He spin round twice, Bip! he fall down*
*Dove start to jump up with glee up and down the pepper tree*
*He said, "Now take a tip from me.*
*Our friendship done because of jealousy."*

And here we drove across North America to see his mother. I looked at him and I didn't even really know him. What did he think about love? What were his life's regrets? Did he think that he'd outsmarted us all with the little effort he invested in our family? Did he ever love my mother? Could I ever forgive this man?

❉

After we arrived, I greeted Aji in my way: I bowed low and placed my forehead on her toes as she stood on the threshold of her house. "Jug jug jiye, beta," she blessed me.

"Beta, you come?" she said to both me and Pap. Her one-bedroom Brampton apartment was just as I'd last seen it, cluttered with pictures sent by her children and grandchildren. I saw a picture of Emile, Emily, and me when we were young and had just moved to Florida. Emile and I were wearing camouflage while Emily was tied up between us as though our prisoner of war.

Pap sat on the crushed-velvet couch. Aji brought him some barah and achar. It was already night.

"Aji, I have to tell you about India," I said. I'd brought several things for her. I handed her an ordhni made of silk and cotton. "Here Aji, I got you this ordhni, handwoven in Varanasi."

Aji took it and opened it up and wrapped it around her head. "Dis is good, t'anks a lot," she said. "Me go wear 'am to de nex' jhandi."

Pap turned his head and narrowed his eyes.

Aji's eyes blinked at me through her thick lenses.

"Also, I learned a song. I met a baba who lived in a Ram Mandir who sang a song just like the one you taught me." I looked at Pap. He was watching to see Aji's reaction.

"True?" Aji asked. "Sing 'am na den leh abi hear 'am?" She asked me to sing.

I began.

*kekahi mange bheje khatir*
*raja ke jaan bachaiyal manchwa par*
*ajodhya tohar hoijai*
*je mango to mango rani*

*ham mange, raja, tohar batiya*
*ham mange ram banbas jaye*
*aur bharat raja chalaye ho*
*je mango to mango rani*

"You hear da a India?" she asked. "Da is like me one."

"I know, Aji, can you imagine? India-man still a sing dis kine song," I said. I looked at Pap. "Aji is singing in Bhojpuri—it's an actual language."

Pap looked at me and at Aji. "They sing *that* broken Hindi song in Varanasi?" Pap asked.

"Yeah—it was an old, old man who recalled the oldest song he could," I said.

Pap looked away from me. "I thought it was broken Hindi," he said.

"No, Pap," I blinked. "It's a language called Bhojpuri." Pap took another sip from his cup. "I'm collecting as many songs as I can."

"That's a nice hobby," Pap dismissed. "Ma, is what time Sonia go come?" He put his empty plate on the floor.

"She go come jus' now," Aji replied. I picked up the plate from the floor and started to hum *Dove and pigeon were two good companions—I said dove and pigeon were two good companions.*

# The Last Time I Cut,
# A Journal

## 12/4/04

I've started seeing a therapist since I came back from Canada. Gainesville is an okay place, but it feels too small for me. I want to get out. I want to be in a city where there are more brown and queer people. I just don't work here. At University Club every guy that I've ever tried to talk to shuts me down. I'm invisible. Well, there is Tom. But he's not for the long term.

We met at UC and have a friend in common. He's getting a master's in literature. We've made out plenty, but it feels like it's just a way to pass the time—he's on his way to Boston soon, so what does it matter?

My therapist gave me a book today called *Living the Mindful Life* by Charles T. Tart. She thinks that I live in the future too much. I began it and it's about being mindful—like bringing your attention back into your body. She thinks that I live too much in my house of anxiety, that my mortar and brick are laid with doubt and steel me against the hurricanes of self-loathing. Every time the text is punctuated with the phrase "the bell is ringing" you have to come back into your body.

You have to feel your feet on the ground and slowly become aware of your calf muscles. Are they tense?

Then feel your knees and thighs, the pressure from sitting in a chair against them.

Your ass.

Your breath. Is it deep or shallow?

Your lower back and arms.

Your mouth and tongue.

It's called re-centering yourself as a way to come back into the moment and to stop living in the what ifs and what happeneds.

I am skeptical.

A book about Buddhist vipassana meditation written by a white man in the 1970s?

✻

## 12/7/04

Jimi is coming to visit me in Gainesville in March. He will stay with me and it will be perfect! We met at a queer Caribana party in Toronto I went to with Leila and danced to the old-school "Lotela," by Sonny Mann. I had just changed out of my kurta pajamas coming from a nikkah—one of Pap's friend's daughters—and there he was inside the club with curly hair and a mole on his cheek. I thought he saw me, too, as I glanced in.

The bouncer said to Leila, "Your cousin can come as long as he is an ally."

Leila laughed. I remember her leather boots up the knee and her curly hair gone mad.

And there Jimi stood. He looked at me. I couldn't breathe. His dark complexion was just like mine, round face, round eyes—eyes like a fish. His trainers were almost new, his T-shirt looked thin and blue.

I pulled Leila over and asked her, "Who is that? He is so beautiful."

Leila said, "He just said the same thing about you. You should go and talk to him."

I put down my rum and Coke and walked up to him. At this very moment "Lotela" started to play.

*Lotela khub lotela*
*Lote bhauji haan lote bhauji khub lotela*

Not the modern version with all kinds of instruments and electronic sounds—the one by Sonny Mann with just tassa drums and his voice. The kind that Aji used to play on her tinny record player, the kind that we dance to at family parties. It was so weird to hear it here where almost everyone was some shade of queer.

We danced and I leaned in and kissed him. He asked me to go home with him and I felt like I couldn't—I hadn't seen Leila since I came back from India and I wanted to spend time with her and her girlfriend. But Leila said that we should just go to her apartment together and that she and Yessinia would meet us there later. The music played on.

*Bhauji leke sabun khub nahayela*
*daru piye lagale bhauji khub lotela*

We held hands and walked down the road. I'm not sure which one—Dundass, Queen? I was still feeling a little tipsy and very giddy walking hand-in-hand with Jimi. A car sped by and a man shouted "fucking faggots." I withered and took my hand out of Jimi's. He held my elbow and slid his palm down back into my hand.

That night he said I was *bad*. In my head, a symphony.

*Lotela khub lotela*
*Lote bhauji haan lote bhauji khub lotela*

Did he mean that I was bad at sucking dick? Did he mean that I was bad as in *good* or *surprising*? Did he mean that I was bad because I was doing this in my cousin's home? Did he mean that I was a bad Hindu? Did he mean that I was a filthy fucking faggot who needs to go back to my own country? Did he mean that my parents would never accept me and that my entire extended family will disown me?

❈

## 12/12/04

I asked Andrei and Autumn whether they thought that if I were bad at sex it would be enough to make someone not love me. There are so many reasons I can think of that make me completely unlovable. For one, I am very hairy. I see people look at me when I have to take my shirt off in public. I try and try to love myself, but I just can't seem to make it work. This hair is like a hindrance to self-love. If only it would go away forever and then the boys at University Club would look at me and think I'm attractive.

Another thing that makes me unlovable is that I am thick. It seems everyone wants to be with a rail-thin blond boy—the complete opposite of what I am. I remember the old Baptist woman in Oviedo warned her daughter against me, telling her to stay away from that "big hairy Hindu monster." Oviedo and Chuluota are filled with this kind of thing. I am a monster—especially after 9/11. There's a white van with the words *BOMB THE RAG HEADS* painted on it that drives around and tailgates me every time I've been home since. *The bell is ringing.*

I feel invisible as a homo. I try to smile when I walk down the street so that white women are not afraid that I am a terrorist, or that I will try to harm them. It's like starting from a negative space. Gainesville is so close to Oviedo, only about an hour and a half away. I know that there are a lot of queer people in Toronto and there must be in New York, too.

❈

## 12/24/04

I came back to Chuluota for the winter break. I don't have to be back in Gainesville until the 28th. They gave me all the time off I needed from working the counter at Hollywood Video. Tonight, I sat across from Pap at Denny's after the Christmas Eve service, alongside Emily and Ma.

Pap's nose sloped into a dagger point and he thinned his lips.

"Na, na, na, na, na. I don't want to hear this."

Ma looked at me. Two years ago she told me to never tell him, that it would give him a heart attack—*he's very sick, don't you know?*

Emily looked at me. She has known since I've known.

"It's an abomination," Pap scowled. He looked at Ma. "This is your fault. You want me to be nicer to the kids. We never should have moved here. This never would've happened!" Pap slammed his fist on the table. The water in his glass trembled then erupted, spilling on Emily's red silk.

"What about Girlie and Dado? Didn't you say that there were two gay men that lived in Guyana that you knew?" Emily tried to come to my rescue. I was drowning.

"That was different. They were cured and married women and now have families," Pap retorted.

"But that doesn't mean they are not gay anymore—it just means that they are lying to their wives and children," Emily continued. It didn't matter. I looked down, imagining I could see my feet through the table and uneaten tuna melt. I tried to breathe deep into my stomach. I deserved to—

"Don't ever call me father again," he said, pointing his finger in my face.

Boys who fail their fathers deserve nothing.

❄

## 1/1/05

*. . . bell is ringing. The bell is ringing. The bell is ringing. The bell is ringing. The bell is ringing. The bell is ringing. The bell is ringing. The bell is ringing. The bell is ringing. The bell is ringing. The bell is ringing. The bell is ringing. The bell is ringing. The bell is ringing. The bell is ringing. The bell is ringing. The bell is ringing. The bell is ringing. The bell is ringing. The bell is ringing. The bell is ringing. The bell is ringing. The bell is ringing. The bell is ringing. The bell is ringing. The bell is ringing. The bell is ringing. The bell is ringing. The bell is ringing. The bell is ringing. The bell is ringing. The bell is ringing. The bell is ringing. The bell is ringing. The bell is ringing. The bell is ringing. The bell is ringing. The . . .*

❈

## 1/2/05 3 a.m.

My legs aren't legs. My eyes aren't eyes. My feet aren't feet. My fingers aren't fingers. My palms aren't palms. My skin isn't skin. My wrists aren't wrists.

*You are nothing.*

*No one will ever love you.*

*You are fat and hairy.*

*You can't even fuck right—an ass virgin at 24.*

*You will be disowned and then what will you have?*

*You can't even think for yourself.*

*You are so miserable, a good-for-nothing.*

*You deserve to be disowned.*

I can't scream with my mouth. People will hear. So I make mouths on my arm to scream their red for me.

❈

## 1/17/05

Today a package from Leila:
  pepper sauce
  stickers from Toronto's women's bookstore
  a rainbow pin
  a handwritten poem
  a book of poems by a gay Guyanese poet

Is it possible that there are others like me? Could gay Guyanese boys write poems people take seriously? Jimi is close—he's South Indian and I have Tamil ancestry on my mother's side. I sat down and began to write.

❀

## 3/17/05

Jimi finally came last week. I have been too busy to write anything down in a while. I wanted to be fully there in the moment. And now that he's gone, I want to remember every last detail.

"I need you to like me," I said. In order for the sex to work between us I needed to be confident that he really liked me, that this was not just some kind of fling that brings a Canadian down to Florida. Autumn and their new partner Kelsey said it was cool if he stayed with us.

We went to Lake Wauburg and rented a canoe. The day was bright, the sky's blue clear and cloudless. Floridian humidity permeated the air, yet it was still too cold to swim. Jimi, I don't think, had ever lake-canoed before.

The water was dark and like cola when we climbed into the canoe.

"There are so many kinds of animals that make homes in the water," I said. "You can't really see anything until it's like a couple feet away from you."

"What kinds of animals live here?" Jimi asked, his neck bruised with hickeys.

"There are herons, water moccasins, gar, all kinds of fish, frog and toad tadpoles, there are also alligators."

Jimi raised his eyebrows. The contrast of the dark brown, almost black irises with the eyes' whites was surprising and alarming.

"Don't worry—if you are respectful and stay clear of them, they won't bother you," I chuckled. I was lucky to have grown up in this deadly and beautiful landscape. Like walking alone in the woods, I didn't have to be anyone's son or anyone's Indian friend. I could see traces of animals, their telltale footprints, and then a white-tailed deer would leap across my path like a poem's volta.

Jimi splashed me with water from his paddle. "Holy shit! I think there's an alligator there!" He pointed to a four-foot alligator afloat on the surface in the sun and started to back-paddle.

"It's okay. You don't have to worry. You can't see what else is in this water very clearly. That alligator is tiny and most likely afraid of us. Its teeth look dangerous and its jaws are super powerful, but it doesn't mean that it will kill you," I said.

Being unforgiven for something intrinsic to me seemed like it would be terrifying, like it would have sharp teeth that could dismember me in minutes and hide my torso in the deep water until it began to rot.

As we paddled by, the alligator took a dive and disappeared into the dark.

But there was so much I couldn't see. Maybe the *bad* isn't so bad. Maybe in the present moment I can look at the alligator and know its danger and behold it. It wasn't biting me. It wasn't approaching. I knew that it was there but so were the sun on my skin and the breeze that kissed my neck. I was sitting in a canoe with another brown queer in Gainesville. I was so happy not to be alone.

We brought in our canoes and started to walk back to our car where it was parked along the road. We passed by a broad live oak tree. On the path a large swamp darner dragonfly fluttered on the pavement. It was dying. I'd seen this before. Dragonflies slow down before they die. But to die alone on cement seemed like a horror.

"The poor thing," Jimi crooned.

I leaned over and picked it up. Its wings buzzed just a couple times then it calmed down, expecting that I was a predator most likely. It gave in to its fate. I placed it on my palm and examined its blue and green stripes, its many eyes, and walked over to the live oak. I placed the dragonfly with many eyes on the grass just under it.

"Why did you do that?" Jimi asked.

"If I were a dragonfly, I'd much rather die under that tree than on the cement path," I said.

We drove home, where I made roti and aloo. We sat South Indian–style on the floor and ate until it was time to go to the Iron and Wine concert. When we came back, I put on a Susheela Raman album. It was the first time I slept with a man. I don't want the bells to ring. I want to linger here for a while. I want to remember this.

※

## 3/20/05

I saw the therapist again today and told her about how I wept when I took Jimi to the airport. I didn't know if we would see each other again. She remarked that my wrists looked great from New Year's and that I was doing a good job of breathing. I don't think I'm doing a good job. I'm just hanging on. I told her that there are brown faggots in the world and that I am not the only one. I could stay in the Orlando area and pray for a brown gay community or I could try to make my way to New York or Toronto to be closer to Jimi. Honestly, I could get a job at Whole Foods or something there and go be young brown and queer in a big city.

I have been checking the phone almost every hour to see if it's flashing with a voicemail. We talk on the phone and Jimi says that he is going to try to come back to visit me after pride. But what if he finds someone by then? June is three months away! What if he doesn't love me? What if he thinks that I am too young for him? He's 30 and I just turned 24. That's not that big of an age gap. My Nana was seventeen years older than Nani. What if he thinks I'm stupid? What if he realizes that I'm no one, a nothing? What if he really thinks I'm *bad*?

❁

**4/30/05**

I haven't heard from Jimi in the last couple of days. *The bell is ringing.* He is coming in June. *The bell is ringing.* I've stopped seeing my therapist. *The bell is ringing.* I'm breathing deep. *The bell is ringing.* I graduate in a few days with my bachelor's degree in religious studies and minors in anthropology and teaching English as a second language. *The bell is ringing.* When Jimi comes back, we will take a road trip to New Orleans. I've never been. *The bell is ringing. The bell is ringing. The bell is ringing.*

❁

**5/1/05**

*Fucking faggot.*
   *Abomination.*
   *Coolie.*
   *Crab-dog bitch.*
   *Brown piece of shit.*
   *The world would be better without you in it.*
   *You are a failure of a son.*

❁

**5/5/05**

Graduation. Who cares? I didn't want to walk, but Mom and Pap forced me. They weren't too thrilled by my degree anyway. I told them that I didn't want to study microbiology in my sophomore year. I didn't even know if Pap really even understood what that was. He heard the word "biology" in it and assumed that it meant premed. I drove to Chuluota to tell them that I had changed my major from microbiology to religious studies and that I wanted to study folk iterations of the *Ramayana*.

"You need to know the difference between a hobby and what can lead to a career," Mom said from the counter. Pap sat on the wicker-seated stool next to her.

"What are you going to do with a degree like that? It's worthless," Pap said.

"At least I will be happy instead of studying something that you were never able to do." I sat on the counter in the kitchen facing them.

"When you're hungry, you'll eat happiness?" Pap looked at me.

"We've sacrificed so much for you already and this is what you want?" Mom said. "At least do something that can get you a job." Mom's forehead lines betrayed her worry. Her own husband didn't have a job. I wonder if she was talking to me or to Pap.

Well, they came anyway and acted like they weren't impressed. I mean, Emile never finished college and neither did Pap. Mom only went to college after I was in middle school, so you'd think they would treat this like something special.

I was accepted to YSS—Youth Solidarity Summer, a program for leftist South Asians in New York in August. But before that Jimi comes. I can't wait until he gets here.

**6/30/05**

How can I be whole again? Jimi came. He and his ex are getting back together. They hung out at pride. And fucked and fucked, I'm sure. I can't believe that he came down anyway and told me "We can have sex if we deserve it." What the hell is that supposed to mean?

He looked at my wrists and said, "Those look fresh. When did you cut?"

"A couple of weeks ago," I said, pulling my sleeves down. I wanted to shut all of my doors to him. I should have kicked him out of the car.

I can't believe I drove him all the way to New Orleans. After I did, he said he wanted to spend time by himself in this city because I didn't know the underground scene here—what the activists were up to. How the hell am I supposed to know what the leftists are doing in New Orleans?

I brought him a piece of cake and he stopped showering to keep me away from him.

When we checked into our hotel room it was on Philip Street—the fucking name of his fucking ex—I fell through the floor. I wanted to vanish like smoke, wispy and feathery here and then gone. I knew this would happen. I knew that he would find someone else. I knew that I was unlovable. Why did he have to come down? Why didn't he just tell me on the phone that it was over? Why did he make me waste my time and money? Why did I give him so much space in my heart?

Leila said she happened to see him in the airport in Toronto as she was dropping off her dad, and he seemed pretty peppy. I bet he was fucking laughing to be rid of me.

One day I will see him again and I will show him just what he's missing. I will do something good and helpful to people. I wrote three poems that I showed Leila and she said that she liked them. I don't know—who writes poems? Not brown kids who are supposed to be doctors. But then again brown boys who are supposed to be doctors aren't supposed to suck dick, either.

✿

7/1/05

Night still. A hollow
dovetailing dark I've made

a home. In Ocala National Forest,
I place a dying dragonfly

under an oak. Under
my shadow, lake water,

an alligator watches.
God of death, Goddess

of hearth when you churn
the milk sea: before nectar,

poison. Before kindness,
ruin.

# Antiman

WHEN I GOT to New York from Florida wearing a Students for the Ethical Treatment of Animals T-shirt I had rescued from a pile of rags, my Pupha arrived with Jake to pick me up from LaGuardia. I'd come to New York for a five-day conference called YSS, Youth Solidarity Summer, in which radical South Asian youth from all over the country could network in a progressive space that wasn't a Hindu marriage camp.

"You look so gay with that headband." That was Jake's version of *namaste bhai*. Jake had always been a bit awkward around people. Most of his friends were his cousins and other family members. His stare stripped me naked in public.

I looked up to see if my uncle had heard, but his head was nodding rhythmically to Mohammed Rafi on the radio: *Sajan re, jhoot na bolo* ("My love, do not tell lies").

"Keep your voice down," I said.

❀

I walked into the long, narrow home in Richmond Hill, Queens. The smell of saltfish frying with wiri wiri peppers and aloo struck me. Pua was up early, her hair grayed in streaks, and dyed back in an electric red—in what I called *Coolie red*, which looked like fire in the sun. The scent of her unique spice mix clung to the walls like oil paintings, perfuming my clothes. It was the smell of ocean, salt, cumin, and frying bread. It smelled like my grandmother—like home. My first day in New

York had a scent of promise. The city's bouquet always enticed when I was excited to be there; its fetor repulsed when life became complicated.

My aunt held a metal spoon and bathed the frying bake in a splash of hot oil. "I thought I'd make a little chikna for your first day. You can eat some now while the bake is still hot. Here, take a plate," she said, a red-lipsticked smile framing her teeth.

She put her spoon down and placed the ceramic plate in my hand and scooped out some fish and flapped a fresh bake onto my plate. The bread was sweet with sugar and the fish salted, preserved in crystal. Such a unity of seeming opposites—just like Pua and Pupha, together in a dish.

Pua came to Canada as a tourist when she was eighteen, having just finished school in Berbice. Her English must have been all kinds of Creole and Coolie—in fact she still talked with a lilt despite her being here for over thirty years. Pap said that her accent was like jeera in the rice; masala in the daal. It's what makes her speaking beautiful. When she was here as a tourist, my father's old classmate admitted finally that he wanted to marry her.

At first Aji was vexed, but ultimately my father, her second-eldest son, brokered their union. Pupha and Pua married in a simple court ceremony and began preparing the paperwork for her green card. They moved to New York City twenty or so years later. It was a simpler time for my family. We were able to come to this country on sponsorships and marry to stay here. Pupha was a mild man, filled with uncle jokes, and had a generous but goofy spirit.

They eventually had a wedding—she wrapped in a yellow sari, he in a pink jama-jorda. The oblations of ghee, kapoor, lawa, and incense fed the hawan's flame. They took their marital steps and traded garlands—something I would never do. Marriage, a marro, a hawan, a pandit. Who would stoke this flame for fags, a marriage flame to feed the bed and the hearth? I was not even certain that *marriage* was an institution worth upholding.

❋

The next morning, I took the A train to 14th Street and 8th Ave to the first meeting in the Brecht Forum, the Lefty space in the Meatpacking District right across from the West Side Highway and the Hudson. When Prahlad walked in, everyone's heads turned. His wild curls bounced to the rhythm of his feet. It was a cultural show, and he stamped barefooted on the hardwood. He brought his ghunghru, his dancer's anklets, that wound as snakes up his wiry legs. The audience intoned the Adi tala while he danced.

He had come in late. *India Standard Time, Brown Time*, I thought. Tucking a curl behind his ear, he looked around and found an empty seat in the corner, right next to me. Goosebumps rose on my arms, feeling the movement of air inspired by his motions. He was slim but sturdy with skin as dark as a date, and most likely as sweet, judging from the scent of attar that wafted in with him. Incense and curry. He was like a daily prayer: familiar and moving.

I don't remember which workshop was happening—maybe it was the one led by Zahir, where we were divided up into groups based on the places in South Asia we were "from." This felt like another way that subcontinental South Asians showed me my outsideness.

For this activity, my group with two others—a queer transnational adoptee from Baltimore, Ryan, and an East African Ismaili, Hayat—drew maps of India, the Caribbean, Kenya, and the US on a length of brown butcher paper. We scribbled in crayon and the paper did not stretch far enough to make the distance between all of these places we were "from" seem realistic. Our countries were collapsible into a wall decoration.

"This shit is so messed up," Ryan laughed. He was tall and stunning, his curly hair cropped short on his head.

"Yeah—like why is it that people from the subcontinent want to tell us other darkies that we're not Desi enough?" I said back.

Ryan looked at me and smiled with his entire face. "Right on, Rajiv—I know, it's so weird answering all the questions. Like where in India are you from, what do your parents do. It's bullshit."

I nodded. "Even in this activity the 'real' Desis literally put us on the outside. Like shit. Why are there no other Indo-Caribbean people here—"

"Right? and why are there no other transnational adoptees here either?" Ryan shook his head. His pierced tragus and long neck shook as if dancing to music. I'd met someone who understood me.

I sketched Guyana by way of the United Provinces in 1890. I know my patrilineal ship was called the SS *Jura* and left from Kolkata and landed in Skeldon, where my family charred in the tropical sun, broke their backs burning cane fields, cutting cane, and hauling it to the punts. They chipped their teeth on the provisions of tinned fish and mutton and drank rum to forget the heartbreak of being exiled from home. Even if they returned to India, their families would never recognize them, so distorted and discolored by toil and sun.

Prahlad's skin was smooth; his smile made my stomach lurch. Our eyes met. I could feel the heat radiating off his neck as he stretched to pick up an orange crayon.

"I'm Tamilian." He looked directly into my eyes and greeted me with a smile.

"Uhh—hi, Tamilian," my voice cracked. I was trying to be funny. Crash and burn right into the cane field.

"No, I mean," he said pointing to the map that my mini group was drawing, "my family is from Tamil Nadu."

"So that would be . . . where exactly?" I asked. Of course I knew where Tamil Nadu was. God, what an idiot I am sometimes.

Prahlad pointed to the southernmost tip of Indian peninsula. "I'm from there." He grazed my pinky with his finger where he touched the map. Our eyes met again only this time he looked down, smiling.

I drew a stick figure with curly hair on the butcher paper.

"Look, it's you. What's your name?" I asked, my smile spreading wide now.

"Prahlad."

"As in the child who sat in flame and would not be burned?" I recalled something about sitting in someone's lap, too. I touched his shoulder and could feel the slight and firm muscles under his shirt.

"So mythological, no? I like being named after a flamer." He winked at me and grinned. He looked at me and touched my knee. On my skin: an explosion of fire.

❀

When I got back to Pua's home in Richmond Hill I found Jake in his room working on his computer. The floor creaked as I walked.

I knocked on the door and sat on the bed facing the computer desk. The room was small, just fitting a full-size bed and a small desk.

"I met some guy today who's totally hot," I whispered. I looked at the door I'd shut when I came in.

"Oh, yeah? What's he like?" Jake turned from his work to face me.

"His name is Prahlad and he's from Jersey," I said.

"Oh. Is he gay, too?" Jake's voice trembled slightly.

"Yeah, I mean definitely." Outside the sky was darkening.

"What does he look like?" Jake asked.

"He has long curly hair and is very slim—his family is Tamilian I think. He's also a dancer—classical Indian."

Jake laughed. "Definitely sounds gay." He turned back to his work. I picked up my book and read for about twenty minutes before getting up to take a shower.

Later that night we went to eat dinner with Pua and Pupha downstairs. Pua looked at me and set the daal and rice dishes on the table.

"Pupha, Jake, and I are going to Toronto to see Ma over the long weekend. That means that you will have to be here by yourself. Is that okay?"

"It's not a problem. I'm sorry that I don't have much time to hang out anyway because of this conference. It looks like they have us really busy. Just let me know if there's anything you want me to do while you're away."

"You can begin with eating! Your food is getting cold!"

That night they packed their Cadillac and left in a puff of non-EPA-compliant exhaust.

✿

The week passed quickly. I got close with Ryan and Farida, who lived in Queens. Farida pulled me aside after one workshop about the differences between reform and revolution: reform being coded liberal doublespeak about maintaining the systems that privilege the upper-casted, the white, the cisgender, straight, normative power. Revolution, instead, offered a whole new ground upon which we could build equitable foundations together.

"I like how you think and speak," Farida's cheeks pinkened. "You and I are a lot alike."

I smiled, insecure in my own intelligence and activist leanings.

Prahlad and I spent lunches and workshops finding moments for our arms to touch, to rub each other's backs—sore from sitting too long in conference chairs—to tease the curls from our hair. On Tuesday he found me and sat next to me in the circle. He drew his plastic chair closer and his thigh heated mine. On Wednesday we walked to the park across from the West Side Highway in the Meatpacking District and I kissed him. We walked side by side discussing the importance of South Asian activism on our college campuses and our respective student body's failures to diversify their political actions, when I grabbed his arm and pressed my lips into his soft neck. We stood on the grass, cars hummed past us in puffs of smoke. We walked hand in hand from then on, along the Hudson overlooking Jersey.

On Thursday, the night before the workshop's final party, we drank Jameson from the bottle and traipsed through the East Village, looking for various queer spots to make out in. Or we made out on the street, and made those places into queer spots. We were fairies that turned public spaces into private ones. Saint Marks and 3rd Ave to Thompson Square Park—where instead of squirrels, rats are the tree lords. We kissed under the honeysuckle and marquees. The red fluorescent lights painted our skins in flames.

"Do you know where we should go?" I asked.

"Let's go to my friend's apartment. She's not there tonight and she's cool with people coming and hanging."

We took the elevator to the roof overlooking the Financial District. As the door closed, we reached for each other. His attar was a perfume dressed in Jameson. We were a tangle of hair and brown brawn. I could feel him bulge beneath his denim. He licked my neck. The wood veneer door closed in front of us and I fell on my knees, back to the door and ran my fingers along Prahlad's zipper. He gasped. I had wanted to do this the first time our fingers touched. He closed his eyes. I could no longer wait.

The door opened on floor 15 to a surprised blonde in a leather jacket. She stammered and refused to get in as Prahlad pressed the "close door" button with a fury. I looked up and we both burst into laughter that did not abate for the rest of the week.

We poured forth onto this landscaped roof now closed to the public, a queer version of privacy, giggling and giddy, walking hand in hand.

We found a place to sit where New York lay before us, spread-eagle and eager. We huddled together, his head on my shoulder and my head on his. We laughed at the sheer impossibility and ephemeral nature of this connection—a Desi and a Coolie on the same roof for a single moment. I knew I would have to put my shirt back on, slip my feet back into my shoes and walk away in a couple of days. I thought of Pua. Would she have any idea what this could mean? I was so excited about this new life; I wanted to share it with everyone. I was getting the hang of being open about queerness. I wondered then, would our own grandparents even recognize us? This connection? We gazed out at the cityscape, looking for clusters of buildings, locating the ones we knew: Chrysler, Empire State, and the Statue.

"I really want to go to the party with you," Prahlad said, I felt his breath on my neck.

"Like, as my date?"

"Yeah."

"Cool." I tried to conceal my heartbeat flapping like a bird in my throat. I didn't care about what would become of us.

✻

The morning of the conference's culminating event involved a direct action. We would circle outside Karachi Delight, an immigrant-owned-and-operated restaurant in Jackson Heights that perpetrated known abuses of undocumented workers. Unfair wages for slavery. Ryan, Farida, Prahlad, and I along with the rest of the YSS participants brought materials for our signs. Markers, poster board, and righteous anger were the ingredients to brew this protest.

We spent three days researching the laws around workers' rights and found that despite their legal status in the state of New York, they were entitled to minimum wage and overtime pay. Karachi Delight provided neither.

A worker named Asif-bhaiya spoke out in Urdu. "I came to this country and my cousin said that I would be able to work in this restaurant where his friend's the owner. I would have to wait tables. When I got here, I was put to work in the kitchen. The ventilation was poor and I was forced to work eighty hours a week without overtime. The manager threatened to report me to the authorities if I didn't comply." He wiped his eyes with his fingers. I glanced across the room to see that Prahlad's eyes searched back for mine.

"Asif-bhaiya, why didn't you go to the police?" one girl asked. "I mean, if you have these rights, you should go and tell them what's happening."

"If I go, bahin-ji, then I will not only be putting myself at risk, but also the other workers. The manager said that if any of us go to the authorities, our wages will be withheld and he will deny that we ever worked there." He trembled. "How will I feed my son and daughter?" He folded his head into his arm.

How could brown folks shapeshift into terrible beasts akin to overlords on the sugar plantations? How could brown folks do this to brown folks? Something about it made sense in my own family history—the arkotiya, or recruiters, for the British were Indians themselves. They made money for every person who stamped their thumbprints onto contracts that bound them to torment in five-year terms. My ancestors were brought to Guyana like this. This current immigrant struggle was related but different. All these oppressions felt resonant with one another.

We listened. I went to stand next to Prahlad and grabbed his hand and squeezed it. Ryan looked over at me and raised his eyebrows. Anger swelled in my stomach. Of the forty of us gathered, we all wanted to take down Karachi Delight—how could someone from our community of South Asian immigrants exploit one of our own?

"How do you say *justice* in Urdu?" I asked, clutching a marker in my hand.

"Insaaf," replied Zahir.

"It sounds like *insaan*, or *human*." I gritted my teeth and thought *nainsaan—nonhuman, antihuman, antiman*. I gripped the marker tighter until my hands were pale with rage.

On a piece of poster board I wrote: *Insaaf Zindabaad! Long live justice!*

✺

Morning in Jackson Heights, the adhan is the only thing missing. Otherwise there are vegetable sellers spraying water on the cement, chai stalls frying jalebis, and even the bhangra music shops playing their songs. The city outside the city awoke to chai and chaat.

There's no street food like that in India and there is no India like that found in Jackson Heights.

At eleven, aunties gathered to buy their food for the day and young men began distributing their leaflets in their tight jeans and paan-stained teeth: Palm Readers/Jyotish by Karan. On Roosevelt Ave: above, the 7 train rumbled along; below, samosas fried to a golden brown. Sweets shone, begging a tongue to lick them.

That afternoon we marched on the Jackson Heights streets from the corner of 73rd Street and 37th Ave to Karachi Delight chanting, *The people united will never be defeated!* picketing with our handmade trilingual signs. Onlookers gathered around us.

Young men with budding beards. *The people united will never be defeated!* Old Bangladeshi men with beards reddened with henna. Aunties in hijab, aunties in saris. *The people united will never be defeated!* Dominican high school kids in backpacks and braces. *The people united will never be defeated!* Young Colombian fags and their queeny friends. Arab and Iranian women, men. *The people united will never be defeated!* From the Filipinos, femmes, and hipsters. Prahlad and I picketed together. He was in front of me. His dancer's frame pranced his indignation in furious stamping. Ryan and Farida also stomped and shouted.

Confused, the manager exited Karachi Delight and looked at us in the face. He asked Prahlad, "What do you mean, coming here? Have you no shame?" He threw up his hand with a flick of the wrist.

*The people united will never be defeated!*

Prahlad's hand clasped mine in prayer. Being in this crowd of people fighting for ethical treatment of others, my heart beat its *dhol* as though I was in a wedding processional. My voice was raw from screaming,

*The people united will never be defeated!* But I didn't care. I screamed louder. My body was exhausted, my knees trembled. I believed in this because I had to. I had to believe that others were willing to raise their voices to stop dehumanization.

Prahlad shouted in return to the manager, "Do you have any shame, riding these people as though they are donkeys?" He furrowed his brows and pointed at the critical mass of brown bodies. I could feel his words echo in my chest.

The manager picked up his cell phone and dialed a number. He paced back and forth speaking with the person on the other end. His Punjabi was fast and his swearing was guttural. I only caught some of what he was saying. Beneath the "mother/sister/goat/pig fuckers" was something about being afraid of the police. The person on the other end must have been the owner, who encouraged the manager to shut down for the day.

With that, Karachi Heights closed its metal grate. *The people united will never be defeated!*

We left with this simple satisfaction.

Prahlad turned to me then and said, "I'm so tired, I will need to take a nap before we go to the party tonight. If not, I'm likely to fall asleep."

Was Prahlad saying that he wanted to go home without me and take a nap or meet up again? I thought of the time we spent together throughout the west and east sides—huddling in corners of the avenues, behind the large subway maps installed as art that divided the subway platforms. I imagined him saying he wanted to suck someone else's dick before we hooked up for the final time that night. Were we over before the conference was?

"Come with me," he whispered and licked his lips.

I cleared my throat.

❖

We slept on the couch of his friend's Financial District apartment after taking a hurried shower to wash the city's grit from the folds of our skin, between the legs and asses. We lay on that couch, naked, hair matting with hair, his left cheek on my right.

Darkness. Insert a surrealist dreamscape of some grand, meaningful connection: a ferry ride to the statue, or perhaps some Delhi or Chennai in New York cityscape of swirling colors, perfumes of incense and potent curry spices, the heart-thrum of bhangra, bass turned up and blasting.

"Fuck! Rajiv, wake up!"

I opened my eyes.

"We're late!" We needed to get ready at seven so that we could be at the party by eight.

"There's no way I can make it on time. You should leave without me and I will go back, get ready, and meet you there." I jumped to my feet, dazzled by the fog of an afternoon nap.

"No. I want to go together—who gives a fuck if we're late?" Prahlad had a point. It was a brown party. I don't think I've ever known a brown party to start at the time written on the invite.

"Okay, maybe you shouldn't shower here. Come with me to my aunt's house to get ready and then we can cab it back to the Brecht Forum."

Prahlad stuffed his deodorant and his pants in a sack. Since both of us were university students, every last dime was necessary in our weekly budgets. We took the A train from Chambers Street to Lefferts Blvd.

We sat silently in the train car. It rattled and shivered its skin, as Shesha shuffles and slithers across a sea of milk bearing Lord Vishnu. From his navel, a lotus blossom. In that lotus blossom, creation. Creation doomed to the destruction of Lord Shiva's dance. All around, the faint odor of something burning—the ghost of engine fuel, building dust. I closed my eyes. Prahlad held my hand and rested his head on my shoulder.

"Faggot terrorists!" someone shouted. I didn't want to move or respond. What could I have said? Prahlad was sleeping on me. I didn't want to think of anything else.

I was about a foot taller than him, fuller in the stomach and hips. Our nipples were the same chocolate—his lips darker than mine. With his head on my shoulder, I was comfortable. The party didn't matter. All that mattered was that we were snaking through Queens in the summer.

❄

I could already smell the curry before opening the door. Pua, Pupha, and Jake were in Toronto—somewhere with Aji or Auntie Rani. Maybe it wasn't a good idea to bring Prahlad home to shower. Maybe I should have insisted on meeting him at the party. Maybe I should have called Pua in Toronto to ask if it was all right. I opened the door. Clarice, my cousin, sat on the couch and turned off the television.

"Hey, Raimie. How are you?" Clarice's eyes widened, then faded into a smile.

"Hey, Clarice, this is Prahlad. He's at the same conference. We're going to get ready real quick and head back out into the city," I said, wringing my hands. I had not told my aunt or anyone that Prahlad and I would be getting ready—in fact, I wasn't expecting anyone to be in the house as I opened the door.

"That's okay, I'm just doing some laundry while Mom is away and I thought I'd come by and say hello. I haven't seen you in so long!" she said, throwing up her hands for a hug. She didn't get up from the couch.

I pointed Prahlad to the bathroom so he could begin his dressing ritual.

"How's your mom and dad?" Her saccharine tone turned my stomach. I watched her eye the bathroom.

"They're good! They're excited for your wedding!"

Clarice was engaged to a Belizean man. "Yeah, I can't believe that the day is finally approaching! We've been together for three years."

"I can't wait for the party tonight," I replied.

"Well, go get ready and have a great time!"

I narrowed my eyes. Something was up. Her voice was syrup. Was she being two-faced? Aji used to say, *All skin teet' na laugh.* She was smiling but definitely not laughing. I went to my bedroom and opened my suitcase to decide what to wear.

❁

We danced and drank. We danced with Ryan and Farida. Farida brought her cousin Sef to the party. He stood tall for a sixteen-year-old and wasn't drinking. We shook hands and Prahlad and I clung to each other. The music played mixes of Bollywood and EDM while lights pulsed in the hall. We drank some more and ran out into the streets of the Financial District. Prahlad's friend's house was closer than Richmond Hill so I decided to sleep there with him. This was the last night that I would see Prahlad like this—peeling off his clothes as he stared into my eyes. With each garment he tossed to the floor he dared me to wrap myself around him.

At night the manholes breathed smoke. Underground the city's Kundalini wound its way into the pockets of immigrants, both recent and established. K-Town, Chinatown, Little Mexico, Italy, Manila, Bangladesh, Guyana, Jamaica, Armenia, et cetera. It was a wonder that I would meet some queer like Prahlad. An artist, a dancer, a great cocksucker.

We rubbed our bodies together until it hurt.

❁

The morning after the party Prahlad and I woke slowly to the sunrise pounding on the glass like an angry neighbor. This was our last morning before he returned to San Francisco. Even if I did see him again, I couldn't be certain of when or if we would still feel the same way for each other at the same time.

He stunk of booze—sweet and personal, of orange juice and morning breath. I would later try to recall this morning's every detail. Two cups of water on the coffee table. His shirt, buttons ripped completely off. The hair sprouting from his chest. His lips. I traced them with my fingers. He smiled and kissed me. I didn't want him to put on his socks, hide his cock in his boxers, and zip up his suitcase. He pressed himself close. I held him closer. The sunlight showed the dust dancing in shafts. Prahlad's skin was gold.

After showering together I waited with him while his cab came to take him to JFK. He was flying out of Queens, close to where Pua lived. I slid my hand into his. He leaned his head onto my shoulder. This felt natural. His attar filled the street as myrrh.

"Write me an email when you get home," I asked, pursing my lips. Prahlad had a tear streaking his cheek. He got into the cab. He shut the door and opened the window.

"It's funny how in Hindi the word for *goodbye* also means *hello*." His voice, full and throaty.

"Yeah, funny," I said, looking up at the stoplight that had just changed from red to green.

✿

I was sitting back in Pua's Queens apartment when the door opened. In the July heat, an unexpected cold gust frisked me. In walked Pua and Pupha, followed by Jake. He hid behind his mother's skirt mostly.

"Hey guys, how was Toronto?"

"Good."

"How was Aji? Did she make barah?" For some reason Pua and Pupha were not looking at me. They answered my questions in single-word answers.

"Yes. Please stop talking now. It's been a long day and I'm going upstairs." Pua climbed the stairs.

Something was obviously up. "You guys must be tired. Jake, want to come with me to get some milk?" We took a walk. I had to leave the house.

"You're in trouble with my parents," Jake said, his straight dark lips stretched thin. "It's not like I have never been in trouble with yours," he leaned in.

We sat on the street, where Lefferts met Liberty Avenue in Richmond Hill.

"But why? What did I do?" I asked, my palms flat on the cement. The nearby shops packed up all their sugarcane and juicers. The only music that we heard was from the tires on the asphalt, from the chutney soca music blaring from passing cars.

"When we were away you used the house like a brothel. You brought that whore here and Clarice saw. Come on, Raimie, you know that's disgusting. How would you like it? This isn't Florida." His eyes narrowed.

"You don't even know him—why do you call him a whore?"

"He probably has . . . diseases. You said yourself he's a little slutty." He folded his arms across his chest.

Had I mentioned that Prahlad was no prude to Jake? *Diseases?*

"It's not homophobia, Raimie," Jake insisted. "It's like you shouldn't have invited anyone into our house when we were not there."

"I know, but it's not like we were staying long—we had to get ready for the party. All my stuff is in your house and he really just wanted to go with me. Like, we'd show up together. It's sweet," I smiled, lost in a far-off look.

"It's disgusting." He sneered, "You're bringing diseases into our house."

"Diseases?" I raised my eyebrows. "Neither of us has any diseases. That's so homophobic! I don't think this would have been any kind of problem if I brought a girl home, and if Clarice saw her instead of Prahlad."

"Don't make this about homophobia, Raimie. You should not have done this *antiman* thing. This is not your house. This is not Florida,"

Jake continued, "You can't do whatever you please and not expect us to be mad."

"But I'm not even sure what happened. All I know is that as soon as they came home your parents were acting like I killed someone." I could hear my mantra invading my mind, praying these words again and again as if strung like prayer beads:

*You are nothing.*
*No one will ever love you.*
*You are fat and hairy.*
*You are good for nothing.*

"You brought that slut into our house, Raimie." They went to Toronto and were having dinner around Auntie Sonia's table—the one in her kitchen reserved for family. They ate roti and baigan. During dinner the phone screamed. It was Clarice. She said I was taking a shower with Prahlad.

"You really have no fucking shame, do you? She told Mom and Dad about what you were doing. You brought that slut into the house. Were you staying with him the whole time in my house?" He continued in his ire. His lips were dry, lined in a thin wisp of dry spit.

"No way!" I shook my head.

"Raimie, you're caught."

I looked down at my feet, now my ankles were properly textured by the cement they rested on. I pressed them deeper into the gray.

"Jake," my voice shook, "why on Earth would I bring Prahlad into your mom's house to stay? We were there to get ready for a party—we fell asleep in the Financial District and wanted to go together. We came to your house to shower and leave. I swear to god!"

"You were using our house as a gay brothel." Jake could no longer look at me. He stared at the A train above the avenue as it coiled in the above-ground platform. This was its last stop.

"Did you tell Aji?" I clenched my fists. I wondered what word he used to tell her.

The only way Aji would have been able to understand what was going on was if they had explained to her what *gay* meant. They must have used that word. The A word: *antiman*. How would they do that? If Aji knew this about me, would it change the way that she told me stories and sang me songs? I was afraid of that river drying up. I feared exile from her poetry.

I used to hear the uncles all talk about the West Village as a place to avoid because *antiman does stay dat side*. I know what they think of us— swishy fags who deserve damnation.

"What did you tell her?" My jaw clenched.

"Well, Clarice told Mom," he said. Clarice told her mother that Prahlad swished about and was very effeminate. And that I was gay. Antiman.

A bus's headlights stunned my eyes before the noise of its horn as it kicked down the street in the night streaked with cigarette smoke and humiliation.

"I never told her anything." Clarice was so sweet to us when we came in. I didn't understand where this was all coming from. I never would have told Clarice anything about who I have sex with.

"Yes, but you brought that fucking *antiman* into the house." He furrowed his eyebrows.

"Stop. His name is Prahlad," I spat, hands held out, palms facing my cousin in the mudra for inner peace.

"You brought *Parminder* into the house," he tried to provoke me in his whiney screech. "Then my mom and Dad with Auntie Sonia, Auntie Rani, and Aji sat me down and asked, 'Is Raimie gay?' I can't lie to my parents."

A car blaring Babla & Kanchan's "Na Manu" guffawed and choked its smoke down the street past where we sat. *Na manu, na manu, na manu, dagabaj tori batiya na manu . . . I can't believe you, I can't believe your words of betrayal. . . .* How many times have we danced to this song at family parties?

I rose to my feet, "Why didn't you tell them to ask me if they had suspicions?" My voice trembled and cracked like a wooden beam burning. "I never would have done that to you."

"Well, you shouldn't have brought that fucking *Par-slut-jeet* into the house. I told them you're gay!" Jake screamed, pointing his finger in my face. The A train hissed on its platform before the automated conductor began in his cheery, mechanical croon, *Please stand clear of the closing doors. . . .*

We both stood in silence, wide eyed. *Antiman.* So foreign and so familiar—familial. I don't think I'd ever heard anyone outside my family use this term. Ever. And now this term was me. If the world lurched on in its orbit and spun or if it stopped causing typhoons and earthquakes I couldn't tell—my knees and legs were jelly, I might as well have been standing on my head. All sound around us ceased.

I imagined a crowd of brown bodies gathering around Prahlad and me, chanting and holding up signs that read *Sharam Na Ave? Aren't You Ashamed?* Their voices picketed as ghosts moaning in unison, Antiman. Anti-man. Auntie-Man. Anty Man. Andy Man. Auntie Man. *Antiman.* Ante, Man. Ant eat man. And T-Man. Ant-He-Man. Against Man. An Team an. Ant Iman. Andtiman. Aannttiimmaann. Aaannnttttiii-mmmaaannn. *Antiman. Antiman. Antiman.* My heart burst from my mouth and ran down the gullies and avenues, New York bared its teeth. It wanted to chew me up. I wanted to be eaten, to not face up to any of this.

I was exhausted. I clasped my hands as though I were praying. Being so alone, who would advocate for the ethical treatment of me? My heart beat out bhangra and chutney as though my wedding processional had arrived unbidden. My eyelids throbbed. My voice was trapped in my chest. My body was exhausted, my knees trembled. I wanted to believe everything would be okay: Pua loved me, right? This was all just a misunderstanding that I would clear up.

*The people divided will never be united!*

After several minutes I had stopped shaking. There wasn't anything I could do. I was staying with them for one more night, and I would have to face them again, at least to retrieve my bags before I left.

✤

Jake and I walked back into the house from the corner market. Silence in the streets, on the stereos of passing cars, from the pigeons roosting on the roofs of the houses. I had taken Jake's bullshit into my pink like a fat cock. Prahlad must have already boarded his plane back to the Bay. I thought of him and our last night. We'd had a hurried farewell after sleeping a second night together on his friend's couch. I should have done something special. I should have told him that this had never happened to me before—meeting someone who was filled with adventure and dosas—someone cool *and* brown.

Jake and I walked through the door and Pua was in the kitchen washing dishes. They had finished dinner. It smelled of katahar and daal. I walked into the kitchen, to that very place I sat on Monday. I looked at Pua. She avoided my eyes.

"Pua, I'm sorry for this misunderstanding. Please let me explain what happened." I showed her my palms.

"I don't want to talk about it," she said. "It's okay."

"It's not okay. Prahlad didn't spend the night here. We just—" I pleaded, choking on my words.

"You're right. It's not okay."

I stood, stunned. Pua threw down her sponge and slammed the faucet shut. She walked out of the kitchen and up the stairs to her bedroom where she shut her door to me. I went to bed. Jake slept downstairs.

The next day Pupha drove me to LaGuardia Airport without a jolly word. I left his house that morning—and the smells of home.

No Hindi songs played from the radio. Just silence and asphalt. I would not hear Hindi music in that house for a long time after that, uninvited to my aunts' homes even upon the death of my Aji.

I would live in Queens and Aji would die and family would gather from all over the world to keep wake, but no one would call me even though I would live only one subway stop west. I would have to wear the name *ANTIMAN* as scales, never able to molt when it no longer fit my body. But this would also mean that I would be a dragon with wings and a tongue of flame. I would have to get used to flying.

I sat looking at the city fade below me, lost to the haze of cloud and atmosphere. It sparkled its lights at me, winking. It knew my secret. It knew that Pua was certain to tell my father. If not Pua then Auntie Sonia or Auntie Rani. My father was going to disown me, tell me never to call him *Pap* again. He would call me *Abomination*. To never attribute anything I become to him.

As soon as I returned home, I told my parents everything—how I remembered it happening. I told them all the details about where I was and where Prahlad was when I was there.

Pap would lie to his sisters over the telephone and through the gossip chain, telling them that Clarice made up lies about me. That she made up this lie because when she was a child my father yelled at her for throwing up on the carpet.

I didn't learn this until much later, though, what he told them. He wanted to save face—to pretend his son was not the antiman that they all knew he was. I would not be invited to family gatherings for being a *lying* antiman. Everyone would whisper about me behind their hands like good Christian converts and thank God that their children hadn't been ruined by the United States in the way I was.

# Aji Recording: How Will I Go

dulhin rowe rowe piya ke ghar jana
kaheki rowe piya ke ghar jana

piya ke ghar jana, piya ke ghar jana
kaheki rowe piya ke ghar jana

sasur mare mare baans danda leke
sasur mare mare nanad gari aawe

saiya mare mare baans danda leke
saiya mare gale mein bahi dalke

kaise ham jaibo sasural
chunari mein lagal daag

kaise ham chipao
chunari mein lagal daag

❋

Dulahin cry fe go a 'e husban' house
'e cry an' cry

Faddah-in-law an' muddah-in-law does beat me
Sistah-in-law does send insult

me husban does gimme lash wid one piece bamboo
me husban does beat me afta 'e grabble me t'roat

mow me go go a me faddah-in-law,
me orhni get one stain—

mow me go hide 'am,
me orhni get one stain—

❀

The bride cries, she must go to her lover's—
she cries because she must go.

My in-laws will beat me,
my sister-in-law will curse me out.

My love will hold my neck
and beat me with a bamboo rod.

How will I go to my in-laws
with a stained veil—

how will I hide it,
the stain in my veil—

# Eh Bhai

Eh eh Raimie, you get so fat; you must kiss all your aunties, we should never have moved from Guyana; no matter what she call you that is your auntie; eh eh Raimie, you must mind you daddy; oh my goodness—how can you say this about your family; don't call me Pap; Ram ram Aji; eh eh Raimie, did you know your cousin Jake learn fe talk Hindi?; eh eh Raimie you get so dark; dis English country speak English; She only knows how to talk broken Hindi; she only speaks broken English; you are so disrespectful; when I was young I wanted to get my siblings out of trouble and here you are trying to get them in trouble; we never should have left Guyana; stop talk Hindi; did you know that Jake is a vegetarian, too?; Did you know your cousin Jake is engaged to a good Guyanese girl?; oh my goodness—I have failed as a father: my first son got his white girlfriend pregnant, my daughter dates Black men, my small son is a bullahman; why did we come away from Guyana. Shanti—your kids are an embarrassment; your hand na reach to wash you batty, how you go seh you turn big man and want take next man?; *You are nothing. No one will ever love you. You are fat and hairy. You are good-for-nothing.* Raimie, you must kiss all your aunties; Raimie, how's your mother?; Raimie na must rude you auntie; Raimie you must kiss you auntie; should have stayed back home; back home na get this kind wo't'lessness.

# A Family Outing,
# Alternative Ending 1

MY FATHER'S THREE sisters, my puas, sat together in Auntie Sonia's Brampton home. As children Jake and I called this Bramladesh since it was so brown—every other person was Sikh, Hindu, or Muslim.

We were so clever.

But now we were well into our twenties.

I was staying with Pua and Jake in Queens while attending a conference. During the week they had gone away to Canada. It was summer. The phone rang its tin.

"Hello?" Pua answered.

*Something on the other end.*

"Oh, hi, Clarice," Pua was smiling into the receiver. Pua thought that Clarice had called to say hi.

*Something on the other end.*

"He brought someone into the house? That's okay—" Pua continued.

*Something syrupy on the other end.*

"He's what? He looks like what?" Pua's mouth gaped.

Outside cardinals flitted between the branches of the tree clusters in the backyard. Pua stared outside at their play. The bright-colored male crushed millet from the bird feeder in his passerine beak and placed his bolus in another male's beak. His feathers shivered.

She dropped the phone from her hand.

Pupha got up from the table and picked up the receiver.

"Hello, Clarice? What's going on?" He took off his glasses.

Pua looked at him with wide eyes, her Coolie-red hair blazing in the afternoon sun.

*Something on the other end from New York.*

"Okay. Just stay there and we will come back just now." He put down the phone.

Pupha stared at Pua. Jake swallowed hard. He was sitting there the whole time.

"What happened?" Jake asked.

"Jake, did you know Raimie's friend?" Pupha asked.

"Which one?" Jake's eyes met Auntie Sonia's eyes before he looked down, picking at his knee.

"The antiman," his voice now shrill. Auntie Sonia looked at Auntie Rani who looked at Pua who looked at Jake who looked at Pupha.

The kettle boiled on the stove.

The kettle whistled on the stove.

The kettle screamed on the fire.

From the other room Aji walked into the dining area in the kitchen. She had been sitting alone in the front room.

Pua chirped, "Clarice says that Raimie had a friend at the house and that he's staying there with him."

Silence.

"Clarice says that he swishes about like a gay," Pua finished.

Pua walked to where Jake was sitting, as did Pupha. They glared at him across the table. Auntie Rani and Auntie Sonia were now smiling, excited by the action.

"Clarice says she thinks Raimie is gay. Do you know this, Jake?" His mother grew three feet taller and looked down at her son who cowered below.

"Did you know that Raimie was gay, Jake?" Spit had whitened the corners of Pua's mouth. Jake looked from his mother's face into his father's eyes.

"Is Raimie an ANTIMAN?" Pua shouted. Aji opened her eyes wide and blinked. Her eyebrows arched high into her forehead.

Everyone put their forks down and looked from Pua to Aji and back to Pua again. This was scandalous news and all of the aunts were drinking it up like the hot tea they would soon take after the burn of their roti-baigan calmed on their tongues.

Aji, usually sitting elsewhere and ignored, blinked her eyes being so directly addressed. She took a sip of water and asked, "What kine ting dat?" Pua huffing before her. She did not know this word, or at least why they would use it to describe her grandson.

"Don't worry about it—na mine da," Auntie Sonia replied shortly, watching with keen eyes. They flitted and flicked as flame from Pua to Jake.

Jake shook, his hands trembled—he knew something, she thought but dare not say aloud. This would be more dramatic if it were to unfurl of its own accord. Nature was such a wretched instigator; its twin, nurturing, was equally as duplicitous and conniving.

Pua sat like a stone.

Pua's pupils were lifeless like a statue hewn of marble.

Pua's face was glazed over, like a doughnut.

Aji repeated to the assembled aunts, uncle, and cousin, "What is antiman?" She could taste the word. It tasted like salt: was it seawater or blood?

"Ma—" interrupted Pua, eyes raining brimstone and sulfur flame, "I was talking to Jake. Just relax. Relax." Her words hung in the room.

"A-you talk 'bout Surj ke sacand son, na? Wha' mek you call he antiman?" Aji insisted. Pua shot arrows from her pupils and answered shortly.

"Antiman is when one man take one next man like he a ooman." The entire room was silent except for the air burst of Jake snickering behind his palms.

"Wha'? Na da cyan't be." Aji laughed. "Man an' man cyan't make pickni," Aji indignantly replied betraying a sad truth, that she did not believe that sex could be for pleasure divorced from childbearing. In her mind, this was the reason for marriage—fe mek pickni.

"Is not fe make pickni—is when one man put he lolo in de next one batty," Auntie Rani said, scorching the room with her Coolie-red hair, dyed cheaply.

Silence of a scorched forest.

Jake looked at his feet.

"What de ass? Me na know what da hell a-you dis a-talk," Aji stammered. No birds chirped outside, no deer, no owl, no fowl at all, no fox—nothing.

"Dem a put de lolo in de next one kaka-hole. Raimie one bullahman, one battyboy!" Pua threw her hands in the air as though in *hallelujah*.

"Even so, na mattah. Da is you bhaiya son," Aji sang in her typical lilt. She grasped a spoon on the table and put more pepper on her plate before she began to eat again, with her fingers.

"DEM NASTY FE SO!" Pua shouted, rattling the perfect pink and white teacups.

Silence.

"Jake, did you know Raimie is one antiman?" Pua clenched her teeth.

"Yes," Jake looked down. He put down his water glass—his hands shook with tiny aftershocks, spilling drops all over the tablecloth.

"How long have you known this, Jake," Pupha now whispered. Jake could sense all of his aunts' eyes on him—the beloved nephew who could do no wrong. He sweat up a storm—he couldn't imagine lying to his aunties.

"For a couple years now." He did not make any eye contact.

"Did you know that he was having a friend that he met at the conference stay over?" Pupha continued.

"No."

A cardinal chirped a summer song before it looked into the window and stammered shut its beak.

"Jake, are you gay?" Pua asked. Auntie Rani looked at Auntie Sonia who looked at her hands twirling a napkin.

"No, I'm not!" Jake replied loudly, his face now red.

"Did you know that Raimie was using this house for this nastiness?" Pua continued idly reiterating. It was time to perform for her sisters, who liked a good intrigue.

They would be gossiping about this for months, for years, for decades— that day when they got confirmation that Surj's son was an antiman.

Pua hemmed and hawed.

Pua brayed and beat her chest.

Pua slammed her fists on the table.

Pua dashed her teacup in the sink and said bad words like *hell* and *damn* and *bitch*.

Pua said *ANTIMAN GO BU'N IN HELL.*

Pua flailed and wailed.

Pua riffed and ripped napkins.

Pua shouted her voice hoarse.

Pua collapsed in a chair next to Pupha.

Aji came up, put her hand on Pua's shoulder, and said, "Beti, you cyan stop rivah f'om run."

*You can't stop rivers from running.*

Outside the cardinals had left their feeder. They were there, some-where, not hiding in the woods but unseen. A bird with such bright plumage can stay hidden in tree shadows for only so long.

# A Family Outing, Alternative Ending 2

JAKE SAT NEXT to Auntie Sonia. Brampton was always a flurry of daal puri and curry. He relished, among other things, how cold the tap water got in Canada. Canadian bags of milk.

*Oh, Canada,* he thought, *there is nowhere in this world better.* Of course Canada is a large place, but he was home with Auntie Sonia's children even though they were ten years younger than he was. These were Jake's best friends.

Auntie Sonia looked at him, her eyes bulging out of her head with affection, and fell into them like a wounded cardinal falls into a pond.

"Here, eat one more roti." She placed the daal puri on his plate. "I made this especially for you," she said and admired him as he ate with his hands.

Jake had just recently started to experiment with being a vegetarian. Auntie Sonia had scoured her house and exorcised any trace of meat she could find. She teased him about becoming a pandit one day.

✻

When we were children, about eight or nine, Clarice and Jake came to visit us in Orlando. We had moved there from New York when we found out that my sister had cold-triggered asthma. Since Clarice was my brother's age and Jake was my age, my parents thought it a good idea to invite them to hang out with us for the summer. Since Jake moved to New York, he had become pretty reserved. I heard the adults speak in hushed voices about the trauma of being shoved into a large city from a nice residential area like Mississauga. But no one ever said that about Aji, who had been forced to relocate to Scarborough, Ontario, after all her children got married for green cards or overstayed visas.

※

Pua and Pupha sat at the table. They were discussing Khadija-Chachi, the latest object of ridicule. She was a Muslim their brother married. Khadija-Chachi came from money. Aji would drink rum and offend her so she stopped talking to the family.

Auntie Sonia was just about to remark on how their son was "wasting his life" following his passion for painting, when the phone interrupted.

Auntie Sonia rolled to the phone and answered. It was Clarice. She was calling from New York. Jake kept eating his curry and roti.

"Take this," she motioned to Pua. She walked across the room and spoke on the phone.

"A gay? In our house?" her voice rose in pitch.

Aji entered the room from the living room. She had been sitting on the floor by herself eating. She wasn't able to follow the flow of the conversation. When she asked questions of clarification—and she asked them frequently—she would become the butt of the joke. Instead of being insulted, Aji found it easier to sit by herself. Her children weren't interested in speaking Bhojpuri anyway. What could they ever have to talk about?

Jake thought he could hear Clarice from the other line. He craned his neck forward and listened.

"Raimie brought this guy into our house and I think he's staying there," Clarice whined from Queens.

Silence.

✸

When they came Jake was a ball of nerves. My parents took us to Chuck E. Cheese to exhaust us so the house would be quiet that night. We must have eaten some bad pizza because when we got home Clarice and Jake both had stomach upsets. Clarice puked all over the carpet in my parents' bedroom. She was twelve years old and my father yelled at her, asking why she couldn't have made it to the bathroom to be sick in the toilet like any normal person. He asked her if she behaved like an animal in her own house.

✸

"And I think Raimie might be gay," she relished those words as she spoke them. She was thrilled to be at the instigating end of drama and to join the ranks of our family by spreading gossip. "Did you know that Raimie was gay? You should never have invited him."

Pua dropped the phone from her hand and sat catatonic. She was horrified.

*A gay in her house?! What the ass?* she thought. Pupha rushed and finished the phone conversation. Clarice said goodbye and smiled into her glass of water. Jake swallowed hard, his hands yellow from the turmeric.

"Wha' happen," Aji asked.

"Na worried." Pua wasn't looking anywhere in particular.

"Wha' you call gay?" Aji continued.

"Is when one man take a next man," Auntie Sonia jumped in.

"Take 'em where?" said Aji, puzzled.

"Like when one man married one next man."

"But—"

Pua glowered at Jake and interrupted Aji, speaking over her. "Jake?" He was only used to loving looks. Pua drawled again, "Jake?"

Jake couldn't handle the pressure. He blurted out, "Yes, Raimie is gay! I've known all along. He has been seeing this guy, Prahlad, since he came to this conference. He told me about it. He told me that he had a crush on a Madrasi man and I told him that he should have never come to New York or come in our house because he was a filthy abomination."

❄

Clarice called her mother and father from Orlando. The next day they packed up all their things after my mother washed their clothes. They were going to stay with Chacha and Chachi, who also lived in Orlando but had no children yet. When they left, I wondered if Jake would be bored there because Chachi didn't cook as much as Pua and my mother. Or she did, but there was weirdness with Chachi, Khadija-Chachi, and my mother. Basically, all of the Puas distrusted their brothers' wives: one was Muslim and two were Hindu, and later one became a Christian. They were all from rich families, which allowed my father and his brothers never to hold steady jobs.

❄

Pua silently stared out the window. She shifted her glance back at Jake. He still couldn't take it.

"I bet he's using the house as a gay whorehouse. We are away and he is just there taking advantage of how generous you are," Jake whined.

Auntie Sonia, not to be outdone, added, one eyebrow arched, "Just look at Raimie's mother. She comes from a different family, I mean, do you even know them? Georgetown people are all kinds of wild. No telling what kind of madness goes on in their house." They both stoked the flames until Pua was in a conflagrant rage.

Pua trembled as she whispered, "Faggots burn in hell." Her voice broke into glass shards. Any word spoken would have ripped through skin.

Looking at the mess, Aji spoke up to Jake, "Nevah mind who an' who a what. Wha' you go do? All bady na get one sense." *Does it matter what he is? What can you do? Not everybody thinks alike.*

# A Family Outing,
# Alternative Ending 3

AFTERNOON BREAKS THROUGH the windows in its liquid and particle light.

Brampton midweek afternoon ramble.

Eggplant mashed into baigan: a purple mass now brown and gold: an inside picnic.

Auntie Sonia opens her mouth: an exodus of bats.

Her teeth are enamel trees, her tongue a grassy knoll.

✿

*Dear land of Guyana, of rivers and plains,*
*Made rich by the sunshine, and lush by the rains,*
*Set gemlike and fair between mounts and sea—*
*Your children salute you, dear land of the free.*

✿

Auntie Rani's hair grays at the temple where she's offered bananas and persad.

Her god of wood is stapled to a tree.

Meanwhile: prayers to the god of loss.

The skies are open and clear—not a single cloud shadow in sight.

❁

*Green land of Guyana, our heroes of yore,*
*Both bondsmen and free, laid their bones on your shore,*
*This soil so they hallowed, and from them are we,*
*All sons of one mother, Guyana the free*

❁

Somewhere a bell rings.

Pua shivers her feathers and begins her voice's creak against the cold plastic receiver.

Jake eyes his mother and melts into a puddle of water three inches deep.

The water is clear and catches the light so well that all felled trees and squirming fish are visible.

There are no secrets in this shallow pool, except that it is poisonous to birds and people.

Pupha stands up and his head breaks through the ceiling of the house.

It climbs the stairs and pokes through the second story and attic.

The sun crowns his head and burns the skin under his eyes.

❁

*Great land of Guyana, diverse though our strains,*
*We are born of their sacrifice, heirs of their pains,*
*And ours is the glory their eyes did not see—*
*One land of six peoples, united and free.*

❁

"A FAGGOT! A FAGGOT! MY HOUSE A BROTHEL!"

Pua collapses into her Coolie-red hair, sprouts bright cardinal wings, and flits off into the distance.

Pua dissociates for twenty minutes.

Jake begins to ripple.

She returns carrying a cutlass.

"ME GO CHOP DIS SKUNT TIDAY SELF."

Jake's surface tenses.

❀

*Dear land of Guyana, to you we will give*
*Our homage, our service each day that we live;*
*God guard you, great Mother, and make us to be*
*More worthy our heritage—land of the free.*

❀

Aji comes up from behind and bursts like a water balloon and flows as a river.

"Try dam meh, you na go hable," she laughs as she winds her way, inundating everyone until, all about, there is only water in flow.

# Amazon River Dolphin

// You unfold your lungs and dive into the dark Queens avenues filled with catcalling men and Oh-hell-no women // You walk into your aunt's house and she puts you out // You walk into your aunt's house and she tells everyone you know it's a brothel // You walk into your aunt's house and when your grandmother died no one called you or invited you to the wake because of your "condition," because of your being "disturbed," because of your blubber // They watch your movie where you give birth to a watermelon and you lick every cetacean seed you have seen // After each man, you lick his seed from your fingers //

// The Amazon river dolphin dries their pink body on the riverbank before dancing at parties, attracted to the din of drums // They are a skilled musician, an expert of communication where human words deflate // Their words pulse throughout the Amazon Basin // You can hear them when you lose yourself in the rain forest // If you look into their eyes you will fall into a fever // They will impregnate you or cause you to impregnate them // Don't blame your own practice of mischief on others //

// From the shore you are singing this song of praise // From the shore you sing to the Lord who is half woman and half man // Your own body's earth in hemispheres: the Ganga, the Jamuna, the Pleiades in your throat // Open your Caribbean lips // Spread them with one hand // Your ass is begging for it // Your song, it's not your fault that men, women, queers drown to hear //

// In the Orinoco River the dolphin is a singer // You practiced singing in six languages since your pubes were seedlings // Your parents are from South America so you can be what you will—half Indian, half mammal, half sea: wherever you locate your whole // Don't bother explaining Indian indenture // Your vertebrae are not fused, capillaries close to the skin // A mollusk with one shell or two or more or not a mollusk at all but rather cetacean pink skin and echolocation //

// You are suited for locating queers // How can you be pink //

// There are river dolphins in the Ganges // There are river dolphins in Guyanese rivers // Your echolocation vibes with both species // How queer for a dolphin to live in a river // Diaspora is a queer country // How can you be at once two species from two places //

// You break your mirror in two // You hear that on the street queers are bashed over the head // Queers are gunned in the village // Queers are queers and queers // One down, *yo ho, yo ho* // You are a pirate // A poker // You are into men up to your balls // You are what your balls say you are // You wear eyeliner and fuck that // You are a nautical mile

// And then the cutlish, the machete // And then you learn to bisect yourself and to throw away the dolphin bones // You stop singing and visiting rivers // Your bones hang in the museum // Once upon a time a man was a man // Once upon a time a woman was part of a man // She was extracted and they live separately // The Bible is the sword in the armor of God // Follow me and I will make you fishers of men // Follow me and I will cleave you in two // Follow me and we will overfish the streams // Follow me and we will starve the boto into extinction //

// On Biologizing Bodies/Desire // A truth that is justified in an epistemological bound that is a tide // Sometimes barnacles and bivalves die from the out-tide // Sometimes being exposed hollows you // You now lapse into the realm of the mythological // You are a folktale warning sons and daughters: beware of pink bodies // It is drawn to one-two one-two drums // Two is a myth //

// Climbing into the Orinoco you feel it first in your feet // Only pain //

// Your ankles fuse and then fluke //

// You enter the river and //

// Below the silt //

Disappear

. . . pajire se kara kara bhaile dupahariya
kholo bahini baja rakhe ho

kaise ke kholo bhaiya hamare lugariya
gaile dhobi ghat paas ho

lewo bahini lewo mor kandha ke kanawar
kholo bahini baja rakhe ho

kaise ke kholo bhaiya baja rakhewariya
gorwa mein lagal mehendi ho . . .

> Da bright bright mahning a-tun black black night,
> sistah, keep a-doh hopem.

> How me can hopem a-doh me clothes gone
> a-dhobi ghat side fe wash.

> Tek dis me sistah, tek dis, me shouldah ke clat,
> hopem a-doh na sistah.

> How me can hopem a–doh
> me foot na get mehendi?

# ANTIMAN

*Early morning, midday, the sky blackens.*
*Open the door, sister.*

    *How can I open the door when my clothes*
    *have all gone to the washer's by the river?*

*Take this, sister, take this my shoulder cloth.*
*Open the door, sister.*

    *How can I open the door wide, brother,*
    *fresh mehndi dries on my feet . . . ?*

# Aji Recording:
# Song for the Lonely Season

aawan yaawan kahe gaye
ke dole barhomas

patta tute daar se ke
legaye pavan urdai

aise chhute yaar se
ki man kahan na jai

kaise kaise zabana
badal gaye re

                              ✿

Jus so Hindi a-change.
Jus so Worl a-change.

Awan-yawan da wind a-blow a-tree
how petal bruk from da lim an fly out.

Jus so me lub gan,
whe me haht go stan?

# ANTIMAN

✺

How time changes
everything. How the world, too,

changes. Wind plays
a folksong. Blossoms shake.

A petal flies, broken from bough.
So, too, my love left me,

abandoned,
where does a heart go?

# Leaving Florida

CHULUOTA HAD NOTHING for me except my family and their judgment. The family legend goes that when we moved down to Central Florida my father drew a circle with a twenty-mile radius from each university in the area. He wanted us to live close to universities even though he'd never attended one; he also wanted his children to experience growing up in the "jungle" as he had in Guyana. What he meant was that he grew up on lands that belonged to the Waraus, the Wapishana, the Arawaks, the Caribs, the Patamona, the Wai-wais, the Akawaios, and the Makusi before the British stole them and gave them to his ancestors to settle.

Chuluota was a town in Seminole County about twenty miles from Orlando. The Seminole people had lived and resisted the American genocide on these lands. Mvskoke, Miccosukee, Alabama, Choctaw, Tamassee, Yuchi, Hitchiti, Seminole, Black Seminole, and other southeastern Native folks joined their forces together under the banner of Chief Osceola and Coa Hadjo in 1837. Thomas Jesup, a settler general, betrayed them under a false promise of peace close to Saint Augustine. Jesup raised a white flag of truce and drew the Native leaders close, captured them, and killed them. He claimed, "The country can be rid of them only by exterminating them."

Of course, in Chuluota there are places named after this murderous settler, venerating him. The land is haunted by this history. Rivers and lakes bear their Native names as though monuments to the Natives' banishment and elimination. If there are no Natives on the land anymore, then it is terra nullius and therefore belongs to the American government to distribute as it so pleases. Settler logic is an invasive species. The truth is that Native people are still around and look after the land. The Seminole Tribe of Florida, The Miccosukee Tribe of Indians of Florida, and the Seminole Nation of Oklahoma are all federally recognized today.

I grew up in this scrubland of tall pine trees and palmetto bushes, magically alive with animals, my family's own colonization beginning around that same time. It was in 1838 that John Gladstone began his Coolie experiments with importing 396 "hill Coolies" to work sugarcane plantations in what was then British Guiana. Part of the agreement was that the planters would prevent any Coolies from assimilation into Guianese society: my ancestors would live separately from others. This is not identical to the North American case of Native removal and genocidal practices but rather a different experience of colonization that I could harmonize with those around me.

In Florida, coral snakes, white-tailed deer, small brown bats, whippoor-wills, eastern cottontail rabbits, bobwhite quail, raccoons, armadillo, otters, bobcats, alligators, buntings, herons, eagles, hawks, and all manner of fish and bug and bird visited us daily. Emile, Emily, and I, very different kinds of Indians, would ride our bikes on barely paved roads that led to dirt paths that led to cow pastures. There were several kids my age in the neighborhood who went to late elementary, middle, and high school with me. One of them at eighteen bought a pair of plastic testicles that he hung from his car with a confederate flag. Another moved far away and fell into his own kind of white supremacy. We lived in the forest, alone and brown. There were no other people of color close by, and random men in pickup trucks would follow me or my sister for miles to finally get out of their cars to tell us to get out of the state. That this state did not need *terrorists* and *sand n—s.*

I had been home for three weeks post-graduation. I packed up my 1999 Toyota Corolla and drove from Gainesville to Chuluota at night.

It was only a matter of ninety minutes, but it felt like a different hemisphere. I would miss the French doors of the room I rented, the way they opened their mouths into the covered porch where I could see in the retention pond the alligator who had become my yearlong companion. I was leaving behind friends and also Tom, the white man I had been messy with. He wanted a relationship and I wanted to be dating around.

Finishing at the University of Florida was my first-generation accomplishment. My mother, however estranged from her own family, was raised in a family where girls didn't go to school. So, her brothers became doctors, dentists, and lawyers, while she became a housewife, disallowed from completing her studies post–secondary school. After my father and mother married in London, bore us, moved us to the United States, and began struggling in Florida, my mother took classes and became a classroom teacher in the public-school system.

*What will I do now that I've graduated from college?* I wondered steadily. It had taken me six years to earn my undergraduate degree in religious studies with a double minor in anthropology and teaching English to speakers of other languages. I needed some time to scheme. I knew that I wanted to work toward some kind of racial equality, immigrant rights, and education. India had politicized me into thinking about structures of power around me, who could have what and why—who could speak what language and why.

I heard about the New York City Teaching Fellows program and a parallel program in Oakland—both big cities to be young and queer in. I would apply for these programs to get the hell out of Florida. The deadlines were not until December and January—for now I had some time to languish in the town that taught me how to shrink into nothingness.

I contacted a friend of mine who, in a new relationship, was busy but excited to put me into contact with her friends at Whole Foods in Winter Park. Mel was a young Catholic woman who in previous years experimented with the Eastern philosophy of Ram Dass and Eknath

Easwaran. We spent time meditating in open fields. Canoeing in the spring-fed Wekiva river to feel the earth's energy move us. She was hoping it would move into my dick, and that I would discover that we were meant to be together.

After drinking at a house party in Gainesville we got naked in bed. Even with the kissing and rubbing, her moaning and Reiki, I remained as flaccid as an earlobe. She cried and cried. This had never happened to her. The next morning when we woke up slightly more sober she made me climb on my roof and shout, *I'm gay!* I did this to make her feel better about my not being able to fuck her the night before. Shouting this from anywhere only made her happy. I didn't care who knew what about me anymore, broken by my family's betrayal. She was another person who had expectations of me that I could not fulfill. One more way that I didn't fit: the square peg in a sea of circular holes.

At the interview with Whole Foods the manager asked me what my life plans were, as though Whole Foods would require everything that I could possibly give. Most of the people who worked the front end were artist-adjacent or musicians.

"I don't see myself being here longer than a year," I replied, quite content with myself. Maybe this was to protect my viscera.

At the customer service desk the liberal white Central Florida crowd gathered like ants to sugar. Well-meaning white women and men routinely asked me my opinions on the frozen Indian food that was sold.

"I don't know," I would say and shrug, and sometimes, "Yes, it's way better than the restaurant at UC7." I didn't know. I didn't care either. This is how I acted in the face of Floridian whiteness. I decided then that I was not going to be anyone's authenticator—especially not at Whole Foods. From my cash register, selling expensive groceries grown with organic processes by people in the Global South, I could see the image that Whole Foods used to market itself: a faceless brown body gripping a hoe and working the fields. Could the workers depicted in such gross images afford five-dollar bottled coconut water? I definitely could not.

I imagined my own great grandparents and the punishment that they suffered for white people. They worked the fields and ate little and drank much to escape the horrors of servitude. The Empire saw them as faceless, disposable, worthless except for what they could do for global capital. And here I was, working under a crass image of someone else's indentureship to an American company. The humiliation of this resounded in the customers' treatment of a brown cashier.

What did this mean for my brown body when white customers would look at my bangles and ask, "Were these your slave shackles?"

What did it mean for the managers to side with the middle-aged white gay man who insisted to me that "all Muslims are terrorists," and that his "saying this is not racist?" I was told not to make a big deal about this, that I don't really know what racism is or what it feels like.

What did it mean when a white customer would tell me, "Go back where you come from," as I rang their groceries up and accepted their cash with a smile, since talking back would cost me my job?

What did it mean that all of these statements of white entitlement aggressively indicated that I did not belong here in the United States— or that I did not belong in Orlando?

It meant that it was time to drink through the bullshit of living in a brown body as an adult in Central Florida. And drink I did.

There were several people in the store I liked to party with: Sandra and her husband George—a semidomesticated couple. Ricky and Maddy, his girlfriend. And Nikki, a woman several years younger than me with a love of poetry and writing. IBar, or Independent Bar, was a club downtown that played music from independent labels. And of course, there were house parties.

❁

On New Year's Eve Autumn and Andrei came to Orlando from Gainesville. Andrei was back from China where he had been teaching ESL.

They showed up at Whole Foods and took me to Sarasota in a friendly version of kidnapping.

We spent the night on the beach listening to folk music and reminiscing about what life was like. I remembered that I was a person who had a past. And just how beautiful Florida could be. I recounted the story of Chief Osceola and how it was rumored that his skull was sold after his decapitation—to add insult to the People of this land—to a dentist somewhere in the Midwest, according to a Linda Hogan poem. How Indians in the United States were called Indians because Europeans were idiots and thought they were in India. Even the name India is fatuous, given to people of the subcontinent by traders and marauders because they lived close to the river Indus. We were named by Europeans for the same river. Indians.

The morning was cool and balmy. Salt hovered over the surface of the aqua deep. Sargasso perfumed the fine sugar-powdery sand as tiny crabs scurried along, busy with their morning mantras. The oceans all connect, my Aji said—the Ganga, the Jamuna, the Pagal Samundar, all were the Kalapani. The black water that baptized us with contracts of indenture and would forever change our stories. That black water that galvanized us into people whose survival was resistance to Empire. That black water that was the sea of milk, Shesha being the SS *Bern* and SS *Jura* that carried my ancestors across, into adventure and punishment.

The yellow light began as orange and then pink until it reached its soft gold fingers across my skin. The ocean rolled slowly and hissed on the sand as its drops fell below the visible. Tiny coquinas burrowed deep into the wet. Sand lice shifted and scurried. Pelicans flew low on the horizon. The beach was a kind of temple—the deity: the sea. It was time for my own crossing, something more permanent.

As Autumn's sibling, Astrid, and I walked along the beach, we found a seagull skull that I picked up and offered to the rising sun. So many beings here have lived and thrived, migrated and passed. Even the water that cycles from ocean to vapor to cloud to rain to ocean. I was a part of this motion. With three scoops of water I remembered my father, my mother, and my Aji. And the words she taught me to say. I turned them inward to the sun rising in my chest. How it began to burn brighter.

I wished to feel whole. I wished to escape into motion. I wished the dawn waves would come and ferry me to a place where every day was not a struggle to be visible, to be happy in my skin.

❀

Down the street from the store Ricky lived with two roommates. He invited me over, and I came and tried to erase myself in spirits and rum. I remember leaving the party to sleep in my car—waking up to vomit onto the curb, and then falling back asleep until I was sober enough to buy some overpriced coconut water with what change I could muster from my Corolla's console.

After trailing my liquor stink into my parents' house and showering I opened my computer and began to fill out the application for the NYC Teaching Fellows program. They wanted essays upon essays. I had to figure out why I wanted to teach ESL in New York City. The answer was not so hard. I wanted to undo the damage that English had done on my family—the cultural erasure that it perpetrated, the turning us into "stupid Coolies." I wanted to be kind in the ways that I helped families and students navigate a system that was stacked against them.

As I submitted the application in the morning, my mother saw me at work. She made me a cup of tea and a piece of toast with jam and cheese. There were perks to living in my family home again.

Pap had been up for hours and turned back when he saw me working. I was in his way, a reminder of his failures as a father: raising an upstart antiman. I was out and into being out. I was vocal about homophobia and racism and the things that made my life difficult. He wanted as little to do with me as possible.

We were happy to avoid each other. He told me constantly how disappointed he was in me but would brag on the phone to whichever of his women from "back home" he was talking to, saying, "My son speaks Hindi." For him, this was something he loved about me and hated. He loved my connection with my Aji—his mother. He hated the parts of himself that were brown. It was a complicated situation to be brown and an immigrant in Klan country. I didn't know how to forgive him yet for this complete disavowal of me except when it benefitted him.

"What are you doing today?" my mother asked, hungry to hear about my plans.

"I'm trying to escape this racist cesspool," I said forcefully. Her eyes widened. I didn't feel like pulling any punches. I was motivated to leave the confederate flags, the regularized homophobia, the unbearable, dehumanizing whiteness. I had on many occasions spoken to my mother about the everyday racism that I faced. She would look at me and sigh.

"The United States is not as racial as England." Her standard answer.

She had been traumatized by the British versions of the "rebel" who wore skinny Wranglers and who believed that "fags burn in hell." She needed to believe that she was in a better place now, that we were safe from the ills that she faced: being pelted with stones and spat on as she walked through London during the reign of Enoch Powell. Here, though, the threats I faced were different. I was a man in a man's body. At least in the United Kingdom Mom belonged to a brown community. Here in the Chuluota and Oviedo areas, there were only a few other brown families I knew who sent their kids to my school. There was only one Guyanese family, and they did not live close by. It was easier for my mother to believe that racism did not threaten the lives of her children here in this forest far away from the English National Front. If only she or Pap would have looked into the history of the American South and the demographics of Chuluota and realized what they were doing.

"Tonight," I replied to my mother's eager look, "I'm going out with Emily and Ronnel to a party."

Another one of the benefits of living at home was that I got to know my little sister as an adult. Emily's hair was fine and slack with curls. In the light it shone brown instead of the black of my own hair. Her face and voice were my face and voice—her register a little higher, her nose a lot smaller. She stood up to my chin and taught me how to drink rum and Coke instead of the cheap Pabst Blue Ribbons and Sparks that I guzzled before entering the club. Every time I mentioned working at Whole Foods she would roll her eyes.

"The people there act like it's the best place on Earth to work and that you have to be a supercool smelly white person with unwashed hair to get in. Like the people there literally stink," she laughed. "It makes sense they drink that piss Blue Ribbon, it's fucking nasty! You should drink things that taste good," she admonished. Rum and Coke was the Guyanese drink.

❁

That night I took Emily and Ronnel, her childhood best friend, to a party as the designated driver. Ronnel was tall and had a beautiful singing voice; we had been in choir together in high school for the one year we overlapped. We both sang tenor one and were both queers. Being three years older than them, I felt like it was an important way for me to show my sister that I approved of her life. I wanted to learn how she was able to cope with living in this place. We blared a mix of Destiny's Child and Alicia Keys on our drive across dark-brewed rivers and live oak forests.

When we arrived at the subdivision, the yellow lights from the street gave the buildings a sallow glow. Our shadows elongated as we walked up the stairs.

We discovered that the host of this party was under the legal age to buy alcohol. I grew uneasy, not wanting anything to botch my application to become a NYC Teaching Fellow.

Emily and I stood outside while Ronnel ran inside to begin his smoke and drink. After a couple of minutes Emily and I decided it was time to leave. "Let's go to Denny's," she said as a consolation.

As Emily braved the inside of the kegger to get Ronnel from the din of bad college music, an undercover police officer approached and demanded that everyone leave at once. He was white and pale, his skin almost translucent. *Did he have a gun?* I wondered.

I waited for my charges at the bottom of the stairs. That same officer in street clothes came up to me and told me, "Leave right now." The parking lot was abuzz with opening and shutting car doors—a night serenade of Top 40 centos, as the music from each car blared and then stifled.

"I am waiting for my sister and her friend to come out. I'm the D.D.," I said.

He repeated, "I said leave NOW."

Emily approached without her friend. As she came, I said to her, "Let's wait by the car, this rent-a-cop needs to flex his muscles."

The officer turned ruddy white. Clearly in his feelings he said, "You in the red shirt, come here. What did you call me?"

"I was talking to my sister." My voice was flat.

"What is your social security number?"

"What? I'm not giving you my social security number."

"Okay, then give me your license."

"It's in the car." I tossed my keys to Emily and said to her, "License mere jhole mein rakhi hain. Is suwar ko dene ke liye le aana."

She approached with my bag and as she gave it to me the policeman looked at her and said, "Drop it. Don't step any closer to him." Was he touching his pocket when he looked at Emily?

"But you asked him for his license. It's in the bag!" she said as she placed it on the ground.

The officer looked at me and then at her and then back at me. "I am going to ask you one more time, what is your social?"

"I thought you wanted my license." I was genuinely confused. It didn't seem like he knew what he was doing.

At this time seven white police officers crowded us and started taunting me by saying things like, "You can't just walk around with a beard speaking Arabic and not expect us to question you. You fucking hear what he is saying? Do you speak English? Just give him your social security number, you fucking idiot, or we will arrest you."

White faces blended together with white faces. How many were there now? Eight? Why were they all screaming at me? I was being responsible here—driving people home who had no business driving themselves.

"What are you trying to arrest me for, exactly? Why are you swearing at me when I am speaking rationally to you, explaining why what you are saying is contradictory and confusing? It would be miraculous if I just started speaking in Arabic."

Their German shepherds barked and pulled at their leashes and the policemen tried and tried to provoke me into an argument so they could subdue me. Our shadows, lengthening and then fading as more and more red and blue lights gathered, stretched out before us on the cement.

They were all white, of course. How many of them were secretly part of the Klan? A friend in high school, just around the corner, confided that he knew of Klan members in the school, in the district, and on the police force. *Police FORCE,* I thought—the right wing of the vulture of racism. Of pickup trucks and *Go back and starve in your shithole* slogans. These were the "protectors." Better than what was in England? I didn't know. I had to get the hell out of Central Florida. It was not a place for me.

I finally gave up my driver's license and the rent-a-cop issued a trespassing warrant against me on any University of Central Florida properties. I looked at the officer, into his cool pale eyes—the eyes of a demon. I wanted to remember as much as I could about this moment. I noted his name in the journal I kept in my bag. *Jenkins.*

"This isn't over," I called back over my shoulder, Ronnel and Emily now safe in my car.

The drive home was uneventful. No music. Just the black of night and the occasional yellow streetlights.

"I need to get the fuck out of here, Emily," I said.

Looking out of the window at the rushing scrubland she answered a simple, "I know."

❄

The next morning I called the Oviedo Police Department to file a complaint. The person who answered asked what the matter was. I explained last night's harassment and that I was a victim of racism and racist profiling.

The officer on the other end laughed. "I assure you none of us are racist here." I asked to speak to his boss, who was conveniently absent that day.

I wrote a letter to send to the precinct and to a community organization that tried to target institutional racism, but after four days, as I was driving along the highway with Emily to Whole Foods, where she had just begun working with me, we heard on the news that an officer in plain street clothes had been shot and killed by a uniformed officer on a UCF property. He pulled a gun and a passing uniformed officer saw it as a threat and shot the undercover officer before he had a chance to explain his situation. The dead officer was named Jenkins.

We looked at each other. I remember him touching his pocket when Emily came close with my bag. I'd been in more danger than I knew. And I'd put my little sister in front of a charging bull.

❄

In a matter of days, I opened my email to read that my application status to join the Teaching Fellows had changed. I was invited to both Oakland and New York City to interview. Could I actually break free from this town without Central Florida chasing me out like a ghost or wildfire?

New York was first: a three-day event during which I stayed with Jegga in her mom's house in Little Guyana. The first day consisted of a timed writing exercise. The second day was a sample lesson delivered to a class of interviewees and two evaluators. The third day was the panel interview with two New York City teachers.

I wrote my essays at a classroom desk in Midtown. Above me hung a student project on Hindu deities and the goddess Saraswati—goddess of learning, of language, of music—showered her blessings on my paper. I recalled Aji's song: *Utho bahini bidya pardho . . .*

My lesson on count nouns versus noncount nouns was directed at an ESL student body. I highlighted vocabulary words that they'd need and led them in a guided exercise.

In the panel interview, two older white women asked me high-pressure questions. One asked me about gender and what I thought about "girls" using the "boys'" bathrooms. I replied something about gender being up to the individual. She furiously wrote notes and laughed, "Well, I guess in the Village anything goes!" Was this supposed to unsettle me?

Right after the NYC Teaching Fellows interview I flew out to Oakland, where I would be staying with Prahlad. He'd wanted me to visit ever since YSS. I also heard that Ryan would be coming and that we would all be hanging together.

I was excited to see Prahlad again, to sleep in his bed again. I didn't want to spoil it by telling him what happened with my extended family—at least not yet. When he greeted me at the door we hugged and kissed. His energy was different. Was he dating someone?

He walked me into the room and introduced me as his "friend" to his older, white roommate, who welcomed me. On the porch Ryan was smoking a cigarette. We hugged and laughed and hugged. The buildings on the hills outside whitened in Greek-like radiance. The sun was gold and felt like joy in the cool air of San Francisco spring.

I don't recall much about what happened at the interviews other than the interviewers asking me why I wanted to teach math when my marks in the subject were so poor.

"I only put it down because we needed five options for the application. Truth be told I haven't taken a math class in ages." Did I answer this wrong?

The one woman who asked this question took off her glasses and smiled at me. "It's perfectly fine for you to want to teach what you feel are your strongest areas." This comforted me, and I was glad for her warmth.

Back at Prahlad's apartment, Prahlad, Ryan, and I smoked and drank, listened to music, and went to several gay clubs. Queen Harish was performing in San Francisco and we decided that we absolutely had to go.

Arriving at the club we all wore our YSS T-shirts that read *Resistance Is Fertile* and made out. Our energy was unquenchable. We danced and sang and watched with giddy tummies as Queen Harish performed move-by-move Rekha's Kathak to "Dil Cheez Kya Hai." The crowd of brown faggots sang along.

*Aap meri jaan lijiye.* "Why just my heart? Take my life." And then in that moment, to these two men I offered my love. I looked at Ryan and then at Prahlad. I was home with these two who could see me. Finally. There were people who could see me.

Prahlad and I had only a moment together alone and I explained some of what happened to me in New York with my family. I didn't want the drama to eclipse our last moment together before returning to Florida, where I was invisible as a brown body.

Prahlad lay on top of me, breathing on my bare chest. Time slowed to two hearts beating against each other in dissonance and harmony. His long curls tickled my neck. I could feel him harden. We were just our whole complicated selves without explanation. He smelled like musk and coconut oil.

I kissed him for a moment, wanting to be with him, but wanting so much more to be part of something big, something brown, something queer as fuck. When I left we promised to keep in touch forever.

❄

I was accepted to the Teaching Fellows program and would be teaching ESL to K–12 students in the city. When I received the letters of acceptance from both Oakland and New York, the choice was clear: New York City all the way. I could be a free brown West Indian queer in Queens rather than remaining almost invisible in a city without a sizable Guyanese population.

Even though Prahlad was in Oakland, I longed for New York—its grit and its community of West Indians. The organization was glad to have a Hindi speaker onboard, since there were so many immigrants who spoke it; I was glad to be able to use this skill to help offset the sadness of a devalued home language that wasn't English. I was excited to go and make a community of badass brown folks.

"Mom, I got in!" I ran to her room, where she was sitting up watching television in bed. She held a small plate with buttered saltines. "I got into the New York City Teaching Fellows program!" I repeated.

Mom was trained as a teacher herself—having gone to school when I was in middle school. Now she was working for the district with Title 1 funding while studying for her PhD in educational leadership in a remote program from the University of Florida.

"Apparently this means that I will have to go in early summer and take summer classes to begin teaching in my own classroom in the fall. I found a way out of Florida!" My words were clumsy.

She put her plate on her bedside table. "That's great!" she said. "You're actually going to New York." She choked on the words New York. Her eyes sparkled with tears. "You're going to be so far away," she trailed off.

"If anyone could understand why I would leave home and go far away, it's you. You did the same thing—your brothers and sisters are mostly in England and Guyana," I said. The television light painted blues and yellows across her face. Her eyes were wet.

I resigned that day from Whole Foods and hosted a goodbye pool party for the five friends I had made.

❀

The day I left, Pap took me to the airport. The radio crooned oldies. The songs reminded him of John Wayne and growing up in Guyana. Yearning for some kind of class status, he and his siblings drank up American music like I drank rum in high school. I had taken the first step toward making myself whole. I was doing something to affirm myself, to affirm my political convictions.

We merged onto the FL 408 toward Orlando. I looked out the window and saw a red-tailed hawk sweeping the sky in broad circles. I took deep breaths to come back into my body. *The bell is ringing.* I felt my feet hum on the car floor. The jiggle of my calf muscles. The pressure of the seat on my thighs, my ass, my back. I felt my arms and slowed my breathing. In for a ten count, hold for a five count, and out for a ten count. In for a ten count, hold for a five count, and out for a ten count. In for a ten count, hold for a five count, and out for a ten count.

And then I had a realization. I wouldn't have to be alone. I could be with people who would value me and think I was exceptional. I was alive and could feel things deeply. Being a sensitive person is like having a superpower. I just knew it. Maybe this was the feeling my therapist wanted me to connect with when she suggested that I breathe deep and allow myself to be in a space. It all sounded too simple.

I gasped.

"What happened?" Pap asked.

"Pap, I just realized that I don't have to be alone. That I can be loved and I can have a relationship with someone."

Pap was quiet then turned off the radio to begin. "You are disgusting. Do me a favor and don't tell anyone in New York that you are my son. You are an abomination, so never attribute anything you do to me, ever. Do you hear me?"

I looked at Pap and then back out the window. This is what he thought of me the entire time that I spent living at home: something disgusting that he had to endure. He had no control over me anymore now that I was a grown-ass antiman. Maybe it was hard for him to say goodbye to me, now that I was moving on from the life that he'd wanted me to have. Maybe his disappointment was not with me but rather with his own failure to follow his heart.

"We moved to this country so you would have the opportunities that we didn't have," he reminded me one day before I was admitted into the program.

"I am doing just that, Pap. I am taking the opportunity to live in the world the way that I want." It was as simple as that. My mother and father gave me the opportunity, sacrificed so much to make sure that my brother, sister, and I could be fully active agents in our own lives. I was on my way to New York to escape this dialogue that I'd internalized. I knew a part of me would always be safe. I was breathing.

# Ardhanarishvaram Raga
## अर्धनारीश्वरम्

Raga: कुमुद्क्रिया
Scale
Ascending: S R1 G3 M2 D1 S ||
अवरोहण: S N3 D1 M2 G3 R1 S ||
Tala: रूपकं

❀

पल्लवि
अर्धनारीश्वरं आराधयामि सततं
अत्रि भृगु वसिष्ठादि मुनि बृन्द वन्दितं

Line of Imaginary:
I bow to the Lord who is half Shakti,
half Shiva, whom the sages Atri,
Bhrigu, and Vashishta exalt.

अनुपल्लवि
अर्ध याम अलङ्कार विशेष प्रभावं
अर्धनारीश्वरी प्रियकरं अभय करं शिवं

At midnight's half-watch,
their adornments are indomitable
and ardent. Beloved of Ardhanareshwari,
they, benevolent, bestow
fearlessness.

चरण
नागेन्द्र मणि भूषितं नन्दी तुरगारोहितं
श्री गुरुगुह पूजितं कुमुदक्रिया रागनुतं

आगमादि सन्नुतं अनन्त वेद घोषितं
अमरेशादि सेवितं आरक्त वर्ण शोभितं

Foot:
Adorned by the serpent-jewel,
mounted on the bull Nandi,
worshiped by Subrahmanya,
praised in Kumudakriya ragam,

extolled by the Agamas
and in the Vedas alike,
their servants are devas like Indra.
They shimmer a reddish sheen.

Your father pulls over as you drive along the Blue Ridge.

It's a black river.

Wildflowers fringe the bank.

You are on your way to some uncle's daughter's nikkah, migrating from
    Florida to Toronto.

On the radio a 1960s Bollywood tape spins its tin and screeches.

You step out and pick elderflowers and black-eyed Susans to tuck into
    your braids.

*Some things are unconscionable*, your father says,

*like the liberties people take with their freedom.*

Why can't we be whatever we want?

*The lyrics of your music are non sequiturs.*

All bady na get one sense.

Consider Ardhanarishwara, papa.

There is a god/dess split down the center, the right side Shiva,
    the left Parvati. Whole.

There's a universe in my throat.

*Nonsense.*

*Are you a god?*

You are not a mythological creature.
It's Caribana in Toronto and Sonny Mann's "Lotela"
beats its chutney soca.
You've only heard this song at family parties.
The queer you're eyeing asks your cousin if you're single.
That night you wear his oil for days.
The first time you mirror someone like you, you are never lonelier.
You hold your breath.
Your face is red.
Your family shifts.
Never mind that when he leaves you will clutch your belly.
Walking into the plane cabin, he will not even look back;
he will mount the steel and iron and sail across the sky.
You will leave messages on his answering machine,
squeeze your lips tight whenever the phone rings.
You will crave his mounting you.
Somewhere is another of your kind.

Crabwood Creek been get one wha' dem bady been a call Girlie.

Hamini oke Girlie bulawe rahe kaheki uu, ka bole ham, uu antiman rahe.

He been lub one nex' man fum 79 village an' all bady been a sabe.

Aur saadi kare, bibah kare ke time aagail.

De night befo' 'e lawa, 'e been tek one bottle Malathion an' sab piye hai.

Da wha' you know?

Jahariya wha' dem pregnant gyal does tek when 'e shame 'e mumma an' 'e papa.

Like when 'e get one pickni in a 'e belly aur saram lagela den 'e go piye da ting an' seh, *O god-o ham aapan mai-baap ke saram de del.*

Well Girlie ke papa na been know 'e son been drink a jahariya?

'E cerry 'em go a haspital.

When dem a bhuje de lawa Girlie ke baifrien' been come 'pon one harse and tek 'em til a New Amsta'dam.

Baad mein dem been lef' mati an' Girlie go back a 'e papa house fe bibah kare.

Ii time okar mai-baap oke jahariya khilawe rahe taki u Girlie ke marro tak le jaye.

Aisan karis ki uu na bhag sake aur laiki se bibah kare.

Til now 'e married an' mek pickni an' dem a stay a Wiscansin.

In my village there was once a man named Girlie.

We called him that because he, you know, acted like an antiman.

He was in love with a man from 79 Village and everybody knew.

Come so it was time for his marriage.

The night before he grabbed a bottle of malathion and drank it.

You know, the rat poison that pregnant women drink when they have
dishonored their families.

Well, the father caught Girlie in time and took him to the hospital.

Later on they continued with the wedding preparations and the night
before the wedding his boyfriend scooped him up on his horse and
they rode all the way to New Amsterdam.

They eventually tired of each other. Girlie returned to the village to
marry the dulhin.

This time his parents drugged him.

This time his father dragged him to the mandap where the priest
started the havan and made sure that he didn't leave.

He's married now with children and lives in Wisconsin.

Mohini is Vishnu's only female incarnation.

When the gods churn the sea of milk and the nectar of life emerges,
the demons, the asuras steal it all.

With quick fingers Mohini picks it back from them.

The master of tricks, she is the slayer of Bhasmasura.

Once when the demon who could turn others to ash with his hands
mirrored Mohini's dance, he reduced his great form into nitrogenous
dust.

This is why there is immortality.

One look from her eye could drive one mad.

Once Shiva saw her, Kama clove his heart in two.

The wild ache stokes a flame. Her eyes, bellows.

Knowing her to be Vishnu-incarnate Shiva trundles the earth over, an
elephant in heat, stamping through rivers and forests.

In his whirl of desire he spills his semen across the land.

Bewitched by Vishnu on earth: the bewilderer of demons, the thief of
immortality, the wo/man seduces Shiva.

Ardhanarishwara is your household deity when you move into the
    Jackson Heights walk-up apartment with your boyfriend.
A mantra plays the first time you see the flat. It's your ringtone.
Your mother is calling *bhur bhuva swaha*.
If there ever was a sign it's this.
He is a drag queen named Lotay.
His catchphrase: *Karma's a bitch.*
Interstitial, his transitions bore into bedroom politics: cocaine dancing
    and fucking with the wig on.
Karma reduced you to ash.
You open your blowhole and take him deep.
Dolphins are prone to sexual experimentations.
When he walks out you call four guys you've known.
You disappear into the dark water, brackish, mixing Scotch with
    saltwater.

# Mister Javier's Lesson Plan

## ESL Standards

ESL 1: Students will listen, speak, read, and write in English for information and understanding.

ESL 4: Students will listen, speak, read, and write in English for classroom and social interaction.

ESL 5: Students will demonstrate cross-cultural knowledge and understanding.

## Objective

Students will be able to listen to, retell, and respond (creatively through illustrations, writing, and song) to the story of *Encounter* by Jane Yolen.

## Lesson Sequence

### 1. Personal introduction

"Hello, class, I know I am starting late and I am so glad that you all left your other classes to join me in this special advanced-level English as a Second Language class! We are going to have so much fun together! My name is Rajiv Mohabir, but you can call me Mr. Mohabir."

My class of twelve students was populated by bright-eyed and happy six-year-olds. They mostly spoke Spanish and were English-language learners. Most of their families came from Mexico, Central America, or the Caribbean.

The students walked in and sat in the "meeting area," where boxes of books sorted by reading levels faced the children. The books were kept in multicolored plastic baskets with the letters. The carpet was patterned to look like a little town from a bird's-eye-view—the road led from the fire station to the houses to the church.

"Mister Javier?" A black-haired, black-eyed boy of six fidgeted, hand raised. He looked like a bird that puffs out its feathers before it poops and then shakes.

"Mister Mohabir," I corrected. "Yes, Alonso?"

"I want go bathroom."

"Do you want to go to the bathroom now or can you wait a moment?"

"Never mind," he said, sitting in a darkened puddle.

"Why don't you go to the nurse's office? We will call your parents and they will come and bring you new clothes. Amanda and Wilson, will you please take Alonso to the nurse?" I called the custodians to come and clean up the mess. They came and pulled up the carpet and removed it from the classroom. The students then sat cross-legged on the hard linoleum floor.

The classroom was a rubble heap, still grimy despite my having spent the last five days on my hands and knees scrubbing the caked dirt out of the windowsills, the cupboards, and the closet. The floor's linoleum had started to peel away in the corners of the room. In the back was a sink and to the left of that the closet where I had inherited all kinds of left-over trash. The chalkboard stretched its brown slate from ceiling to floor, the windows were barred with iron rods and only opened six inches, the wooden furniture was mouse-chewed.

I picked up a big pad of chart paper from the floor in front of the door to make a little space. Rays of dust darkened the morning beams of sun that broke through the grime that covered the windows and guard bars. Making this classroom safe for six-year-olds was going to be a full-time job in itself. It was like a filthy cage in which no bird would ever sing.

The assistant principal in her skirt-suit had grilled me with her light eyes during my interview. She hired me, she later told me, for an answer that I had given. Part of my teaching philosophy included treating the students with compassion. Mrs. White loved this answer.

The Teaching Fellows program was a maelstrom of dos and don'ts for teaching. Do speak in the positive while making rules. Do validate the backgrounds of students in the city. Do believe that every child can learn. Do work yourself into the ground. Don't talk to other teachers in the school because they will not understand you or your work. Don't look to us for support outside of the summer session.

It took two trains and one hour fifteen minutes to go from my studio in Jackson Heights to Bushwick. P.S. 45: a concrete block without any green space inside or out. There was, however, a cherry tree that bloomed in the spring as a promise of better fortune to come. The real color of the school was shocking and beautiful. The faculty was as varied with predominantly Black, Dominican, and Mexican students.

## 2. Read Aloud and Active Engagement

We sat in the meeting area, the students on the linoleum and me on a child's chair up front. "How many of you know who Christopher Columbus is?" I asked, holding a picture book.

"He discovered America," five voices chirped in unison. The light from outside shone into the classroom, brightening the space. The students' hair glowed in the light; it looked like each was crowned with a halo. I was so happy to be in front of the class.

Cardo, the smallest student in the class, wore a shirt with a parrot and "Puerto Rico" in red, white, and blue. He stood up and said, "He discovered Puerto Rico! That's where my daddy comes from!" Shorter than the other six-year-olds, he sang as he spoke. Cardo, himself, was birdlike—delicate with a singsong voice.

"Well, there were already people here when he 'discovered' the Americas. Do you think that someone could 'discover' something when there is already someone who lives there?" I asked. The students looked around at each other. "Today we are going to learn about Christopher Columbus by reading a book called *Encounter* by Jane Yolen."

"Yay!" came a cheer from Nicole. This felt good, loosening the knot in my stomach on my first day of teaching. I was flitting about, not sure if I would make it. One student had already pissed himself. I felt as though I might do the same.

"Let's sit crisscross applesauce and fold our hands in our laps," I said as though I were leading a guided meditation. "Let's look at the picture on the cover. What do you see?"

"A man and a boy." Amanda was very bright with her dark Dominican curls and wide eyes.

"Yes, and what is the man doing?"

Amanda now got to her knees and didn't bother raising her hand. "It's a man who looks like he is mean in a big hat and the boy is half-naked and he wants to hug the man."

"Very good, Amanda! Can you show me how we are supposed to sit in the meeting area? How do you think the boy is feeling?" I wanted to see what others thought, too. "Victor?"

"He is feeling happy. When my dad comes home, I like to hug him," Victor was a skinny child with swagger.

"Well, let's see what the boy is feeling as we read the book," I began as I opened the picture book and began to read. It concerned Christopher Columbus first arriving in Guanahani—the island where the little boy lives. Everyone in his tribe is happy to greet Columbus, but this little boy dreams that his zemi tells him to beware. He soon learns that Christopher Columbus is a gold-hungry demon and he kidnaps the boy to go back with him to Spain. The boy escapes from the boat by jumping overboard and goes to other islands to warn Native groups that invaders are coming and that they should be on guard against their deceit and greed.

The wide eyes of the twelve second-graders were sparkling planets. I could see the cognitive dissonance fogging the room. I wondered, *Am*

*I going overboard? Can these kids handle this truth?* I was afraid of what the students' parents would say about their new teacher. I had pulled these students out of their former classrooms where they were taught by middle-aged straight women and they were now in mine—a brown queer teaching radical history in ESL class.

"Okay, please turn to your partners and talk about this book: what happened? How do you think the boy feels about Columbus after reading it?" The students each sat next to someone who would become their reading workshop partner. I counted out three minutes, watching the clock and overhearing snippets of conversation.

"... mean and evil ... scare ... monster ... brown ... Puerto Rico ..." *Good,* I thought, *they are making connections between colonization and their own histories.*

"One two three all eyes on me," I said.

"One two three all eyes on me," the students chanted in unison.

"Nicole and Natalia, what do you think the boy is feeling in the picture?" I asked.

"He is feeling sad because Columbus stole his family away and he will never see them again and he wanted gold and hurt the people," Natalia's voice quivered, brown pigtails bouncing as she moved her head. Her hands motioned as she spoke, flapping like a fledgling testing out her wings. I felt pride tightening in my throat.

"Yes, very good—"

"My daddy is from Puerto Rico and says that Columbus came to our home," Cardo interrupted.

My heart sank like a ship. Was I doing something wrong by teaching this boy whose last name was Colón—Columbus' Spanish name—that this "explorer" was evil?

"What do you think the boy is feeling, Cardo?" I asked, trying to steer the conversation away from a brewing maelstrom. Did Cardo's family identify as Spaniards who happen to live in Puerto Rico?

Cardo put his forefinger to his chin. He was the fairest student in the class—most other teachers read him as white. The teacher in the classroom next to mine commented on him in the morning: "He's so handsome," she said as she greeted her students into the classroom.

Cardo looked at me and said, "I think he is scared. But my daddy says that Puerto Rico people are nice, and he doesn't understand why people are so scared of him." He got to his feet and approached the picture book. "He also said that Puerto Rico is not bad, but this book makes it look bad."

I had to say something. I looked at my hands. I knew what it was like to be profiled for how I looked—understood as a threat for no reason and unable to change it. I looked into his brown eyes. Maybe Cardo's father had been racially profiled in the city and communicated his frustration to his son. "Sometimes people like Christopher Columbus do bad things, but that doesn't mean that in Puerto Rico people are bad."

"But why are you saying that he was a monster?" Cardo was clearly distressed. I hadn't told them about Christopher Columbus's bloodthirst: the way he chopped off brown hands from brown bodies if they didn't bring him enough gold.

I thought back to when I flew to New York City as I left Orlando International Airport—how the TSA agent relished patting me down, placing his fingers in my underwear band, questioning me about my carry-on luggage that held a laptop and a few books on radical pedagogy. When I landed, I found the official slips in my luggage that told me that airport security had rifled through my bags. They'd seen my last name and read me as a threat of terror. The agent searched me because he saw my skin. I wanted to affirm Cardo, to tell him that he was beautiful—not for his fair skin but for something deeper—and so was his father, and it was the American imperialism, the social realities that were distorted, messed up, and evil. I didn't know yet how to translate this into language a second-grader would understand.

"Your dad sounds like a very smart man." I looked at the clock. We had to move on. Reading workshop was almost done. The principal wandered the halls making sure that all the teachers in the grade were moving at the same pace to the next lessons for the day. I looked at the class and asked, "Would you want to celebrate a man like Columbus?"

## 3. Student Practice

Part of the writing lesson was to make protest signs against celebrating Columbus Day. I came to school prepared with ten packets of markers, poster board, and sentence strips for the students to write their slogans on.

"Today we are going to make posters about Christopher Columbus based on Jane Yolen's book *Encounter*. What words do you want to write? Tell me so I can write them on the board." I picked up a piece of chalk.

"Evil," came one voice. "Monster," cried another. "Guanahani," "Columbus," and "Taíno" were words that the students called out. I wrote them all, excited by the sound of chalk on a fresh board: new knowledge on a young mind.

I split up the class in mixed writing and reading levels and had them come up with a slogan and write it on their sentence strips. Some students wrote *Columbus this is NOT your land!* or *Columbus was greedy for gold* and *Celebrate Taíno memory not Columbus's greed,* asking for my help spelling words that I did not have written on the board. My heart sang like a parrot freed from its cage.

"Now on your poster boards please illustrate parts of the book that you liked," I instructed. Cardo drew a picture of the zemi, the Taíno god; Nicole's group drew Columbus's ship that landed in Guanahani. Natalia drew a picture of a gold sovereign with the scene of Columbus's men behind it. I was surprised, as I floated about, that these students were talking about the story.

When they were done, I called the students to gather back at the meeting area. We needed to review our work and practice retelling the story.

I took out chart paper as the students obediently crossed their legs, their marker-colored hands folded in their laps.

"Let's tell the story of *Encounter*," I said, "but let's tell it in ten syllables," I repeated, clapping with every beat. The students had practiced phonemic awareness with their previous teacher.

Cardo called out, "Do not welcome them, my dream's a warning." He was a poet, composing so quickly. I wrote in blue marker on the chart paper.

"Very good." I looked around. "The next line should be six syllables," I said. "Turn to your partner and come up with a line."

Amanda raised her hand. "They want to steal our spice, they want all of our gold."

"Very good, Amanda," I said as I wrote *They want spice, they want gold* on the paper. "I've changed what you said but only a little. Is this okay?"

Amanda looked at me, pleased with herself and nodded. The lesson continued until I elicited responses from the students. I wrote down the words:

*Do not welcome them, my dream's a warning.*
*They want spice. They want gold.*
*Christopher Columbus*
*Enslaved the Taínos*
*and stole their land, stole their land.*

When I told the students that they could sing this song to the tune of "Frère Jacques" they gasped in excitement.

### 4. Share Out

"Now," I said with a full grin, "it's time to go and let everyone know what we've done."

The students lined up and marched down the hall into the main office holding their signs high in the air, singing the song that we had written based on the summary of *Encounter*. We took over the main office and interrupted classrooms along the way, stopping in to sing our song and to share our signs. The students taught the other teachers and the other students in various grades the story of Christopher Columbus and why we shouldn't be celebrating Columbus Day—that instead we should celebrate Taíno heritage and memory. Columbus Day was fast approaching, and the students didn't want any part of it. *This is critical pedagogy,* I thought, satisfied with myself.

## 5. Reflection

The next night was parent-teacher night. I learned phrases in Spanish like *Tu hija se comporta bien en la clase; tu hijo necesita practicar de lectura.* I wanted the parents to trust me, to see me as an ally in their student's education in a racist system. I dressed up for the event in khaki pants, Timberland boots, a gray button-up shirt with a yellow paisley tie. I wanted to look a little older than twenty-five.

It was strange being at school at night. No light crept past the bars and into the windows. The classroom was illuminated only by the fluorescent lights that hummed their halogen glow overhead. Cardo ran into the classroom. "Mister Javier?" A deep voice boomed behind him. Cardo sat in the meeting area and picked out a book about the parrots of Brooklyn to read.

"Mister Colón," I held out my hand to shake his. He grabbed my hand and nodded slightly without a smile. He was a broad man with a full head of brown hair, his skin as fair as Cardo's. He was striking and attractive. I felt a little giddy. I wanted to seem trustworthy. I wondered if he read my queerness. I had worried about this for a while—what would the parents think if they met me and were disappointed, not wanting their students to be in my class?

I directed Mr. Colón to sit in a chair where the students sat. I sat opposite of him with a notepad and pen ready to take notes on anything he wanted me to find out for him.

"Mister Javier," he began. "Is that your name? You Dominican?" His strong jawline and lips did not betray his thoughts.

"Oh, it's actually Mohabir. My family is South Asian and not Dominican. But in fact, my parents and grandparents are from South America."

He let out a *humph* and folded his arms across his chest. I looked out the window. There were no birds, only bars. The streetlights bled their jaundiced yellow onto the pavement. "You're the one teaching my child about Christopher Columbus?" he asked, furrowing his eyebrows.

My heart beat out of my chest. My mouth dried and my palms sweat. My leg started to shake. Maybe my leftist politics and penchant for critical pedagogy seemed extreme. I mean, what second-grader is ready to hear the story of the destructive hurricane that Columbus and the Europeans brought into this hemisphere?

I took a deep breath. I had to tell him my plans for this class; he would find out anyway. I planted my feet on the ground and blurted out, "Yes, I taught Cardo about Christopher Columbus. It's part of a larger unit where I trace the invasion of the Americas by the Europeans and end up looking at immigration in Brooklyn today. I want the students to understand the connections between anti-immigrant sentiments and an anti-Native feeling all over the country."

Mr. Colón sat back in his chair. It creaked under his weight. He raised his eyebrows. I was sure that I had angered him. I was certain that he would demand that his son be sent back to Mrs. Rossi's classroom where the students were writing thank you letters to Christopher Columbus for "discovering" America.

He motioned to the posters pinned to the chalkboard with dinosaur magnets. "Which one is Cardo's?" he asked. I pointed to the zemi. "He's been singing that song nonstop since yesterday," he said as he relaxed his eyebrows and leaned forward in his chair.

"It's based on the book *Encounter* by Jane Yolen," I said, emphasizing that I was working from the state-approved curriculum.

Mr. Colón put his face in his hands. Was he crying? He took a deep breath. The lights flickered with a tinkle.

"Thank you so much Mister Javier for teaching my son my history," he said, drawing back upright. There were tear streaks on his cheeks. "Since I moved to this country, I have had to forget so much of where I'm from. I am worried that Cardo would not learn about where he's from, about his people. Even though there are no Taíno people around anymore, I have Taíno blood—we all do who come from Puerto Rico. The Taíno didn't disappear, they are us. We live in cages here in New York. We are no longer allowed to be free."

My arms were stiff. Was he really thanking me for teaching his son this history? It never occurred to me that there would be parents who would feel affirmed by what we did in our second-grade classroom. But it made sense. So many of my students were Mexican or from the Caribbean— so many had indigenous lineage. Traditionally the American school was the place that sought to un-Indian the Indian. I wondered about how many parents must have feared that in order for their children to succeed in school that they would be forced to abandon their identities as Native.

I looked at Mr. Colón and then at Cardo sitting in the meeting area by himself. Were my parents afraid like this for me when my brother, my sister, and I went to school? Was this why they didn't want us to speak Creole? Was this why they had resisted learning Guyanese Bhojpuri from their parents? Were their parents afraid, too?

Mr. Colón looked like he could have been my age. I wanted to reach across the table and give him a hug and tell him that I understood what he was saying and promise to do my best to teach honestly and reflectively. I wanted to assure him that my classroom was a safe space. I wanted to give him back his wings so he could fly. I reached out and placed my hand on Mr. Colón's shoulder.

# Islamophobic Misreadings:
## Some Queens Definitions

**Islamophobia - (n) from:**

*Islam* – Arabic: surrender to the will of God

*Phobia* – Greek: an irrational fear

**Islamophobia** is the irrational fear, prejudice against, hatred for Islam or Muslims: a contemptuous way of viewing Islam or Muslims that existed before the crusades, endured past World War II, and was reimagined in country songs after the Twin Towers fell on September 11, 2001.

**Misreading - (n) from:**

*Mis* – Old French: prefix to denote wrongness

*Reading* – Old English *rǣdan*: to advise or interpret

**Misreading** is the basing of judgement of a person on preconceived notions: literally *to read incorrectly*: a way of racially profiling brown bodies.

❀

**Islamophobic Misreading** is when a parent of one of your former students approaches you outside the schoolyard and emulates their version of what Arabic sounds like and talks to you in Ecuadorian Spanish saying, "*Mahalahama, pareces uno de los hombres del once de Septiembre que atacaron las torres.*"

She laughs and tells your friend standing next to you not to translate. She continues, "*Para esto tu ves gordo.*"

You catch *gordo* and you ask your friend to translate.

She says, "Some people are so ignorant. She said that you look like one of the bombers from September eleventh and she asked me not to tell you."

You say, "And she called me fat."

❀

**Islamophobic Misreading** is outside on the cul-de-sac in Chuluota. The white neighbor woman asks your sister, "What will God think about a brown girl with Islamic writing on her arm?"

Your sister replies, "First of all there is no such thing as Islamic writing, and this is Hindi. And I'm pretty sure that God loves this little brown girl with or without tattoos."

❀

**Islamophobic Misreading** is a Facebook post on a photo of you with a beard.

*Comments from a high school classmate: Wow! That beard puts the Arabs to shame over here. R . . . You remind me of a character from a movie. It might be* Aladdin *or another Disney movie. That facial expression is hilarious. I can't place it yet, but it will come to me.*

❀

**Islamophobic Misreading** is when you are an ESL teacher and your assistant principal says that he wants the newcomer hijabi girl to remain in your class because you may speak "Islam" and that you will know "how to handle these kinds of parents."

When you explain that you don't know any spoken "Islam" and your Arabic is limited to only a couple of phrases from Bollywood movies, he says that any commonality is sufficient.

At testing time (when the students are required to take their high-stakes tests even though they've been in the country less than a year) he says that as the student took the test (with the Egyptian Arabic speaker hired by the district as a translator) he noticed the student did not write in "hieroglyphics" but rather wrote in "normal" language of English letters in "fucked up phonetics."

✿

**Islamophobic Misreading** is when the Dominican man working at the restaurant called Caridad says to you, "Why you have a beard, no tienes calor? Where are you from?"

You answer one at a time, "I just like it. Yeah I get hot, but I'm from Florida. I'm of Indian descent."

"Oh, India? You are trying to look like a real Indian?"

"Well, I'm not sure what you mean."

"You should shave your beard, you're a handsome guy. You are Muslim, right, you don't want to look too Muslim."

"Well, actually no, I'm not Muslim."

"Oh, so you're telling me that I can trust you." He laughs at this for a loud thirty seconds.

✿

**Islamophobic Misreading** is the public response to the death of Osama Bin Laden. You recorded in your journal:

i didn't want to hear american reactions, or see the joy in the people dancing on the pavement rendering flags in a nationalist seizure.

a friend posts on Facebook "may god protect all the american troops and the christians in the middle east. and bomb those rag heads."

obama says, "thanks to the tireless and heroic work of our military and our counterterrorism professionals, we've made great strides in that effort."

while this is happening another drone dropped a bomb— dropped on the tribal waziristani hills raising the death toll to 109,895 civilian deaths.

i don't understand words like *collateral damage* and *civil*.

whose agenda is this mysterious sea burial serving, why wouldn't the body be sent to the family.

*dear christian god teach me to turn the other cheek or to love my neighbor.*

※

**Islamophobic Misreading** is when you are singing your Aji's song and the words are Ultan-Sultan. You sing for your aunts and uncles and your father laughs and says to his brothers and sisters, "They must have been fullah with names like Ultan and Sultan," unaware that his Muslim brother-in-law is sitting right there.

*Fullah*, or *fullahman* is the Caribbean Bhojpuri word for the Hindi *mussalman* or Muslim.

Your father profusely apologizes and your uncle says, "It's too bad you think our relationship is so fragile that I wouldn't be able to heal from the wound of your comment."

When he leaves, the whole family starts laughing.

❖

**Islamophobic Misreading** is when the principal at your school asks if you are allowed to shave your beard, asking also if you are keeping it for "religious" reasons.

The security guard in full police regalia, complete with a pistol, at the entrance to the elementary school says she wouldn't know if your name wasn't *Mohammad Singh*—her version of an arbitrary brown name.

She points out whenever she sees you that you look "more and more traditional."

❖

**Islamophobic Misreading** is sitting around a table with seven of your New York City Teaching Fellow cohort buddies after a day of intense swimming in the Pacific on a random beach in Costa Rica and one of your "buddies" says, "Islam is the worst religion, it's so oppressive to women and the Koran is evil for promising murderers virgins in the hereafter."

You ask him if he has ever read any of the Koran outside of the surahs the media publishes for its own ends, if he's ever heard Hadith, or whether he's considered the fact that women are objectified and suppressed in the West—that the covering, the hijab and burqa, can sometimes be liberating. In places where there is a growing atheism, virulent and itself oppressive when imperialistic—the new religion of the educated white people who once told brown folks that we were ani-mals based on "science"—a woman who covers herself is clearly aligning herself with something, be it a belief in god or an identifier to say that she will be subjugated by neither a Western norm nor a meta-narrative where she must display her own body for the pleasure, enjoyment, and consumption of men.

He moves on to say that the Indians in Trinidad make a farce of Indian culture—that they are not *real* Indians.

❁

**Islamophobic Misreading** is when people observe your skin color and beard and hear a non-American accent in your voice. You walk into a store to buy yogurt, cheese, and bread and three women in hijabs smile at you and ask you in Urdu if you could help them get the paper towels down from the top shelf.

As you check out, the young white clerk asks you if you need a bag, and when you tell him, "Oh, it's okay, thanks, I have my own," he asks again in a loud and slow voice, pointing to the bags and to the three items he just scanned. You laugh and say in a slow loud voice, "THANK YOU, NO BAG, I HAVE MY OWN."

He rolls his eyes and sighs, "I don't speak Islam."

❁

**Islamophobic Misreading** is when a friend hears you say, "I'm from Guyana," and says, "You can't say you're from Guyana, you were born in London."

You feel it's a bit imperialistic for a white person to tell you so defini-tively what you are and where you're from. Your friend sometimes tells others about how "untraditional" your family is. Your friend has never had to explain a long history for people to understand where he's from.

He simply has to say, "My family was from Michigan before we moved to Florida."

You have to say, "I was born in London, my parents are from South America, but we are actually of South Asian descent." You cut corners by saying things like, "I am South Asian, I am Indian, I am Guyanese." These answers change when you talk to different people. If the person is South Asian, you say, "I am Guyanese." When you talk to a white person you say, "I am Indian," to avoid their questions.

❀

**Islamophobic Misreading** is when a white New York poet asks why you're afraid to board the subway and then proceeds to ask, "Is it because you're a terrorist?"

❀

**Islamophobic Misreading** is the question, Can South Asian—presumably *Muslim* families—ever accept queerness without having first *assimilated*?

A New York therapist asked you what it was like "coming out" to your parents in your culture. You tell her that it was okay, even though your father will never fully come to terms with it.

She says with the understanding, do-gooder sparkle in her eyes, "That's not good enough. You deserve a family that supports you despite what Allah thinks. You may have to eventually stop talking to them until they can accept you."

You say that your mother's cool.

Motioning to a picture of your family she replies, "Your mother is very modern, she even wears jeans!"

Your mother wears jeans, skirts, salwar kameez, and bathing suits. She often points out to you other South Asian men who may be queer whom she thinks you would find attractive. You joke about marrying doctors with property in the Virgin Islands.

❁

**Islamophobic Misreading** is when Christians mock the Muslim belief in the Prophet's flight to Medina, his literacy skills, or his conversation with Jibril, because Christians don't rely on other people's translations of texts done centuries ago, because Christians don't handle poisonous snakes claiming to be protected by the holy spirit, because they don't deny their children health care, believing either God will heal them or that an illness is God's will, and because they don't believe that they are waiting for a god to come from the sky and take them all "home," like aliens to a mother ship.

❁

**Islamophobic Misreading** is when the teachers responsible for the fifth-grade graduation ceremony move the only girl in a hijab from the front row that faces the parents to the back of the auditorium, claiming, "She doesn't know the words to the songs very well and she is hunched over." They keep, however, the newcomer Dominican boy in the front row who has just come back to school after several weeks of sick leave. He doesn't know the words at all and will not be able to master them by the graduation ceremony two days from now. The newcomer Dominican student does not wear a hijab, often referred to in the school as a "headdress."

❁

**Islamophobic Misreading** is everyone expecting you to shave your beard since it's not a religious act of devotion for you. You are trapped into elevator conversations by WASPy women saying things like, "Are you going to trim it with a buzzer first and then shave it, or are you going to just go and have someone else remove it for you?"

You obviously will not keep it since it makes you "look too Muslim," (and "you're an American, aren't you?") as a coworker points out as you leave the elevator.

❈

**Islamophobic Misreading** is always being the person who is randomly searched by the TSA airport security guards. You start a collection of airport security slips that read, "Your luggage was chosen randomly to be searched"—two for every trip you take.

❈

**Islamophobic Misreading** is your complicity when you ask your sister to cover her shoulders and bra straps with a sweater in eighty-six degree weather because you are in a very conservative neighborhood and you assume she will be harassed on the streets. She refuses to see your point and replies, "Don't tell me what to do, this is America. I thought I was free."

❈

**Islamophobic Misreading** is when your one student who usually wears a hijab takes it off to put on a baseball cap for the fifth-grade field trip to Chelsea Piers and another teacher says to you, "Wow, she is becoming more American. I almost didn't recognize her without her headdress."

You tell her it's a hijab and that she and her sister wear it of their own volition. She says, "Someone should tell them that they are free now that they are in America."

❋

**Islamophobic Misreading** is when you do not "pledge allegiance to the flag of the United States of America" because you don't believe that "with liberty and justice for all" is true at all and another teacher watches you and asks you to stand outside so none of the students sees a teacher not pledging, modeling dissent, due to your "religious reasons."

❋

**Islamophobic Misreading** is President Obama refusing to go to the Swarna Mandir, the Golden Temple in Amritsar, because he didn't want people to see him covering his head "like a Muslim."

# American Guyanese Diwali

I buy marigolds and paper pictures of the three devas, I light the diyas into prayer, that every new home is a Diwali. To feel home, the art of where I'm not from, the batiks, the women playing three instruments, I wish I had that many hands, one would be fully in my pants, the others would be at the chowki and belna, the others would be a mystery, what books would they thumb through and realize *this is no mirror.* I have never been vain enough to think *everyone here is a guitar* or the fingerpicking "Born in the Land of the Mighty Roraima" was an actual creation story. A loud outer metronome keeps the boys in line. Even now I keep my Aja's scissors sharp enough to keep the boys in rum line. Every time I strike a match *om* my *om* breath *om* blows it out. Every time I intend to fulfill dharma, I pick up a flute and play *jai jagdish hare, victory to god of the universe* and my navel string aches from a garbage dump or an animal's belly. I am as inauspicious as a vulture: a father's son who is not a son. Every time I strike a match it is not a sun.

# Aji Recording:
## Love Beat Handsome

LOVE BEAT HANDSOME. Na care how yuh deh. But when you love somebody you love 'am. You Aja been get twenty-two year an' me been one lil chile wha' jus' a grow up. Dem days me been happy. When me live a me muddah in law house, me been real happy.

*pardesi sajanwa ke aaya re*
*adar karo pardesi sajanwa re*

An' when spring wata does come, rivah side wata does come 'e been a swamp. Whe' abi house been deh been a one swamp. So battam de house wata does always come. When a spring come, 'e a full a battam house. So much wata 'e does get. Me does take one piece a sal'fish an' tie 'em pan twine—bab twine. An' me does sit doung pan de step, de house step an' does get one bucket an' one basket. An' me put da hook, da bait pan de twine an' duck 'em in de wata.

An' big big sharigah does come. An' when 'e a bite de bait, 'e a run wid 'am. Yuh lif' 'am easy easy an' tek a basket an' yuh a swim 'am out. You a cetch 'am an' take a grass knife an' bore 'am an' yuh put 'am in yuh bucket. Leh 'e na run. When 'e get a bore 'e na run. So yuh bore 'am an' put 'am in a basket.

An' in de bucket. An' when yuh get half bucket an' come a yuh house—yuh come out from de wata an' pan de step an' yuh come pan

214

de landing now. You clean 'am, you wash 'am, yuh cook, an' you eat. Me does bail 'am wid coconut milk. Sometime you a fry 'am wid black peppah. Same kine sharigah wha' bite yuh han'. Da same kine sharigah.

If yuh see a big big one, too—yuh cetch 'am an' you a cook. Dem days a done. Yuh cyan' get dem back. De battam house. Wha' dem a call a basement he' abi call 'em battam house. When de wata gan an' de place a dry, yuh a dab 'am—dab da battam house wid cow dung an' mud. 'E does be shine shine. Every day abi does siddung an' eat righ' deh, me an' you Aja an' 'e faddah an muddah. An' Lalloo, too. Cook upstais an' eat a battam.

So when wata come in now, a ting na mess up? 'E na nasee? So you cyan' do nutting. You cetch de crab an' t'ing an' you a cook. One time me an' you Aja been cetch about one hundred crab. You siddung pan de step wha' you come doung fe go a battam—same step you siddung. De wata been so much so you take a sal'fish an' tie 'am an' so crab a come an' hook onto de sal'fish. An' so you na cetch 'am?

Abbi been get one barril, punchin abbi does call 'am. So me does full 'am in deh. An' every time you a mek soup you tek about five-six a dem an' me a clean 'am an' me a wash dem an' me a mek soup wid 'am.

When nobady na deh a house. When you Aja alone—me does cetch 'bout three-four a dem from de barril, clean 'am, an' fry 'am wid black peppah. An abbi two been siddung pan de coungtah an' abbi two a eat like a hell. Me faddah in law na been vex. But you know, you mus' respec' zat you na go show dem wha' you a do. Abbi been get a respec' like da—dat you cyan' eat in front a dem. So when dem come me a t'row 'way all de crab bone an' ting.

Me muddah in law does tell me, "Beti a you cook crab tiday, right?"
Me tell 'am, "Yes, Ma."
"Arright"
"You want it? Leh me cook fe a you?"
'E sah, "Na beti, me go cook." So wha' she wan' she go cook. Buy hassa sell every day.

Me been a de only datah in law far 'em, 'e na been get no more. Lalloo been married when 'e done dead an' t'ing. So 'e na know none. Me a de only one. An' me been a lovin' fe all 'e family, all 'e cousin an' ting. But dose days done.

*gayi jawani phir na aye*
*chahe dudh ham litah kha*

Days gan, you can do wha' you want to but you na go get back da. Da gan.

# Sangam / Confluence

LIVING IN QUEENS, my love for Bollywood reawakened and I remembered how much the color and dance enticed me. At eight I'd been bewitched. I sat with Aji in her Scarborough tenement eating phulauri and drinking Kool-Aid. On her TV, a bootleg VHS copy of the 1964 film *Sangam* hummed. Aji told me that sangam was the confluence of not two but three rivers: the Ganga, the Jamuna, and the mythological Saraswati River, which dried up, or perhaps never flowed, but is a crossover from the universe that guides our decisions, where stories live and breathe. This merging of three dark bodies of water is sometimes translated as "confluence," where waters mix. In the film *Sangam*, Raj Kapoor, Vyjayanthimala, and Rajendra Kumar play out what would become, in my mind, an archetypical love story—one of the ways that brown people like me are supposed to lap one another with their waters into a confluence. More than this, I would realize later, the undertow pulled the film's threads of homoeroticism out into the open ocean—something that would happen to me.

Aji interpreted the Hindi in the film, giving me the gist in Guyanese Creole. This was the first Hindi movie I'd ever seen, and her translations were not exact.

What haunted me about this film was that Sundar and Gopal—both men—seemed as though they wanted their brown bodies to meet, though Radha was the object to be desired. At eight years old, I could see but not yet fully understand how this love could work, or what it could actually be.

"Dis bai seh he go sit Radha 'pon he plane," Aji said of the quarrel between Sundar (played by Raj Kapoor) and Gopal (Rajendra Kumar) who attempts to seat Radha (Vyjayanthimala) on his plane. These two men love the same woman. Sundar grows up to become a pilot for the Indian Air Force, and Gopal, after returning to India from studying in London, stays behind as Sundar goes to Kashmir on a dubious mission.

Aji explained: When Gopal and Radha hear that Sundar's plane was shot down and that he is MIA, they allow their love for each other to bloom. But Sundar lives and returns to demand Radha's hand, who acquiesces. Eventually Sundar finds a letter from Gopal to Radha and is so vexed, he vows to kill Gopal. Eventually Gopal shoots and kills himself with Sundar's gun so that nothing will come between Sundar and Radha's love.

❉

With eyes wide as a tuna's, I sat on Aji's velvet couch.

"Akhiya bandh kar. Shet you eye, beta," Aji laughed.

"I don't want to close my eyes," I said as I drank in all the Hindi and Creole.

Radha bathes in a river, hiding her clothes on the bank. She knows what Sundar is up to. A pervy Sundar, having climbed a tree with his bagpipe to sing the movie's title song, finds her clothes and thieves them with a fishing rod.

"I will give you your clothes back when you answer my question," says Sundar to a bathing Radha.

"What do you want?" Radha replies, eyes besmeared in Ganga and kohl.

"Just pretend for a moment that I am not Sundar, that I'm Gopal, and Gopal wants to ask you something." Sundar sings.

*mere man ki Ganga*
*aur tere man ki Jamuna ka*
*bol Radha bol sangam*
*hoga ke nahin*

*My heart's Ganga*
*and yours of the Jamuna*
*Tell me Radha,*
*will the sangam happen or not*

❋

Jackson Heights was bright with South Asia. Along Kalpana Chawla Way, also known as 74th Street, Pakistani and Bangladeshi stores and stalls lined the streets. Bright red and yellow silks on people and in shop windows, the smell of frying samosas, the metered rhythms of the dhol beating out bhangra beats, and a swirl of brown faces made up Jackson Heights. I was perfectly comfortable in my brown skin in this South Asian enclave. My American Guyanese-ness made more sense in Richmond Hill, the Little Guyana of Queens, where I had family. My father had told me that I was pretending to be an Indian rather than Indo-Caribbean, that people from India or Pakistan or Sri Lanka or Nepal didn't understand me as similar to them. But I was not convinced. Yes, I was not Indian, but neither were Pakistanis nor Bangladeshis nor Nepalis nor Sri Lankans. My living in Jackson Heights added another dimension to the South Asian contingent of the area.

All my life I had been told by my family that "Guyanese are different. We're not like de Indiaman"—we were Coolie, great grandchildren of indentured laborers for whom India was only a myth. But I felt a kinship with other South Asians. I spoke English, learned Hindi, and loved Bollywood. All these things peppered my life like Aji's pepper sauce, adding flavor and the burn to learn as much as I could. I moved to Queens—rather than Manhattan, Brooklyn, or the Bronx—because of a visit to Jake in Richmond Hill when I was eighteen and the trip we took to Jackson Heights to eat at a famous Indian restaurant. I saw a billboard with the Bollywood film star Shah Rukh Khan on the corner of Broadway and Roosevelt Avenue and decided, yes, this is where I wanted to be—in a brown community where grocery shopping would be easier, where I wouldn't be profiled as often by neighbors. But now, these days of closeness with Jake were over. Though I lived in the same borough our friendship could not be mended. In fact, since moving to New York I had neither seen nor heard from any of my father's family, despite reaching out to them when I arrived.

Soon after I moved to my studio on 37th Avenue and 80th Street, I got a call from Farida, my friend from the Youth Solidarity Summer.

"You are living in Jackson Heights? Wow. You win Desi of the Year Award," she teased. We made plans to meet for dosas on 73rd Street, along with her cousin, whom I'd met at the YSS party. I remembered him as a cherub, with a round face and pink lips, who was learning leftist politics by hanging with his cousin's friends.

We had protested together, chanting our throats raw, "The people united will never be defeated!" in front of that same restaurant. It had since closed and reopened, rebranded, with new owners.

"Rajiv!" Farida shouted across the room as soon as I entered the restaurant. She got up from the booth to give me a hug. Her cousin watched us from his seat, with wide eyes and a faint smile.

"It's so good to see you, Farida!" I said. As we embraced, I bumped the table and water from a copper tumbler spilled, her cousin jumping up to avoid it.

"You remember Yusef," Farida said as I moved to wipe up the mess with a napkin.

"Sef," he said, correcting his cousin. He grabbed a napkin from the neighboring table and wiped up the water with me. His hand brushed mine.

"Hey, Sef. Good to see you again." Straightening up, I looked at his eyes and saw what looked like a man. This surprised me. When I met him before, his hair was messy, his face round. Now, Sef had a jawline and stubble. He smelled of attar al haram and musk. I could feel my stomach churn as my attraction to this man pulsed through me. He was muscular yet still soft, his voice deep and kind. His broad shoulders would intimidate if not for his gentle eyes and lips as pink as cotton candy.

We ate Pondicherry, rava masala, and butter dosas and laughed about having to finish college and how I would never leave school now that I was getting a master's degree in teaching. I watched Sef's lips as he ate, two pink clouds I wanted to jump into.

Farida worked as the leader of her college's South Asians for Justice organization, queering the Desi population with her radical politics. "It's funny how the belief that everyone should be equal is radical," she mused into her salty lassi. "I mean, just because I am a Muslim queer and I believe that I should be safe—how the fuck does that make me 'radical'?"

I nodded. "It's so true."

"At least I can do something in the world to make it easier for others." Farida finished her stainless steel cup of water.

"I sometimes think that teaching is the easy way out—like it's not really activist work," I replied.

"Actually, you're at ground zero. I mean ESL? You're helping people navigate the system from the stem." Farida's raised eyebrows arched into bows.

"I never thought of it that way," I replied.

"How do you like Jackson Heights?" Sef asked.

"It's great, though I feel like I don't really belong. . . . I'm Coolie, not really Desi. . . . Being Indo-Guyanese is different." I looked at the table. "Even dosas are different for Guyanese. They are floppy and sweet, not crispy like chips."

"I know what you mean—we are Pakistani but there was no India and Pakistan until 1947. And before that we lived in what is now India," Sef said. "Borders are bullshit."

We all laughed in agreement. Farida left, having to catch a bus back to Baltimore.

"I am totally free, Rajiv, if you want to still hang out," Sef said, eyebrows raised. He was tall and beautiful. I wanted to keep smelling him. I wanted to keep smelling him in my house.

"Want to come to my place and have chai?" I said.

He followed me to the building at the corner of 80th Street and 37th Avenue. The stone lions that guarded the entrance glared down at me as I walked by. I felt their judgment, like summer heat. *I'm not doing anything wrong*, I thought and wiped my brow of sweat. It was humid, with a few clouds hanging their black bellies low in the sky.

My studio was bright and warm. The hardwood floorboards gleamed in the sunlight that shone through the kitchen window. In the afternoon, the light painted orange and gold shadows on the prewar molding.

Sef walked around then sat on my futon—I didn't have a proper bed. I hurried to the kitchen to boil milk.

"This place is great!" he said from the other room, crossing his legs.

"Yeah, especially the location. I have never been so close to so many brown people." I laughed. I was glad that he couldn't see me grate the ginger, then, giddy, grate my finger as I placed the grater in the sink.

"But don't you feel like you don't really belong? I mean you said you are *Coolie*—I mean Indo-Guyanese—and these folks are Desi."

Desi. That word burned like too much chili when he said it. Desi—from the Punjabi, meaning "from the country." My parents used to say, *Indians from India don't see us as Indian*. My father's own insecurity bled through my body like spilled water through a napkin.

"Well. . . ." I shuddered.

Sef got up from the futon and grabbed my shoulder with his large hand. "What I mean is that I have a complicated history." His hand was steady and warm. "My father's side is Punjabi from Amritsar and my mother's side was originally from Sindh and stayed in Pakistan after the partition. I have a hard time explaining to Desis that I am not just Sindhi, or I am not just Punjabi. I couldn't imagine how you have to keep insisting on your place of origin."

I was stunned. Sef was insightful for his age. He welcomed me as a South Asian with my own particular migration story and told his story as a parallel—a likeness that intersected with mine.

Sef sat back down on my futon, one leg curled under the other. He was relaxed and his lips were dry. He licked them now and again and I imagined how soft they could be when wet.

I pranced back into the kitchen and sang quietly to myself, "Mere man ki Ganga, aur tere man ki Jamuna ka." I emerged from the kitchen with a tray carrying two cups of chai and chaat to eat.

"Chai leejiye ji," I sang.

Sef laughed at my formality and took his tea. "I'm bi, by the way," he added coolly. I looked at him. Was this really happening?

"Oh?" I sat down next to him, almost missing the futon. My hands were sweaty and shaking. I spilled my chai. Sef was coming on to me and I wanted him to, but if anything happened with him what would his sister say? What would the other people from the protest think? The clouds let out a low rumble.

"I've been out to my family for about four years," I said, "though I had a couple boyfriends before that." I put my cup on the ground. "Are you out to Farida?" I asked, trying to remain as cool as Sef. My leg shook and my throat balled up in anticipation. I looked at him. I was into his dark eyes and wide smile, his comfort and openness. Something about him was very familiar to me despite us being from worlds apart—my growing up in Chuluota and his young adulthood in Queens.

"No. I am new to all of this. But I have a friend, his name is Dilip, and he has been showing me a few things." The room was getting hot. My ears were burning and I scalded my tongue on my chai, like swallowing fire. Sef's face pinked into his lips' shade.

"Dilip—he's Desi?" I said. "What kinds of things is he showing you?" My heart beat fast in my chest and my skin warmed.

It started to rain outside. The sun was swallowed by gray, and the air smelled of copper and electricity. Sef and I both paused to look outside.

"Some . . . things . . . you know," he smiled, looked at me, and put his chai cup on the ground.

"Oh, your poor parents who have to deal with two queers in the family!" I chuckled. Sef let out a belly laugh and touched my thigh. He trailed his finger up to my zipper and unbuttoned my shorts.

"Is this too much?" he asked. Sef placed his fingers on my skin.

"No, it's not." These were all the words I could manage.

Jackson Heights was a rush of water, a deluge.

❁

Gopal and Radha enter a party. She wears white silk—flowers in her hair—and he, a black suit. Sundar enters the room, carrying an accordion. Sundar sings a song for his beloved Radha and Gopal. Sundar circles Gopal, then Radha as he plays his accordion.

Gopal, avoiding eye contact with Sundar, begins to sing.

Gopal:
*Every heart that loves*
*will sing this song*

Sundar:
*You have stolen my heart*
*my eyes are next*
*but don't you know*
*that wherever there are flames*
*moths gather?*

Radha, sitting at a piano, sings:
*Those forgotten memories of our childhood*
*spent laughing and singing*
*now at night steal my sleep.*
*I will confess, but how many monsoons*
*have come and gone? Who knows when*
*the shyness will leave my eyes?*

In the next scene, Radha and her friend read a letter to Gopal at Radha's house. Radha's salwar kameez, white with gold borders, contrasts with her long, black, tapering braid. Her friend snatches the letter out of her hand and runs out of the room to call Gopal.

Gopal comes in and says, "Radha, you wanted to see me? Is everything okay?"

Radha fumbles for her dupatta, the scarf to cover herself, and sees that it's across the room on a couch. She runs to get it, ashamed of her state of undress.

✿

For months, Sef found excuses to come to my place and take off his clothes. We were a mess of late summer, our skin like afternoon's gold light on the mattress.

Once, we lay in bed together, Sef's pink lips smiling into the early evening.

"Did you know that I'm related to Dilip Kumar and that he was supposed to be in *Sangam* until Raj Kapoor vetoed his editorial decision?"

"But isn't Dilip Kumar a Hindu name?" I blinked.

"Yes, but back then, in the 1940s, Muslim actors took on Hindu names. Have you seen *Mughal-e-Azam*?" He asked.

"I'm really bad at this game," I admitted.

"There's a song that you should know. 'Teri Mehfil Mein Kismat Azmakar Ham Bhi Dekhenge,'" Sef said.

Sef still hadn't told his parents about me. Once, rolling back the sheets, he told me, "I will marry a woman and have children one day," and popped a mint into his mouth.

Why tell his parents that he slept with men too? What Coolie and Desi parents don't know won't kill them. I wanted to give my immigrant parents the benefit of the doubt. My own mother was finally okay, though only after she had cried for two years every time we spoke. Sef's situation was different. His parents were different. He was the only son. I was the second son. My brother already had children, so the pressure was off of me to make my mother an Aji or my father an Aja. Sef was bi and the only son in his family and this meant something to his mother. I trusted that he'd figure himself out one day.

"Isn't your friend named Dilip?" I asked. We had agreed to remain casual—Sef and I were free to fuck whomever we wanted. There was no need to put a name to anything. I wanted to embody New York City and keep my options open.

"Oh, yeah—his name is Dilip Kaniyar. His first name is Punjabi but his last name is Malayal," he said.

I yawned and mumbled, "It sounds like Dilip Kumar! Is he hot?"

"He's pretty okay; I think he is new to all of this stuff himself," Sef said, not daring to name it. I distrusted him. I knew Sef liked me, but I didn't want to like him just yet. He was young and naive. I looked down at the floor. Sef propped himself up on his elbows.

Was he trying to spare my feelings? He used to tell me stories about things that he'd done to impress me. He said once he jerked off with two other men he met on the train and followed to their apartment, where they all got naked and stroked one another's cocks. His story had several inconsistencies—mainly the timeline. He would have called me immediately after this happened, his voice trembling with excitement. We were very eager to tell each other our sex tales. Maybe he thought mine were better—the random hookups at parties, the meeting guys on subway platforms. Maybe he was trying to keep up with me, as though sexy stories made him more sophisticated. When I asked him later about particulars, he had conveniently forgotten.

I was ready to call his bluff about Dilip. I stroked his nipple with my finger. "Do you think that he'd want to join us sometime?" I asked coyly. I wasn't expecting anything.

Sef stroked his stubble. "Hmm . . . I could ask him," he said, tilting his head up. "This could be a lot of fun—three of us," he said.

I wondered if Dilip was real, or whether he'd mysteriously be unable to join us. Was Dilip mythological—that spectral lover whose presence would make Sef seem more appealing to me? I wasn't jealous. I wasn't.

I was jealous.

I thought of the movie *Sangam* and sang, "Sangam hoga ke nahin." *Will the meeting of these three rivers happen?* In my mind, Dilip was the Saraswati River.

"Tell him that he should come over for chai sometime." I laughed. "I will add extra spice and cardamom when he comes." I was excited at the prospect of three naked brown bodies on my bed, and that meant more masala. Sef grabbed my boxers and disappeared under the sheets. His face was red and he giggled nervously.

"I will give you back your clothes when you answer my question." Sef's half-smile was daring and flirtatious. I pulled the sheet from over his head. He took a few seconds to open his eyes as he smiled at me. And then he asked, "Sangam hoga ke nahi?"—*Will our rivers meet?* "You ready to go again?"

❀

Sundar sings from his boat to Radha who is on the shore. She is in love with Gopal. Sundar, seated in the Gondola with Radha in his arms, looks into her eyes and sings:

*O mehbooba, O mehbooba,*
*Your heart is my only intended destination—*
*That's the only place you are not present.*

*What makes you angry? What makes you glum?*
*In which thinking are you drowning—*
*there will be a confluence.*

*One day I will hold you tight*
*and everyone will be astonished.*
*I will bring you to me one day.*

Radha runs along the bank while Sundar sings. At this point, Gopal is looking longingly at Radha, wanting so much to tell her how he feels. He tries to tell Sundar.

"I have fallen in love, you know."

"With whom?" Sundar asks.

"With Radha."

Sundar runs toward Gopal with his hands in fists. He is going to spill his friend's blood like he did when they were children.

"With my Radha?"

Gopal gulps and answers, "Is there only one Radha? I'm in love with her, who came to be with Lord Krishna."

Sundar believes—or pretends to believe him. He thinks, *Gopal is not in love with my Radha.*

❁

The rain fell in April, blotting out the sun for twenty-one days. Back home in Florida, in the late summer, the rains would fall for an intense twenty minutes—fat raindrops the size of ikura: salmon eggs. In New York, it rained like this, but mostly the rain was a spitting mist that blocked out the sun for weeks at a time. The collected trash heaped on the curbs baked in the humidity. The gutters turned into charging rivers. What I would have given for some lightning. I took to drinking Jameson. At least I could feel the heat inside my chest if the sun refused to kiss me.

Sef came over but my buzzer was broken, so I took the elevator to the ground floor. With him was his friend, Dilip. He wore wire frame glasses and was shorter than me. His skin was darker than mine. We hugged and I pressed my hands into his back. As we stepped inside, the two stone lions that had previously glared at me seemed to smile with open mouths. I winked at them. The three of us stepped into the elevator. I pressed 6 repeatedly until the silver doors shut.

Once in my apartment, I made chai and counted each ingredient I put into the boiling pot. It felt like something was lodged in my throat. I counted: one, two, three, four cloves, one whole stick of cinnamon. One, two, three, four, five cardamom pods and about an inch of grated ginger to one-and-a-half cups of water. I shook my head like a school child in a Bollywood film: tilt left, tilt right. Two naked men at once. I counted: one Coolie from Orlando, one Pakistani from Flushing, and one South Indian from Great Neck. We were about to stew in our own pot: dark tea and light milk.

I said, nervous, "New York City water is the best municipal water in the world."

"For sure, and did you know Dilip, that Rajiv is so shy?" They both laughed. Sef looked down at his shoes and then up at me in a private smile. It was true. They knew each other long before I knew Sef. I fluttered about like a pigeon shaken in a cage. This wasn't only today, but always. I'd only ever been shy initially.

I laid out sweets and salty snacks for our chai—spicy sev and chocolate katli, a specialty of one of the mithai shops on 74th Street.

"Your name is from the South," I said to Dilip.

"Yes. I've only ever been to India once," Dilip replied. "Where's your family from?"

"We are Coolie—Guyanese. My father's side is North Indian as is my mother's father's family. My Nani was Tamilian, so I am a mix of North and South Indian. She may have been Muslim. It's the Coolie way. I have family that are Hindu, Muslim, Christian, and Buddhist."

"That's like if Sef and I made a child—it would be like you," Dilip mused.

"My body is like a landmass where borders don't really make sense. I mean if my left ear is Ganga, and my right is Jamuna, then where is Saraswati?" I touched his ears starting with his left and then his right. My hand lingered on Dilip's right ear and I could see him flush. He raised his skinny hands to mine.

Dilip and Sef laughed. Dilip said, "It's in there somewhere. Let's find out." He got up and pushed in his chair and took my hand. He led me to the bed where he pushed me against the wall and started kissing me. Sef followed. As Dilip and I kissed, Sef undid my pants and put me in his mouth.

Sef kissed my mouth and I unzipped Dilip's pants. By then, Sef had taken off all of his clothes. His hair had been freshly cut for today. *He must have been so excited for this moment,* I thought, *for his two lovers to meet.* I was impressed and wanted him even more than before.

Outside the rain swelled. It was a fat rain. Yet another reason I was glad to be inside. We moved to the bed. Sef and Dilip were body to body and I saw a tender look in Sef's eyes. I wasn't supposed to see that look between them. I thought that our brown bodies would transcend petty jealousies. Outside, the distant peal of thunder.

❊

Gopal writes a letter to Radha. Cut to fantasy: It's spring, and they are in the Swiss Alps, as Bollywood logic goes. Dream times happen far from the reality of India.

Gopal:
*Don't be angry if you read my letter. . . .*
*I would call you the moon*
*but it's pocked.*
*I would call you the sun*
*but it's fire.*

*I will understand you as Ganga*
*I will understand you to be Jamuna*
*You are inside me, I will*
*understand you to be my own.*

The two frolic in the exotic European countryside.

❀

I didn't want to do it again. Sef was sorry.

"How come?"

"I think I just want to have you to myself. . . ." I paused. "At least when we are hooking up. I've tried the polyamory thing before, and it didn't really work out for me." It was true. Tom was a great person, but I didn't think that I could stay with him. He was white and from a world of pastors and Protestants. I wanted something browner, something siltier. I wanted to be with Sef, and I didn't—though I was lying to him.

"I think that I'm not really that ethical—I tend to hurt people." I was bruised and torn. I fiddled with a button on my shirt until it popped off. I didn't want to fuck only Sef, yet I didn't want to watch Sef fuck someone else in front of me. I thought about this as a boundary for now.

Sometimes rivers divide countries and states. Guyana and Suriname are carved like this by the Courantyne's brown water. Bangladesh and India are separated by the Ganga. But these are human demarcations mapped onto the geological. Cultural divides are not so exact.

Sef shrugged. Clouds rolled off his shoulders, crawled across the floor, and entered my throat. His apathy choked me. "That's so sweet." He smiled, taking off his sweater.

# The Lover and the Chapbook

I PICKED UP my cell; its blue glow pricked my eyes. I tossed the sheets away and stood up, dizzy.

"It's 2 a.m." I could smell my own breath. It was Ryan.

"Rajiv? I don't know what to do." Silence. Then a sob. I was used to the occasional phone call and check in, but never at this time of night.

I turned on the kitchen light. I sat at the breakfast nook table and gazed out of the window. The courtyard of my apartment building glowed in the night. Rats scurried from the sewers into the garbage piles. I lit a cigarette.

"Are you okay? Are you safe?" Ryan was fragile—his alienation in Baltimore was jarring after the promise of a South Asian community of activists in the city. The organizers promised us that we would always have space with them, that we would be welcomed into their circles if we moved to New York. I had moved to New York and no one wanted to hang out. So much for promises.

"Steven and I broke up."

"Isn't this a good thing? Ryan—haven't you wanted to break up with Steven for some time now?" I rubbed my eyes and shook my head. Why was he waking me up on a school night?

"I am just so frustrated right now—I told him to leave my apartment."

"How did he take it?"

"I don't know."

"What do you mean you don't know?"

"I wrote him a letter that said, 'I don't have the emotional strength to continue this relationship anymore. I need you out.'"

Ryan broke up with his boyfriend of two years with a letter he left on the mantle.

"Is there anything I can do?" I asked, understanding his grief and relief. He finally had the courage to let this fucker go and he was overwhelmed with fear of being alone and manic joy.

"Can you come here?"

It was Thursday, I had to teach in the morning. "I will come tomorrow for the weekend," I said, and we hung up.

❄

Several months earlier, Ryan had come to visit me in my studio for the weekend. Ryan's hazel eyes and long frame lumbered toward me. The city had assembled guardrails on either side of the street.

"What's going on?" Ryan asked the waiter at Seba Seba.

"The gays march," he replied and scurried back into the store.

Ryan's eyes met mine. "Queens Pride!" we both said and laughed.

Jackson Heights was a swirl of brown bodies and brown languages. C'était possible quitter la maison sans parlant anglais. Bahut log vaha rehete the jinko Hindi, Urdu, Bangla, Fransisi, aur Spanish ati thin. On 74th Street between Roosevelt Ave and 37th Ave, the vendors came out. Hot jalebis, perfumed with rose, oranged the stalls. Samosas, fresh fresh and hot-hot, piped their steam into the mix of people. By Roosevelt Ave the LGBTQ Center set up a stage. There would be performances. I bought samosas.

"Fuck, dude. You live here." Ryan bit into his samosa.

"It's so familiar yet not at all." When my mom made samosas, it was with egg roll wrappers and ground beef. Not this potato and pea mix.

"I totally get it," Ryan smiled with cumin in his teeth.

I rubbed my head to pat down my hair. Shit. My bald spot was starting to grow from its quarter-size disk.

Ryan probably had it harder than I did—I had a community, or at least there were other Guyanese people about. Ryan was born in Kolkata and orphaned. A white American family adopted him, hoping to do good, and they did for the most part. But it's impossible not to feel alienated as the only different one in the room. I looked at him. He wore a yellow T-shirt, a fluorescent pink belt, and blue jeans that made his ass pop. I had my brother and sister to complain about racist white people with.

The parade started, as did the rain. The marchers held their banners as glitter and eyeliner ran streaks down their cheeks. The sky did not relent. It had something to say, too. The group called SALGA—South Asian Lesbian and Gay Association—passed by and we cheered extra hard. I felt like I belonged when I was with Ryan. I cheered for him and me. I cheered for our friendship—our queer familial bond.

The rain relented and the sun shone bright. A rainbow broke out and danced its wet body across the sky.

❄

I boarded a Chinatown bus from Midtown to Baltimore. In my notebook I kept a record of my thoughts. I was thinking of Aji and her songs—translating them into a language that I could use. I carried a cassette player with me and transcribed the lyrics to one of Aji's songs as I sat on the bus. I stopped the tape and wrote down one word at a time. There was one particular Kabir poem that she sang when I saw her last. It was a chutney song that she said had a deeper kind of meaning than just dancing.

*Chunariya pehenke piya se milbe*
*Saiya, tum ho chatur saiyana*
*sasur ghare jaana*

*I tie my veil to meet my love.*
*Love, no matter how clever*
*you will have to leave for your home*

This kind of song was a nirgun: a song about death—but really about living. I had heard these kinds of songs in Varanasi. The overarching metaphor of the body as a veil permeated my thoughts. My body is a veil that I wear and discard. Or at least this was the philosophy behind this kind of poem. New Jersey raced by the window as I considered impermanence.

I liked teaching, but I wanted to leave it before I became a bitter teacher. The students deserved better than that. The department of education was a mess. Funding issues. Racism. All of the things to put the onus of making children learn on the shoulders of individuals instead of the system. I just didn't know what I wanted to do. When I moved to the city I only wanted to live in New York for several years. There was somewhere else I could be.

My cell phone buzzed. It was Sef. I silenced it. *I'll call him later*, I thought.

Outside, Jersey rushed past. I thought of the road trips that I had taken with my parents and siblings in the past. This was different.

The bus was peopled by travelers like me: those who wanted to save a dime and those who wanted to bring on old-school boomboxes to blast the latest Chinese hits for our long crawl down the Eastern Seaboard—those who were finally meeting themselves in a big city. The road lasted the length of this translation and I began to write my own nirgun poems.

The bus dropped me in the parking lot of an abandoned grocery store. Ryan came with his friend Shayna. We hugged and crawled into Shayna's car and sped off to Ryan's apartment. She dropped us off and went home to get ready for the evening. Ryan's two-bedroom was dark and smelled like grief. He went to the kitchen without kicking off his shoes and poured us both whiskey gingers.

I walked from the living room to the bedroom. The brightly colored furniture helped to alleviate the sense of mold and despair that crept in the shadows, poised for descent the moment the lights switched off. The queen-size bed was stuffed with pillows. Ryan walked in and handed me my glass.

"On the other side of the wall," he motioned to the other side of the room, "was where Steven slept before he left. I could feel his evil emanate from the wall." Ryan took a sip. "Drink up," he continued, "we have a lot of work to do."

I sipped and looked at the photos on his dresser. Steven was a white hipster with blond-brown hair, blue eyes, and stretched earlobes that fit blue plugs.

"He could make me cum real fast," Ryan admitted as he turned the photos down. "Now he's gone."

"Are you going to stay here? Why don't you move to New York?" I was hopeful—it would be great to be able to stumble home drunk with him after nights of dancing.

"No, I'm going to stay in Baltimore. I gotta get the hell out of this place, though."

"Are you okay?"

"I'm great."

"No. Really. Are you really okay?"

Ryan bowed his head. Sweat collected at his temples. With a laugh he flung his head back and shot the rest of his drink down his throat.

"You know, Rajiv, I've started to write poems about him." He pointed to the bookshelf that housed a dusty stereo and five books. Under a figurine of an elephant a pile of papers gleamed. Ryan walked over and pulled them out. "I have about thirteen done," he said.

"You have to read them! Invite your friends and you should have a reading in your living room." My excitement grew at the prospect of Ryan writing poems.

"I am hoping to make them into a book—like a small book that can fit in my back pocket."

"I would definitely buy that book." I took out my own journal. "I've been jotting things down, but they're only scribbles for now. I wish that I could make them more a part of my life."

"Rajiv—you totally can. No one is in control of what you want to do." Ryan opened his eyes wide; it was his serious face. "You already are a poet." He picked up my journal and read for a few seconds that felt as though he was looking into my ears to examine my head.

"You will have to leave for your home . . ." he mouthed. I knew what he was reading. He closed the journal and put it on the table. "Yep. Just as I thought. What's the hesitation though?"

I looked at the floor. "I'm not sure. I've been teaching for a while now and I don't know. . . . I don't even know who will read it."

Ryan grabbed my hand. "I will read it," he looked into my eyes with his serious face again. He meant business. "Write for people like you and me."

I thought of the present that Leila had sent me three years before. There was a queer Guyanese poet who wrote. I could do this, maybe. I said, "But I want to hear your poems first!"

"Yes—but after I read, we are going out because I need to dance," Ryan said.

❊

Jonathan and Shayna arrived at the apartment within minutes. Jonathan greeted Ryan with a firm hug and offered me his lily-white hand in greeting. Shayna's hair was aflame with red and orange and her very presence scalded me.

"Hey there. You both look a little dry," Ryan said and slipped into the kitchen to prepare more drinks. He had changed into a short, pink T-shirt and a darker pair of Levi's. I wrung my hands and my palms started to sweat whiskey.

"Hi, guys," I said.

"You're Rajiv from Queens. I've heard so much about you," Jonathan whined and passed by me to sit on the couch. His thin frame looked like his shirt could break his shoulders. His milky skin betrayed his blue veins hard at work.

"Rajiv!" Shayna said and slapped my hand, palm to outside hand to palm to outside hand to fist bump. I fumbled and did the handshake wrong, confounded by her beauty. "Do you also write poems?"

"I do, but I definitely don't show them to anyone." I looked down at my silver-and-black sneakers.

"So how exactly do you know Ryan?" asked Jonathan from the couch, one leg crossed over the other. "I mean I know that Ryan goes to visit you in New York and that you're a second-grade teacher—but I never heard the story of how you met." He narrowed his ice-blue eyes.

"We met at a conference for South Asian activists in New York a couple of years ago. Our being outside the 'South Asian' norm brought us together and since then we've been connected."

Ryan emerged. The ice clinked a song in the whiskey gingers he handed to his guests: the promise of fresh condensation and a dulling of sadness.

"We were both on the outside, not really fitting the mold of who we should be or what people think we are, you know? You don't lose a connection like that when you make one," Ryan said with a grin and a laugh.

It's true, I thought—in some way we saved each other from expectation and disappointment. Ryan must have felt like a three-headed green monster who wore a mask. What could this white Jonathan know of being on the outside?

"That's very *nice*," he said. *Nice*. He could have also said the word quaint or exotic. I glared at him and then at Ryan. I could feel veins erupt on my forehead and my eyes redden.

"*Nice?*" Ryan laughed. "It was more than just *nice*." Ryan loved this boy as a friend for some reason and maybe I should give him a chance.

I was reading meaning into his words—call it a post-traumatic response or the wild bird of jealousy beating against my throat.

"Psht—" Shayna said and put her hand on Jonathan's knee. "You know that being outside of the norm makes you close to others that are freaks like you." She went in for a hug. Jonathan tightened, then loosened his posture. These three were a unit. Shayna and Jonathan took care of Ryan while he was going through this breakup and I loved them for it, despite myself.

"What about these poems?" Shayna asked, looking at Ryan and then at me.

"I was hoping you would forget," Ryan laughed into his drink. He took a sip and put his glass on the coffee table, ringed with marks of cup sweat. He reached his hand into his back pocket and pulled out a stack of poems that he unfolded. Ryan stood up in front of the fireplace that had been painted over.

"I wanted to make this a kind of book that fits into your back pocket," he said, his voice trembling ever so slightly. I wondered if Jonathan could hear the slight falter—how well he knew him.

Ryan began. "This one is called 'Birth' and it's about my birth parents." I noticed his stance, its posture, and his voice's tremble. He delivered the poem in a musical cadence. His poem asked his parents if they knew about him, if they thought about him after leaving him. His poem asked the birth parents questions about living, puzzling through what he could have inherited from them.

I looked at Jonathan and he was wiping his eyes. Shayna was staring at Ryan, her eyes two full moons. My throat was a collapsed mine shaft. Ryan was dealing with many nuanced layers of abandonment as he called out to his parents.

Ryan read another poem to his audience. The room was silent. We were enthralled with his metaphor. His delivery was half spoken-word and half poet-voice. He continued reading his poems to his silent audience about his breakup and how Steven fucked another guy in the bed where they built their own nest.

Ryan shot his drink and put his glass down. Who needs another one? He trembled after he finished and zipped to the kitchen for more alcohol. I had lost count of how many drinks he'd had. He was exposed. He stood naked in front of us and we looked at his parts, inspecting them and thinking of our own burns and scars.

"That was so brave," Jonathan said, standing up and rushing into the kitchen to hug Ryan. I sat on the couch and reflected. I stared at my own journal that was on the coffee table from earlier. I had not heard many other queer South Asian poets. Something about Ryan allowing himself to write his stories felt freeing. Something broke inside of me. It was fear of being seen. If Ryan could be brave, so could I—at least in front of my friends. He didn't care what the end game of his poems was. Maybe I could be free to just write them and not care. My parents' words haunted me, *You need to know the difference between what's a career and what's a hobby.* I was the one policing this message. It was injected into my thinking and I was the one who polished the idea until it gleamed, outshining any ideas that I had for myself.

I got up and held out my hand to Shayna, who with a flourish stood up. We trotted off to the kitchen. Ryan and Jonathan were still hugging.

"Well it's time for me to go," Shayna spoke up, eyeing me. "That was really exceptional, Ryan. You have a gift." I'd never thought of writing as a gift, but a skill and a bravery that you have after refusing to burn up in flame. It was an act against death.

"Let's walk together," Jonathan said to Shayna, loosening his grip on Ryan's waist.

"You guys don't want to go out? We are going to go dance," Ryan's words started to slur together.

"Nah—you guys go and slay 'em," Shayna said. They put on their jackets and left the apartment.

As soon as they left, I looked at Ryan and said, "Jonathan is in love with you."

"I know."

"And?"

"I'm done with white boys for now."

"Come on. . . ." I began, smiling into my glass as I drained its last brown flame.

"Steven used to like to fuck me when I wore a bindi," Ryan said blankly.

There was no arguing with this. This was pretty unforgivable.

❀

In the Baltimore gutter scene Ryan and I danced and danced. By the time we left the apartment I had no idea where I was or what I was doing. None of it mattered. Baltimore was a sticky city with an electronic "gutter music" that kept us sweating and dancing for our lives. I was celebrating the breakage in me—the permission to write the ugly and to share it with my friends.

Amidst the din and fog of the club I remembered what an astrologer had told me in India. He said that I have an artistic palm, but my problem was that I had to commit to one form of art and that if I did that then I would go far. I thought the art that I would commit to would be astrology, originally, but now something else was happening. I was moved by Ryan's openness and was now moving my way through this process by dancing. Something else broke for me, too: I wanted Ryan.

At seven in the morning we stumbled back over the cracked sidewalks to Ryan's apartment. We had stopped drinking and were exhausted. We crumbled into heaps on his couch.

"I really loved your poems tonight," I said. I leaned in. "You are amazing and I love you so much." And I meant it.

"You keep writing, too. I see you—always writing things down in your journal." He was an artist and restless, like me. It was bright and we were both ready for bed. I kissed Ryan. As he came the church bells tolled 8 a.m. outside.

❋

I boarded the Chinatown bus back to New York. I was glad to return with my new resolve. I could allow myself to be a writer. I could be a poet. Ryan had held me tight and told me that he loved me, too, and that he was lucky that I was in his life. We didn't have to tell each other this. We were so close that my tasting him didn't complicate anything.

As Baltimore began its blur I reached up and pulled off my hat and fixed my hair. The bald spot was big. Outside a hawk flew high above the bus and followed us. It felt like a message from the divine: that I must allow poetry to be a reality of my life. I felt my head again.

I pulled out my journal. What would I write? I flipped through my notebook and saw my translations and trans-creation of Aji's folk songs.

I had been writing this entire time. My head swam. Through translation, journaling, or writing poems and fragments—I had been writing all this time. Since Emily gave me my journal before I went to India. Since I sat with a tape recorder with Aji and penned down her lyrics for translation. I hadn't been able to see myself without my reflection through a beloved until Ryan held up a mirror to my face. It felt as though my consciousness was looking at my life from a hawk's perspective. I could see that this whole time I had been alive on this Earth that I had been writing. I was tied to poetry from my umbilicus, I just hadn't recognized it.

Aji's songs and stories were poetry that I was working with and it was working through me. This was the poetry that I descended from and I could hear its music inside me as I read my own words. Had I always been surrounded by poetry in many languages? I was so used to overlooking what I was doing, thinking that I wasn't able to write—that I was not good enough. That I was not enough. I rubbed my head and was frustrated by the hair loss.

I made a promise to myself right there on the road from Baltimore to Jackson Heights, this hawk as my witness. I would shave my head when I returned to Jackson Heights as a reminder that I would dedicate myself to poetry.

# The Outside Workshop

IN MY AQUA kurta, jeans, and yellow-orange cowboy boots I touched the ground of the hardwood stage and then my heart. This was my first performance since I started to call myself a poet. Hollis Kam from CARIB NY arranged this performance for Caribbean poets to come together and read from their latest work. The lineup included other poets and performers who were recent immigrants from the Caribbean or the children of immigrants.

The stage was black except for one spotlight that shone on the woman who was emceeing the evening. Her dark hair curled like waves about her shoulders.

"Next up this evening is Rajiv Mohabir, who calls himself a Coolie poet. We in Trinidad pronounce the word like *coo-ly*. Y'all Guyanese say *cuh-ly*. I don't know—if someone called me *Coolie* I'd pop 'em in de face," the emcee said. "I hope you will read in English and not in Hindi!" she joked.

I thought of the sound of Hindi and Bhojpuri—the flick of the tongue's tip on the alveolar ridge, the gentle retroflex, the aspirated consonants. I thought of the way my Aji pronounced words like *pizza* as "pihxa," and how there was only ever Caribbean Hindustani for her when she was younger. I thought of my own tongue, my alveolar ridge, made up of the same stuff as Aji's and her ancestors and how English language was new to our family—erupting in my father and mother's generation as a first language.

The audience laughed as I walked on stage. I could see very little except for the slope of chairs beyond the stage as darkness hid its secrets. I stepped up, gave her a hug, and took a deep breath. The poems that I clutched were good enough to get me into VONA—Voices of Our Nations Art Foundation's yearly weeklong workshop—and the Queens College MFA program. I was unsure of so many things.

*Good thing I can't see the audience,* I thought. But they could see me. *What if they saw me and knew that I was a fraud? What if these poems aren't good enough? Can I really do this? I am a nobody—the grandson of illiterate rice farmers. I have no business pretending that I am literary. You are nothing. No one will ever love you. You are fat and hairy. You are good-for-nothing.*

I looked out into the spotlight as if I could see my friends sitting there. All I could see was a burning light—purifying, and I was naked for the first time in front of strangers.

❁

I went to San Francisco holding joy in my chest like a wild flame. I was going to a workshop for writers of color that my cousin, Leila, turned me on to while I stayed with her in Toronto for Aji's eighty-eighth birthday celebration.

Leila, on her purple couch, said, "It's the place for freaks like us." Her large eyes were framed by black curls of hair. She raised her eyebrows in seriousness and continued, "I will be there, too, but as an administrator."

Leila was the writer in the family. She grew up in Ontario and lived part of her life in Quebec, where she learned French and lived with a woman. The aunts all raised their eyebrows.

"I can't wait to go!" I had been warned that most MFA programs in the United States were hothouse factories of white supremacy—that I would never find a whole community or belonging.

"I can tell you that VONA feeds my soul," Leila said. Outside tires screeched to a halt and a car ran into a telephone pole. The sound of crushed metal mixed with Leila's words.

"It's a safe space," she said as we both got up to look out of the window at the wreckage below.

&#10058;

I boarded a plane from LaGuardia to San Francisco. I clutched two books of poems tight through the gates: Joy Harjo's *How We Became Human* and Suheir Hammad's *Born Palestinian, Born Black*, and submitted to the profiling of the TSA. I thought of Suheir's poem "Mic Check" and how the process of being screened, by always being "random" at the TSA checks, was the story of my life.

I landed at SFO in the afternoon and Leila picked me up from the airport with Thomas Glave in the car. He'd recently published the book *Our Caribbean: A Gathering of Lesbian and Gay Writing from the Antilles*, which Leila had gifted me. As I sat in the backseat with this celebrity asking me about my life, Leila handed me an autographed copy.

"Where are you coming from?" Thomas asked.

"Queens, baby." I said and laughed nervously.

He turned around and smiled at me, got out of the car and said through the window, "It was nice meeting you."

As Leila wound up the window, she looked at me and said, "He was flying out as you came in. I'm so glad you got to meet him!" I climbed out of the back seat and sat next to Leila. "I'm so beyond glad you're here, cousin-brother."

I lit a cigarette and we drove off to Mills College, where the workshop was to be held. Leila came up to my single room with me.

"It's Pride today, Rajiv. Let's go check it out." She smiled and arched her brow.

"I'm totally in," I said as we both ran down to the parking lot and drove to the closest BART station.

San Francisco was a rainbow flag of shirtless muscle men, leather daddies, brown bodies, dykes, beer and alcohol, body odor mixing with blunt smoke, and techno music. I had drinks on a slope and we walked hills and took trains and buses and streetcars and ended up at the ocean. We sat in the sand.

"If I am ever sad, remind me of this time when we were both in San Fran for VONA and how we sat at Ocean Beach and watched people surf in the mad cold waves," Leila said as she stretched out her hand for my cigarette. She didn't smoke but she took a long drag. It curled like a prayer into the sunset.

❀

In the workshop I was surrounded by voices of color. I was the only Indo-Caribbean. I've always felt like a nilgai: a rare antelope. I'd sent ten pages of poems with my experimentations with writing in and out of my three languages, intent on cadence and lyric to carry my message. I wrote about New York City, about Liberty Avenue, about Jackson Heights—the scent of Diwali, the way that people strung up Christmas lights for Eid, Diwali, and Christmas. How Patel Brothers always had extra sweets during these times. The loud bang of bhangra music on the avenue, the Hanuman Chalisa being prayed in the Shri Laxmi Narayan Mandir, and the pulse of chutney music where bake and barah fried.

Other students submitted their poems that held phrases in Spanish and other languages. Suheir Hammad's book *breaking poems* had just been released by Cypher Books, and she wove words transliterated from Arabic into her verse. I was finally beginning my writing life and was excited to be in a workshop with like-minded students.

Suheir was the workshop leader for the week and I had long admired her writing and activism. "I am going to decide who goes first," she said from behind her beautiful and wild hair. "It will be Rajiv and Seema." We were the only South Asians in the room. "Let's pay attention to how both of them write about mangoes," she said.

The class pulled out my stack of poems that they scribbled comments onto.

"Rajiv, why don't you read a poem that you like the best." Suheir looked at me. I was nervous. I looked through my own stack and settled on "Bismillah." As I read slowly my classmates made marks on their papers.

Suheir continued, "And what do you like about it?"

"I like it because it felt like it came to me like a prayer," I said, ready to write down every single word she said.

"Well, who are your favorite poets?" She looked at the other students in the room.

"I really love Joy Harjo." There was a brief silence.

"Well, that is a *different* aesthetic," she said.

Wait, I thought—wouldn't Joy Harjo, a Native poet, be held high in a place like this?

"Who would like to begin the critique?" she asked.

One poet in the workshop who wrote mostly prose spoke up. "I get what you're trying to do here with putting in Hindu words, but it's just not working."

"Can you explain that more?" Suheir asked.

My mouth was dry and my palms so sweaty I had trouble holding onto my pen.

"When people write in Spanish it's allowable, but unfortunately Hindu is not on the level that Spanish is in public consciousness." The room nodded in agreement. "It would work if you took out the phrases in Hindu and made it more accessible to the rest of us."

Was she really saying that I was too ethnic? Didn't VONA say that it's a place for the people who are constantly told that they are *too ethnic*? I hadn't even written in the language she called "Hindu"; I had written in

Bhojpuri and Awadhi, quoting my grandmother's songs, the names of foods, lyrics of prayers, and place names. I was writing Queens, impossible to do without referring to my people and how I lived there.

The room was silent with agreement. Even Suheir was silent. Sweat dripped from my forehead and tickled the back of my neck. I wanted to hide. I wanted to run into a wall and have my ghost leave my body—I wanted to float above and watch. My internal monologue continued to punish me as people discussed my work, how my lines needed help, and what my poems should look like.

*Everything that I've written is shit. I shouldn't be writing. I'm terrible and only pretending. Coolies like me belong on a plantation, in a field cutting cane and drinking rum and cussing up. I don't belong in this workshop. My father's generation was the first of his family to be able to read fluently. I am a total no one. Everything about me is obscure—I come from Crabwood Creek and most people mishear Ghana or Guinea when I say I am from Guyana.*

*You are nothing.*

*No one will ever love you.*

*You are fat and hairy.*

*You are good-for-nothing.*

Seema spoke up and said, "You know—the parts that I had the most trouble with were the parts where you wrote English words for the Hindi phrases." Seema was Punjabi and pronounced Hindi with a dental *D*, correcting the other participant's Hindu and modeling the right way to say it. "If you look on page seven, the phrase 'immovable bow' didn't make sense to me until I thought of Ram in the *Ramayana* and the task of moving Shiva's bow and then it made sense."

My poetry was bad. There was nothing redeeming about it, or at least that was the consensus. I had to allow myself to be a beginner and listen to the workshop's critique.

❈

I sat in the garden, smoking and watching the scrub jays fly back and forth, baring their sky-blue and rust to the dawn. I was on east coast time. The cement picnic table where I sat was underneath two tall trees. The bird looked at me and I felt like it knew me. It cawed and clucked, and I mimicked it. He flew closer and tilted his head to the side.

Relief. This bird brought me a feeling of connection. I belong on this Earth. This bird was saying so. He sang his song and didn't care if I understood his craft, he wanted to communicate his music to me. He flew up to a low branch just as I heard footsteps coming my way. Diem Jones walked up with his camera. Diem was a tree of a man, tall and gentle. He looked at me and smiled.

Diem stared at my cigarette. "You been smoking long?" he asked.

My ears started to burn out of embarrassment. "I've been smoking for about ten years," I replied. God, I thought. I am all wrong for this place.

Diem continued, "You know, if you put the effort into writing that you put into smoking you will go from performing thirty percent to one hundred percent."

I stared at my feet. He had a point. If I took the energy and time and money and kept it for writing only, then it would probably pay off somehow—at least I would stop smoking.

Cynthia, a poet from the workshop, came up to me as Diem walked away.

"Hey, can I have a light?" she asked.

I handed her my lighter and had a hard time looking at her in the face. I coughed and sighed.

"So you like Joy Harjo's writing?" she said.

"She's simply spectacular."

"I've never read her."

"I can lend you my book." I said as the scrub jay alit and looked in my direction. He flew closer to where Cynthia and I sat. She noticed my new friend.

He spoke.

I answered.
He spoke.
I answered.
He spoke and I answered.

❖

Each person in the VONA workshop got to meet with the leader one-on-one for half an hour sometime during the week. Suheir had told us to bring our packets of poems with us when we came. She sat in the near-empty dining hall. Suheir greeted me with a warm smile.

She looked directly into my eyes and said, "I don't agree with what was said in class. In fact, I believe that if you can get your reader to trust you, you can get away with a lot."

I pulled out my poems from workshop, hoping that she would tell me what I could change to rescue my poems from their hideous state. I wanted to know how to make my reader trust me.

Suheir looked at my packet and then at me. "You're a new writer, I know. These poems," she sighed through gritted teeth, "I think you are beyond these now." *You are nothing. No one will ever love you. You are fat and hairy. You are good-for-nothing.*

I looked at her and wanted to save face. I could feel the tears start to tickle my eyelashes and my throat start to close up. I changed the subject.

"Tell me the story of how you came to poetry," I asked, feeling sucker punched.

I went to my room that night without eating dinner and cried for an hour until I collapsed from exhaustion. Being a poet was tough. I thought I had found my community, but instead I found a friend in Cynthia and the scrub jay whose words only made emotional sense.

❁

I left San Francisco, unsure of my steps. *If these people didn't think I was any good, the people who were supposed to understand a person of color's struggles, what would the MFA be like?* I wondered.

I had applied to NYU's MFA program, to the New School, and to Queens College. NYU rejected me outright and I was waitlisted for the New School. But one day while I was teaching, I got a call from Nicole Cooley at Queens College. She left a message.

As soon as the art teacher came into my classroom to take over for a period, I listened to the message in the office adjoining my classroom, where I wrote my lesson plans and graded papers.

"This message is for Rajiv Mohabir. My name is Nicole Cooley and I'm calling from Queens College to let you know that we are excited to welcome you into our program. Please call me back if you have any questions and to let me know if you will be attending. We hope the answer is yes."

I was stunned. I dialed her back.

"Hello, Nicole Cooley? This is Rajiv Mohabir."

"Rajiv! Thank you for calling! I wanted to tell you how impressed we all were by your application. We really think it's special that you love Queens so much and we will be glad to have you come aboard." Nicole's voice was true and unfaltering. *Could it really be?* I could do my graduate work while teaching full-time.

I called my mother right away from the closet.

"Ma?"

"Hi, Raim, everything okay?"

"Yes. I just wanted to tell you that I got accepted to Queens College to do my MFA!"

Silence.

"An MFA?" she asked. "What's that?"

"A master's of fine arts," I laughed.

"Finally . . ." she said, "finally, a degree that makes sense!"

I was puzzled by her support for my artistic inclination—I was always told to be *practical*. To know the difference between a *career* and a *hobby*.

"Thanks, Ma, I never knew you would be so happy about this."

"A master of finance will serve you well." She was smiling on the other end of the phone.

"Fine arts. A master's of FINE ARTS," I clarified. "The exact opposite of what you thought," I said.

We both laughed at the mistake and hung up. She couldn't hear fine arts, perhaps because it was so outside of the realm of her world—arts in America? Who would want to read my Coolie poems?

❁

I walked into the orientation, a kind of meet-and-greet. Nicole Cooley stood by Roger Sedarat, who was on his hands and knees attempting to plug in a microphone to a speaker.

Nicole took my hand and shook it. "It's so very wonderful to meet you. Roger, this is Rajiv—remember his application?"

Roger smiled and nodded. "Yes," he said. "We were all so excited to see your writing about how Queens is an important part of you."

Nicole sipped her wine and nodded agreement. "I am excited to see more of your multilingual poems. Kimiko, come meet Rajiv, he's an incoming student in poetry."

Kimiko Hahn came over and took my hand with a "good to meet you" smile. Her scarf was light cotton and looked like a dupatta. I looked around at my future classmates.

*So many people of color*, I thought as I poured wine, smiling to myself. I couldn't believe the professors remembered my application so specifically. They even liked my multilingual poems. I took a deep sip. I'd always felt most at home in Queens.

# Brown Inclusion:
# Some Queens Definitions

**Brown - (adj) from:**

Old English – *brūn*: dark, shining
**Brown** is a color produced by mixing the three primary colors together in equal amounts. It is the color ascribed to people who have dark skin, often used to refer to people whose ancestry is not just European or African.

**Inclusion - (n) from:**

Latin – *inclusionem:* to be made a part of
**Inclusion** is the opposite of exclusion in that a person is seen as having in-group status, though sometimes temporarily, within a larger group. In acts of solidarity, disparate people can unite against a common oppressor.

❀

**Brown Inclusion** is when Zeke—a guy you'd met while out dancing in Manhattan—and his two friends, Analisa and Cindy, come to your house to celebrate Diwali. You drink chai and share stories. You tell the story of the *Ramayana* and represent it with all of its problems. You mention the fact that your grandmother was the last one in your family to speak her language.

Zeke says, "We tell special stories on certain nights, too. The funny thing is, my grandmother is also the last speaker of her language and she's trusted me with some of her songs."

"You should record as many as you can," I said. "Tape recorders, journals, everything. Make sure you don't forget."

That night he spends the night with you in your studio.

❀

**Brown Inclusion** is the watch billboard in Jackson Heights on 73rd and Broadway where Shah Rukh Khan shows off the white gold and diamonds on his wrist. *Chak de, Jackson Heights!*

❀

**Brown Inclusion** is being Mister Javier.

❀

**Brown Inclusion** is stumbling with Sarah toward a bar, through the crowd accumulating on 73rd Street, after reading through poetry submissions to the literary magazine you edit, *Ozone Park Journal*. You met in your MFA program and connected over astrology and your love of dive bars.

South Asian men and women are crowded outside the wooden doors, dressed in colorful salwar kameez, saris, kurtas, and pajamas, watching a musical group set up tabla and microphones on a small makeshift stage wreathed in police tape.

Sarah asks, "What's going on?"

Since you had just been talking about the pomp and glory of Jackson Heights in the festival season, you feel compelled to answer.

You turn to the bearded man to your right just as the tabla starts introducing the tala. The man wears a short-sleeved button-down with a pair of khaki slacks.

"Yahan kya ho raha hai abhi?" you ask in Hindi. "What's happening here?"

"Naba Barsho," he replies in Bangla.

Behind you, three white men exit the last Irish bar in the neighborhood raucously, disturbing the street celebration with swearing and drunkenness.

"What's that?" you ask again in Hindi.

"Bengali New Year, these people are Hindus," he answers laughingly in Urdu.

It occurs to you that he read you as a Muslim and that your Hindi wasn't Hindi but the spoken form of it, which was simultaneously Urdu and Hindi.

❀

**Brown Inclusion** is the Pakistani woman at work who asks you where you're from. You say Guyana and she assumes that you are Muslim because your last name ends in -*ir*. You don't correct her. Every time you run into her in the hallway, she greets you by your last name and speaks to you in Urdu to explain the goings-on of her family life. She asks you if you know anyone, any man between the ages of twenty-seven and thirty-five, who needs to get married. Since you are not native-fluent in Urdu or Punjabi she automatically disqualifies you for some things.

❀

**Brown Inclusion** is the Punjabi cab driver who picks you, your sister, and mother up from the corner of Lefferts and Liberty in Little Guyana to take you back to Little India in Jackson Heights. He speaks to you in English at first then slips into Urdu, assuming you and your mother and sister all speak it because of what you look like and your destination.

When you reply to his questions (in Urdu) and explain that you are not recently from India or Pakistan, he is surprised to hear that you are Guyanese. He says, "You are tall and with your beard you are looking proper Punjabi."

Your sister asks in Urdu, "If you thought we were Punjabi why did you speak to us in Urdu?"

❉

**Brown Inclusion** is the eighty-four-year-old Trinidadian uncle with the henna-red hair in Flushing Meadows Park in Queens whom you meet at the Hosay reenactment and who approaches you out of a crowd of a hundred and talks to you about Islam and its true meaning. "Islam is not a violent religion, people make bad choices, you know you must contact Pritha for my number and I will tell you everything that I learned. The Koran says that men and women are equal. It never says that women are less. But today everybody is mixed up."

# E Train to Roosevelt Ave
# Making All Local Stops in Queens

### 14th St (Transfer Here for the A, C, L)

Tonight Union Square was a whiskey wheeze. A curtain of second-hand smoke and steam rose from the manhole. I looked onto the street, clutching my Johnnie Black on the rocks and gritting my teeth. The door slid open. The bald Punjabi man next to me made eye contact and smiled. Tonight was the Sholay party—the monthly queer South Asian party—but instead of the Prince Street location, it was at Webster Hall.

I'd never been to Webster Hall before, its three-floored circus packed with young college students was a nightmare I could do without. But I loved to dance.

"Buy you a drink?" I asked.

"Is it payday?" he sneered. "Sure." I closed my H&M jacket tight around my chest.

The bartender brought the whiskey ginger.

"You Punjabi?" he asked.

"No. Guyanese."

"Oh," he sounded disappointed. "A darkie. I'm Nav."

I smiled at Nav and downed the cold fire of my drink, ice cubes nearly slicing my throat. "I'm Rajiv," I said.

DJ Bobby started spinning "Beedi" from the new movie *Omkara* starring Saif Ali Khan. I fumbled to the dance floor, not giving one fuck who was here or that I was by myself, or whether Nav thought I was an idiot, dancing chutney and not bhangra.

A man sidled up next to me and we began to dance together. He was tall, broad-shouldered, with long hair. Clearly, I thought, this man was Punjabi. Were there only Punjabis in this city? I fingered his hair.

"Tussi jat ho?" I asked in my broken Punjabi.

"What?" he asked. The music bumped.

I could feel it in my temples, throbbing—my blood thinned by alcohol. I repeated my question.

"No. I'm not Indian. I'm Guyanese."

"I'm Rajiv."

"Hi Rajiv, I'm Zane," he said and placed my hand on his crotch. He went outside to smoke a Newport. I got another drink and fell down a flight of stairs. Somewhere that night he gashed his leg. Our meeting started with pain. I knew I was going to fall in love with him. I decided that tonight would be perfect.

"Let's take the E train to my place. It's going local though," I said.

## DELAY: WE ARE BEING HELD MOMENTARILY AT THE STATION

"I'm seeing someone else," I said. I wanted to be cruel to Sef. "I met this guy at a bar, his name is Zane and he's Guyanese, too." I puffed out my chest and locked my knees.

Sef got up from his side of the bed and went to the bathroom. "What does that mean for us?" he asked. "Will we still hang out sometimes?" A chill hung about the room; the air conditioner kicked into high gear and frightened the pigeons perched on the windowsill.

"I don't think so," I said. "I am going to try monogamy with this guy. I think he wants it and I'm ready to try it, too. He's out to his family at least."

Sef's eyes opened widely and his jaw dropped. He mumbled, "I thought you didn't believe in monogamy. Sher kabse nali ka pani peene laga?" *When did the proud lion start drinking water from the gutter?* He washed his face with water so hot, the mirror fogged up.

※

Sundar, depressed, sings to Radha as he plays the piano.

*You embraced me trembling*
*quaking breath—*
*If it wasn't you, then who was it—*

*the one who wept tears as pearls*
*at our parting. If it wasn't you,*
*then who was it? It only could have been you.*

*The night's intoxication leaves*
*no trace of our joy.*

Radha looks confused. She doesn't know what to do. Will she marry Sundar? Will she fuck Gopal?

## 34th St–Penn Station (Transfer Here for the A, C)

"Karma is a bitch," Zane said of his drag persona, Lotay. The name recalled that of a long thread of a holy mantra that led to nirvana. Or at least it led to a better rebirth if you said it right and often enough. Zane's thread dealt exclusively with his eyebrows. But the way Zane changed it from Lotus to Lotay had different connotations—either lotay as in lotela, or as in water pitcher.

We moved in together in the summertime. My Jackson Heights flat was closer to his work than his five-bedroom three-story house on Long Island. His house was excessive, a mess of cheap Playboy memorabilia and tchotchkes. He had a room devoted to "Asia," an Orientalist fantasy of paper fans, Ming-style vases, and dull katanas. Zane lived in this palace of excess with his brother and his brother's then-girlfriend.

"I bought this house with my mother because it was important to her that her sons be well off," he said.

"That's really nice. I don't think I'll ever have that kind of help from my parents," I replied.

"Well, they wanted me and Lisa to be happy together and start a family," he spoke looking off, past the tacky, cheaply made vases. "I was married to Lisa for less than a year and we are getting a divorce."

"You mean you're married now?" I tried to keep the earthquake in my chest still. My cell phone vibrated against my leg. Sef was calling. I sent the call to voicemail.

"Yeah, my father didn't want me to get married because he knew, but my mom didn't care. She thought it was for the best. So, I got really stoned with my father and brother and went through with it." He smiled, "It's not a big deal."

"Does she get half of your assets?" I asked. "How involved are you both at this point?"

"We will be fine if we move in together and I don't put my name on the lease."

We decided to live in my place until the lease was up and then we would find our own place together. I paid all of the rent and all of the bills while he continued to pay the mortgage on his house; his brother and his brother's girlfriend paid almost nothing.

"Why are they not contributing?" I asked once.

"Rafi is young. I wish I had the opportunity that I am affording him now when I was his age."

"No, instead you married a woman and bought a house ten times what you make in a year." I was vexed. "What about this life we have together?"

"When we move in together it will be a different story," Zane promised.

## 42nd St–Port Authority (Transfer Here for the A, C, N, Q, R, S, 1, 2, 3, 7)

The first time Zane attacked me was when he came to my parents' home. We had been dating for four months. I hadn't been home in about a year, and I was excited for him to meet my mother and father. My sister, my young cousin Clara, and my sister's gay friends, Justin and Ronnel, were planning to go to Parliament House—a gay bar in Orlando. Ronnel had been begging me to go with them. I knew Ronnel and Justin from the time they were eleven and I was fifteen. Now they were man-size and had blossomed into delicious twinks.

We got to Parliament House and I lost Emily almost immediately. She had more gay friends than I ever did. Zane and I went to get a drink at the bar. Britney's "Toxic" played in a trance mix. All of the gay boys were sweaty with excitement. Justin came by and stood next to me and Zane.

"Have you seen Emily?" I asked him through the din.

"Yes, come with me," Justin said in my ear and took my hand and led me into another room where there was a stage with go-go dancers winding their hips on the bar top. I looked back and Zane was trailing us. Justin smiled, his teeth, his perfect jawline, his six-pack under his button-down sparkled more than any disco light.

Emily glowed like a ruby, ruddy from dancing and gin. Zane grabbed my hand and led me to the corner. He pushed me against the wall, hands choking my throat.

"Don't you ever let another man fucking touch you in front of me," he hissed. The club music beat like a pulse. I could feel the blood flow slowing and my veins pounding around where his hands grabbed my neck.

I didn't know what to do. "Let go of me!" I screamed. "Don't you ever fucking touch me like that again!" I hit his arms away from my neck in the one defensive move I'd learned from television.

"If you ever let someone touch you like that . . ."

His hands were in my face and he frothed at the lips, drunk.

"Let someone touch me? Justin grabbed my hand to bring us to Emily." Why did I need to justify anything?

In the corner table my cousin Clara sat. She was the daughter of my aunt whose husband died of alcoholism. He used to beat Clara's mother when he drank. Her eyes were two glassy orbs in which I could see my face. My eyes, half-closed, sweat staining my collar. My phone pulsed against my thigh. Sef was calling. I sent it straight to voicemail.

On the way home Emily was silent, glaring at Zane in the backseat from the rearview mirror. She played Babla & Kanchan and Zane wept in my lap.

"I never meant to put my hands on you."

## Lexington Ave/53rd St (Transfer Here for the 4 & 6, Making All Local Stops)

Thanksgiving: Zane's mother's house. I was in disbelief that Zane said his mother wanted me to come for this holiday. Zane's aunts and uncles and cousins crowded Zane's childhood home, each family packing Tupperware to bring home what food they could. His uncles and father snuck off somewhere to snort coke.

I didn't want to answer anyone's questions about who I was since Zane was not out to many in his extended family. I busied myself washing dishes while his mother entertained.

"But who is this, Dolly, washing all the time? I hope he's getting paid!" one of Zane's aunts said. Zane laughed along and returned to his drink, making straight-acting comments to his cousins like, "Remember Elisha from Adams? She was hot."

The water was so hot it scalded my skin. I peeled blisters off my hands for the next week.

"I don't know who he is," Dolly began. Her upturned nose and short squat frame made everything she said sound hostile. "He must be one of the boys' friends."

The steam rose from the stainless steel basin. I looked at Zane who laughed along, pretending that he hadn't just swallowed my cum an hour before we got there.

## Court Sq–23 St (Transfer Here for the G, M, 7)

Two weeks later. The steady pulse of the water from the showerhead matched my step as I crossed the oak floorboards to get the guitar. I pulled out my acoustic Ibanez and sat on my bed, feet on the cool floor. The bathroom door slowly creaked open on Zane, drying his left ear with a faded blue towel and staring at himself in the mirror.

I sang an old Bhojpuri tune written by Sundar Popo and sung by Babla & Kanchan, a song every Coolie from Crabwood Creek to Kingston knows.

*Chadar bechao balma,*
*chadariya, chadar bechao balma*
*nind lage chal soi rehena*

The guitar strings stung my fingertips. My words: ocean and backdam.

"We dance to this song all the time at the cookouts in my parents' backyard," Zane said.

I continued to sing.

"I don't think I can remember hearing this song for the first time," he said as he joined me on the bed. "When you play it slow like that, it feels like it has another kind of meaning."

"Yeah," I said. I thought about his mother and how Zane's father was an addict. I thought of her disavowal of me on Thanksgiving, how it was really a denying of her son. "I like it because it's about a daughter-in-law singing about her lover."

"Oh, god," Zane said and sang along.

"Do you think your mother will ever learn to love the people you love?" I asked.

"She had a hard life. She wants us to be successful." Zane put his hands behind his head and stared at the ceiling, "She used to like this song."

"But not anymore?"

Zane sighed and got up. He walked back over to the bathroom.

My phone rang. It was Sef again. He wouldn't understand this song in the same way that Zane did.

Zane could understand the color of this memory: stained boards of the SS *Jura* in 1890 bound for New Amsterdam from the Kolkata port just after the monsoon rains. Singing, my body was a ship swaying on the Kalapani that separated families from one another.

"What do the words mean?" Zane shouted from the sink's mirror where he beat his face.

"A woman is asking her lover to lay a sheet down on the grass so that when they're tired they can lie together," I said. That they could find rest in each other.

Zane pulled me down onto the bed, smiling.

## Queens Plaza (Transfer Here for the M, R, Making All Local Stops in Queens)

It was Zane's dream to perform onstage at Stonewall Inn in the West Village. The black-and-white chessboard floor in the downstairs was sticky as we walked up to the second floor where Chutney Pride had arranged a drag show and party. Zane and his friend had been organizing the West Indian parties in the city under the banner of Caribbean unity—a different and more personal aim than the Sholay parties for South Asian subcontinental and second gen queers.

Zane asked, "Wouldn't it be nice to dance to our own music like 'Chadar Bichao Balma' without the subcons calling us *darkies*?" The Stonewall Inn not only had historical significance, it was a space in the city that had embraced queers of color. Zane and his co-organizers knew the perfect DJs to request: queer, brown, and Black. Black, Indian, Chinese, and white West Indian queers from all boroughs came out and marched into the pink and purple lights to watch three Caribbean drag performers.

Lights flashed and Lotay climbed onto the stage. Lotay's Tina Turner wig was a wild forest of light brown flame atop her head. Her stiletto boots climbed to her knees. Fishnets, panties, and a bustier. Lotay had mastered the tuck.

"And now for the main event of this evening: Lotay!" a woman's voice cried into a microphone. A cheer arose from the crowd at the Stonewall Inn. Black and brown hands clapped and turned pink and yellow in time with the music and strobe lights.

Lotay came out on the stage as Lady Gaga's "Bad Romance" blared from the speakers. She did the Trini wine and dropped low. It was if Gaga herself were West Indian.

## 36th St

"You spend too much time writing. Who are you writing to?" Zane reached over and grabbed my phone and scrolled through the messages first, then my call log.

"I am writing for school," I lied. I was writing because if I didn't I would dry up and turn into sand.

"Who the fuck is Hoyt?" he asked.

"Hoyt? He's a guy in my MFA. We are both poetry editors for the school's journal," I said.

"Don't make me fuck you up," Zane threatened, narrowing his eyes.

I had just published a chapbook of poetry—I was called a "poet of note" by the editors at Pudding House Press. It was about removing the evil eye. In the acknowledgments section I thanked Zane for buying me my first broom, the special one that maijis and pandits use to jhare—to banish evil.

"That's all you wrote for me? How are people going to know that I'm the inspiration for this book?" he demanded.

He wasn't the inspiration for the book at all. The only thing he inspired was anxiety and my dropping all my friends. He didn't want me to talk to anyone. Not Jegga. Not Autumn. Not Ryan. Not Sef. Not even my classmates. If I didn't mention Zane in my chapbook it would have meant more fighting. Another empty rum bottle thrown at my foot.

To Zane, writing took me away from time with him. He saw it as a selfish act. He threatened to steal my hard drive and computer, to smash them when I wasn't home—he wanted to destroy my writing if he couldn't control it.

I hid my hard drive at Mae's apartment.

### Steinway St

In the fall, my mother wanted to have a party to celebrate my brother's birthday and my sister's graduation from her master's program. My sister witnessed our father beat both me and my brother with his walking cane and belt when we were children. Our purple welts were dark butterflies on our dark skins. She was never hit. This made her want to heal those with this kind of familial trauma. Zane and I packed our bags and went to Orlando.

Zane had just started doing drag and I bought him his first sewing machine—a Singer. I liked my gifts to him to inspire creativity.

My brother Emile invited his Lutheran pastor to our house for this party. Pastor Pete came in, all Central Florida with frosted tips and a ball-chain choker. His bleached blonde wife followed close behind.

"You are from New York, Emile tells us! When I visited New York," the pastor's wife began, "we stayed in the Radisson in Maintown."

"Maintown?" Zane repeated.

"You know, where the Met is! I just love museums! Especially the mock Egyptian temple there! It's definitely a place that makes me proud to be American—if it were in other A-rab countries God knows what would have happened to it. I heard they hate art."

"Oh, MID-town!" I interjected, straining for politeness for my brother's sake. "But the Met is more like Upper East Side." The foundational base of her face paint was starting to bubble with slight perspiration.

"Yeah, you should go and see it! I mean, I haven't seen anything like their idol collection before. You'd absolutely love it! They have all of the Hindu gods, too." Zane glared at me. I smiled meekly into my drink. It was bitter and warm like piss.

These kinds of tourists are usually terrified of Queens. Queens was brown, Midtown was white, and the Upper East Side was where the money was. Queens was where the working-class immigrant people lived and Midtown was where they worked for a mainly middle-class population who still squeezed their bitter melon and drank the juice to prevent diabetes.

The song "Ham Na Jaibe" by Babla & Kanchan began to play.

*Ham na jaibe sasur ghar me baba*
*I will not go to my father-in-law's house*

The "chune" played and wound itself around my hips and feet like kudzu. What a good escape, I thought. That woman is as awful as her husband's hair. The windows in the room where we danced began to steam.

The pastor's wife wore a rouge tank top and a pair of blue jeans. Her lips were painted with mandarin orange lipstick. Stumbling to the dance floor with a pineapple in her fist, she shouted in a bawdy Southern accent, "You know, I can't tell the difference between Indian dancing and Persian dancing!"

At this, Emily looked at me and then exclaimed, "Then don't dance, just watch!"

The pastor's wife rolled her eyes, then lifted the pineapple she'd taken from the kitchen and placed it on her head and started to snake her arms. The pineapple held in place while her alternating hands grazed the ceiling fan.

"Is this really happening?" Zane asked.

"Welcome to Orlando," I said.

"And who are you?" she screeched at Zane.

"I'm Rajiv's lover," he said. She opened her eyes wide. Globs of black mascara clumped beneath her waterline.

"Oh," she replied, turning and walking away from the Florida room where the music played. I could see her whispering to my sister-in-law in the kitchen.

Zane looked at me. "I'm glad I witnessed what you escaped," he said. Zane was an escape. I reassured myself that our life together was a reason for me not to be in Florida.

## 46th St

Zane and I had a whirlwind relationship. He was all fire and alcohol; I was brooding. He was the faggot-child of drug abusers and learned to defend himself when threatened. Our apartment echoed with shouts.

I didn't talk to Sef for about a year and a half. At first, he tried to call at least once a week. Once I picked up the call and answered in Hindi, "Haan kya haal hai yaar—what's up?" I was casual, as Zane sat next to me.

"Just wondering where the fuck you've been."

Sef's hurt reached its tendrils out and choked me. "Yes, fine. Talk to you later then."

I kept ignoring Sef's calls and deleting his messages before Zane could see. Sef called when Zane and I were at dinner, when we went to the movies in Forest Hills, when I was at poetry readings in Manhattan. His calls came when I was in class and when I went to Orlando to visit my mother. He called when I slept and when Zane and I fought. I never picked up.

Eventually his calls dried like a creek, slowing down to once a month and then to silence. There were no traces of where this river once flowed. He sent me several emails about his confusion. *Why don't you write to me Rajiv and tell me if I did something wrong.* I read his letter with clouds in my eyes. I wanted so much to reach out but didn't because Zane promised me that I would be his only. I wanted to be someone's only—someone's favorite. I wasn't Sef's. I'd seen it in his eyes that day in my studio two years before with Dilip.

❊

Three months had passed since I'd left my studio to move into a flat with Zane. He dodged questions about paying half of the rent, saying that his mother needed the money and that he would take care of it soon.

"It's not fair, Zane. Why am I paying for our entire life together when all of your money is tied up in your house? It's like you're paying for your brother's girlfriend to live in all five bedrooms." I was angry. The pipes in our one bedroom ran with rust-colored water. The windowpanes shook with each passing car.

"Why do you get to have a financial investment when I don't?" I asked.

"I always felt as though this apartment and our life together was your investment and my house was my investment," he said.

"We need to come up with a plan. I can't afford this one bedroom and if you don't want to pay for shit then I am moving back into a studio." I was shaking.

"I don't compromise," was all he would say.

### Northern Blvd

"No."

"You have to."

"I said no."

"Don't be such a tease."

"I said no."

"I'm going to find someone else and you're not going to know about it. Someone better who will put out more."

He pushed his dry fingers inside. "Stop! I said . . ."

Zane laughed.

## DELAY: WE ARE BEING HELD AT THE STATION MOMENTARILY

Lotay screamed at me all the way down Roosevelt Avenue. Past the blue-and-red flashing lights. As we walked Lotay picked up her skirt and undid her belt. Past Lydia's Bar. She took off her right heel and then her left. Past Friends Tavern. She pulled off her scarf. Down 81st Street. Until I crossed 37th Avenue and entered the corner building. The checkered linoleum on the flooring of the building gave it the look of a David Lynch film—surreal and haunted. Inside our apartment Lotay pulled off her foot-high blonde lace-front and revealed her sweat-soaked, bobby-pinned hair.

She cluttered our apartment with baubles: old Chinese-style vases, figurines, fans, and Playboy paraphernalia special-ordered from magazines. Mementoes of an old life where she hid from sight pretending to be someone else. In the light, the scene played out on a vase front, inverted, white and blue, cold as winter. I looked at my ghost.

Another bottle flew from the counter. Its glass now colorless, its black already sucked out. It hit my right foot.

I fell over to clutch my pain. This was not the first time Lotay pelted me with something. There were good times that I shelved deep inside myself.

"You want me to dash things you fucking muddaskunt?" Her eyelashes were falling off of her face. Her eyeliner once curved up at the ends now streaked down her cheeks. Lipstick only colored the cracks in her dry lips. She was drunk again. Fucked up. She had fucked up. I stood up but my foot could not bear any weight.

Looking up at Lotay I knew that our relationship was disheveled and knotted like the pile of Yaqui frizz on her white Italian leather couches. Our connection had the velocity of a porcelain doll on the shelf collecting dust.

"I'm going to leave you and you will never find anyone like me," she screamed at the top of her voice. *You are nothing. No one will ever love you. You are fat and hairy. You are good-for-nothing.*

I felt something break inside me. *I am something. I will love myself. I am beautiful. I am worthy.* It was the smallest bone in my body. The bone that tapped the imprint of her voice on my internal timpani. I had heard enough. It was time to clean the hoard. And I thought, *Good. I don't want to find anyone like you.*

## 65th St

Mae was going to India to visit her in-laws. She had married Atin, our other Hindi teacher's son, and moved to New York to pursue her master's degree at Columbia University. Atin was a student in the New York Film Academy. They lived in a one-bedroom walk-up on the Upper West Side. Mae and Atin were my last remaining friends, the only ones who Zane had let me keep in close contact with. He liked their connection to India and the potential silks they could bring him from Varanasi. This time, Zane wanted to ask her to bring back glass churiyaan—bangles that he could wear for his drag costumes.

"I think that might be asking for too much from Mae and Atin, they don't really have very much," I told him.

"We will pay them," Zane said, though he never gave them any money for all the shopping they did for him in India. I paid them back. Zane and I were not sharing accounts because as he said his "investment" was elsewhere—not in this relationship. He didn't want to be put on the lease just in case his ex-wife could claim my income as her own.

We spent that fall in a string of clubs—Zane drinking and screaming at me in the street, me drinking and crying, heaped in the corner. One night Zane left after screaming at me—a loud FUCK YOU in my face. I figured he went back to Elmont to fix up his house for his brother and his brother's girlfriend. After nine days, Valentine's Day came in like a lion. I never cared about Valentine's Day, but Zane did. He wanted roses, gold, and expected sex.

He called me to see what I had been doing. When I told him that I was writing poetry, furiously arranging my manuscript, he hung up on me. An hour later he texted, "I will pick you up for Valentine's day." I could feel my ears redden and my face flush.

Zane picked me up in his 2001 Mazda. I watched the city fade into a cloudy background as he drove me back to Long Island. Rain formed bubbles on the window like some kind of disease whose scars linger. *Hard water,* I thought.

Once in his house Zane sat down on his bed and pulled out a box.

"What did you get me for Valentine's?" he asked, his voice unnaturally shrill.

"Zane," I said, "you're lucky I'm even here after the way you left."

"This whole time you've had to yourself you didn't buy me a gift?"

"You know the kinds of gifts I give are not for things like Valentine's. You left so quickly and so angrily that I didn't feel generous. I don't feel like I need to buy you anything on command. You have been a total ass to me, why would I spend my time buying things for you with money I don't even have?"

Zane was stunned. "You've been writing this whole time?" he asked.

"Yes." I'd been glad to have time to myself. I could write. I could revise. I could read. No one was yelling at me to do this or to stop talking on the phone.

Zane bared his teeth and spat, "I guess it's over," and threw down the box. Inside was a gold ring that looked like a Guyanese bangle. "I'm going to pick up my things when I drive you home."

The car ride was quick. Zane sped his way down the Long Island Expressway despite the rain. We rode the elevator silently. Inside, the prewar elevator looked as if it was lined in tinfoil. I could feel Zane's anger like heat. Zane stormed into the apartment and shoved his clothes into trash bags. Saris, lehengas, dresses, mirrored skirts, khakis, jeans, T-shirts, shoes all in one junk pile.

"Don't forget your jewelry," I said, pointing to the bedside table. Over a year and eight months I'd spent over a grand in costume jewelry for Zane.

Zane slammed his bag to the ground. "You only think of yourself," he screamed as he grabbed the bangle rack that held the rainbow churiyaan. "Go to fucking hell," he yelled as he threw twenty-five pounds of blown glass bangles at my head. I ducked and it smashed against the wall. There was a rainbow rain. Glass shards everywhere. On the bedclothes. On the couch. On the bedside table. On and inside the open drawers of the dresser. In my eyebrows.

He stormed out with two bags of his clothes and didn't turn back. I followed him to bolt the door behind him. My feet bled from the glass shards.

The door slammed and finally there was peace.

❁

I had to make up with the people I'd dropped. First would be Sef, then Zeke, then Jegga.

Sef picked up the phone and replied with short, huffy thunder. "What do you want?" he rolled.

"Sef, what I did was cruel, and I'm sorry," I groveled, swallowing my own hurt. I did not want to be alone. He was silent for a minute. He came over that night.

"No, this is for you," he said when I reached for him. I laid back thinking of all the things that I wanted to say to Sef. When we finished, he said, "It's good to see you. I've missed you. But I'm not sure this can continue."

He insisted the television remain on, playing *Sangam* in the background. Gopal shoots himself to prove his love and loyalty to both Radha and Sundar. I wanted to change the ending. I wanted them to all live together and fuck and love, all three of them happy and complicated with indistinguishable waters. I wanted to take back refusing to answer Sef's calls. I wanted Pakistan and India and Bangladesh and Nepal and China to erase their borders. I wanted to be a river with him so swollen and tangled that the thought of us as separate would be mythological.

Sef kissed me. His plump lower lip tasted like sweat and chocolate. He put on his shirt and walked out my door. I never heard from him again. Was he only dating women now, or did he find another man to sing Bollywood songs to? I tried contacting him, writing him poetry—a love letter that I never signed, pieced together from Gopal's letter to Radha.

*If you read this, don't get angry*
*that I've understood myself to be Ganga*

*and you Jamuna. I once thought*
*us close as this. One day*
*we will see this and laugh.*

And silence—

### Jackson Heights-Roosevelt Ave/74th St (Transfer Here for the F, M, R, 7)

Zane came inside that first night we met. Webster Hall pulsated until four in the morning.

We kissed and something grew inside of me. I had been waiting for a moment like this—I was young, brown, and queer in New York City, ready for a first, real boyfriend, ready for something that would last. I swore that I would never date another white man, and here was this Guyanese guy from a town just outside of where my mother's family was from. Our ancestors may have even been contracted and bound to the same sugar plantation of Lusignan.

My phone rang. I looked down and silenced it. It was Sef. I could call him back later.

"Bai, you does like fe tek plenty man," he said playfully.

"Me one real antiman," I joked.

"I am so glad I found you," someone says—it could have been either of us. For this moment, in the beginning, everything was perfect.

## Ganga and the Snake: A Fauxtale

## Ganga aur Saamp

agar raga punnagavarali raat ke samay accha se gawe ho ta ii gaana naag ke bulawai jai. uu tohar sange naache khatir aaibe. uuhi dudhwa je tu chardhawe uu saamp piye khatir aaibe. saamp jekar aakhiya malin hoyke chamrdi nikale samay ke kabhi nahin maare. ham puraan bhasa ke kenchul ke chamakaaye baki ham ii bhasa na bol sake hai. lagela ke ham dur se aaili.

The raga Punnagavarali, if performed correctly at dusk, draws out snakes. They will come and dance with you. They come to drink the milk you offer them. You must never kill a snake whose eyes grow milky before shedding scales. I polish the scales of the erased Tamil, the oldest language in the world that's still spoken, native to my mouth country but a visitor from diaspora.

tambe se lotwa ban jaila. lotwa kasti ba. kasti ke matlab jahaaj bhi hai. ganga khet mein janam le leis, muluk chhorde samay chinidad jaye khatir uu betiya indrani aur seegopal ke nahin bhail. chinidad mein bahut ganna rahe. jab ganga ke chaar saal ke rahe uukar patiya-bibah bhail.

The lota of copper sheets pound into a vessel. A vessel is a jug. A vessel is also a ship. Ganga, a plantation baby, was not yet born to Indrani and Seegopal when they left India for Chinidad. It get plenty cane in Chinidad. As a patiya, Ganga married when she was four.

jab terah saal bhail ganga sasural chalal gayal. ganga ke mai ke ordhniya bidesiya geet se bhig gayal. uu tambe ke lota aapan kamar par rakhke chale lagal. okar payaliya ke jhankar sunyai del, ekgo tara jaise chamakela. nathiya, mangal sutra, gale haar, aur kangan—uukar var ke pahiya—jangal mein jaila raga punnagawarali bajawat. nadiya kinare jaye paani laaye khatir ekgo tarah ke sangeet ba.

At thirteen she lives with her groom's parents, her mother's ordhni wet with bidesiya songs. She grabs the copper pot with a pinched neck and bares it away on her hip. Her anklets tinkling the way a star would sound, nose ring, mangal-sutra, necklaces, and bangles—the reigns of her husband—playing raga Punnagavarali as she disappears into the forest line. When she walks to bring water from the river, it is a type of music.

*gulbul gulbul*, paani lotwa mein bharat bole. raja dasrath ke smaran karela—uu jab sarawan paani piyat piyat ke baan se marela. kitne nariya nadi ke kinare se gayab bhaila? jab uu kinare paar kharde hoi gagariya uthaike, aapan ordhniya paani mein girela. nadiya ke darpan mein ganga aapan muh ke dekhila aur aapan chunariya naagin ke sir jaise phailela. manasa devi ke jaise. aapan tambe ke lota paani se bharal.

*Gulbul gulbul* de guglet deh in de wata. She thinks of Raja Dasarath shooting the innocent Srawan as the river water rushes to fill the cavern in lumping bubbles. How many women have gone missing from this very bank, their ghaghriya hiked to their thighs, their orhnis falling into the water? Ganga looks at her face in the river and holds out her veil like a cobra. Like Manasa Devi, the snake goddess. Her copper lota is filled with water.

nariyal ke perd ke niche, nadi ke kinare par, khardela ganga.

In the coconut grove by the beach Ganga stands on the sand in wait.

ragwa bhi kasti ba. nila saamp lotela bhura nadiya ke chamariya ke niche. jab bulawe ta khoon aaila. ii badan ke andar ekgo nadi ke tarah jaal hai je saamp ke tan se banayal ba. chinidad mein nadiya samundar tak jaila. muluk mein ganga samundar jaila. chinidad mein samundar ke kinare ke ganga ghat bulawe hai.

The vein, too, is a vessel. An indigo serpent under the river of brown skin. When invoked, the blood rises. The body is a lattice of rivers snaking under the skin. In Chinidad the rivers flow to the sea. In India the Ganga is a seabound river. In Chinidad all the sea is the Ganga.

aapan sir par ganga paani se bharal lota rakhela aur maurela hiya se chute khatir. sanjh bhail aur okar jehewar ke sona-chandi sangeet suru lagela dubara. uu gaana gaaila. nadiya aapan sir uthaiyela aur ruh ba ruh ganga ke dekhila. nadiya ke aakhiya kanga daant jaise hai aur uu nadiya aapan jubaan ke ghumayela, jaise kahin se adi taal bajayal jaila. ganga saamp ke dekhila. uu nariyal ke perdwa ke barabar lamba ba lekin okar wajan tani kam. ganga aapan lota jamin par rakhela aur saamp ke sange jhum uthela.

As Ganga places the lota of water on her head she turns to leave. It's dusk and her music of gold and silver begins again. She sings. The river raises its head and faces her as a large snake with its eyes like fangs and its tongue lolling and twisting to the beat of the raga. Ganga sees this snake. He is as large as a coconut tree and is light as a puffed puri. She puts down her burden of copper and water and sways with the serpent.

ganga ke kenchul nilam mani jaise chandani mein chamkela. roshan ke jhalak ke jhalak.

Her scales all sapphires and emeralds in the moonlight. A reflection of a reflection of light.

saamp aapan muh kholela aur sab daant dikhayi deila je chawar jaise masurde se ughela. ganga aapan jok chordke saamp-nadiya ke kholal muh mein chalela. phir oije andherwa. phir oije naksatrwa. phir oije akaas ganga.

The serpent opens his mouth to reveal his rows of teeth erupting from pink gums like monoliths of rice. She leaves her yoke and walks into the river-snake's widened jaws. Then dark. Then constellations.

simone aapan khisa pura karela: chinidad chute se pahile britis wale sipahiya red river mein ekgo barka saamp payal. uu saamp ekgo narke aadhi raat jab pesaab karat kate ke kosis karis. jab sipahiya uu saamp ke maarke aur okar pet khol del, uu pachaas kilo sona aur chandi ke jehewariya payal: payaliya, kanganwa, nathiya, mangalsutra, aur jhumke.

Before de English lef' Chinidad, some soldier find an ole ole anaconda in the Red River. It attack one man who get up middle-night to piss into the stream whe' they camped. When dey tore into the body of the great snake dey find fifty kilo gold and silver anklets, bangles, nose rings, mangalsutras, and earrings.

. . . pajire se kara kara bhaile dupahariya
kholo bahini baja rakhe ho

tohare bhaujiya toke pahur petaile ho
kholo bahini baja rakhe ho

kaise ke kholo bhaiya baja rakhewariya ho
bhaujiya hamar orahan petai ho

pajire se kara kara bhaile dupahariya
kholo bahini baja rakhe ho

ultan sultan howe dono bhai ho
ultan sultan tare ho

> Da bright bright mahning a-tun black black night,
> sistah, keep a-doh hopem.

> A-you sistah-in-law send chowr an' daal,
> hopem a-door na sistah.

> Me na go hopem a-doh,
> me sistah-in-law go send complaint.

> Sa bright bright mahning a-tun black black night,
> sistah, keep a-doh hopem.

> A buddy-sistah been de,
> dem been nast like a-star.

*. . . Early morning, midday, the sky blackens.*
*Open the door, sister.*

*Your sister-in-law has sent rice and daal.*
*Open the door, sister.*

>*How can I open wide the door, brother,*
>*my sister-in-law will send a complaint.*

*Early morning, midday, the sky blackens.*
*Open the door, sister.*

A brother and sister's bond is backward,
even the stars are broken.

# Aji Recording: Asirbaad, Blessing

ja dhire se beta
toke bhagwaan bhaalaa kare

jo chahat hai
aapan kaam sikhke
lauteke aaja baap ke gaud mein

bait phir se
mata pita ke gaud mein

❁

Go good
an' may god bless you

da wha'sorevah you wan'
learn you wuk done
you go back to you papa home

you go go back again
to you faddah an' you muddah

❁

# ANTIMAN

Go, son,
and may God put you right

that what you want
after learning your work
you return to your parents' lap

to sit once more
at the feet of your mother and father

# The King and the Koyal: A Fauxtale

# Raja aur Kokila

bahut pahile ke baat hai. ekgo raja rahe aur ratiya mein oke nindiya nahin awat rahe. raja ke kamra ke baahar ekgo perd rahe. perdwa ke sakha par baitke ekgo kokila raat bhar aapan gaana gawe rahe.

A long time ago a king was unable to sleep at night. Outside the royal window a koyal bird sat on a tree branch and serenaded the king throughout the night with its song.

bechara raja—okar jiw jard gayal etna ki raat mein oke kuchu bhi saanti na pa sakal aur uu kokila ke awaaj nahin sahen sakal. uuhi raat se dare lagal. raja ke ghabaraahat ke baujud, rani aaraam se letke jaldi so pard rahe aur ii baat se raja khisi-yaial bhail.

The poor king—he was so disturbed by having no peace at night that he could no longer bear the koyal's song. From that night he began to fear. Despite the king's distress the queen was able to fall asleep quickly having lain down, and of this the king was jealous.

sochal raja, "ham hai raja, sab chijwa jaun ham khoje hai hamke milejai, ii hamaar hak hai. aur ii rani le—uu aapan samne letke so gayal, dust nariya. uu hirwa jaun ham khoje haath mein nahin awe hai."

The king thought, *I am the king, I get every single thing that I want, by right. And this queen—this evil woman sleeps so peacefully in front of me. The very diamond I desire is beyond my reach.*

phir koyal ke ratiya ke gaana shuru lagal. uu gawat rahe ke asmanwa mein urdat urdat kitne ajaadi aaye ki bata na sake hai. Time se bhi uu alag bhail.

ke har raat aasmaan samundar ban jaila aur okar pankha nauwa ke lakrdi ban jaila, aur na jane aadhi raat ke laher par baitke kaha tak le pahuchawela.

Again the koyal began to voice its
night song. It sang that aloft in the air
it was so free, untethered to time.

That every night the sky becomes an
ocean and his feathers become the
boards that make a boat, and having
set course on the midnight waves,
there was no telling just where it
would sail.

ke ajaadi kitne mitta hai ki ekgo bar
chatke rajkumar aur kisaan sab jingi
bhar okar khoj mein aapan sari jiw
gawa deila.

lekin raja koi kokila ke boli ke samajh
mein nahin aail. uu khisiyaial hoike
baja tak bhagat khol del aur dhyan se
sunal baki baja ke khole par kokila ke
gaana gaayab bhail.

raja aapan beswa tordke ii kasam kha-
yal ke, "ekgo din uu julum rakshas-sa
kokila ke rahuwa ham pi jaib!"

That the freedom was so sweet.
That having tasted it once, princes
and peasants alike waste their whole
lives searching for it.

But the king didn't understand the
ramblings of a koyal bird. Vexed, he
ran to the door and threw it open,
yet as soon as he opened it the song
disappeared.

The king tore his raiment and swore,
"One day I will drink this demonic
koyal's blood!"

> raja bolal:
> uu jaun ii dust kokilwa ke mar dalke
> hamke dew, uuhike hamaar sare
> dhanwa mil jai.

The king spoke:
"Whoever kills this evil koyal and
presents it to my court will receive
the entirety of my wealth."

> dhanurdari aapan cutlish taja karela.
> uu ganna ke katat katat jab uu rajah
> ke baat sunal. uu kosis ta karihai baki
> ii ke matlab hai ke agle janam aacha
> na hoi.

> okar khet, bacche, stri, mai-baap,
> bhai-bahin sab gayab hoijai.

> ii kare ke baad ghare nahin laut
> sakihai.

uu aapan palwar ke sab naam ke
yaad hirday mein rakhal ki naua
bacche agar paida hoi ta oisan palwar ke nam debe bacche ke.

A sure-shot archer sharpened his
blade. He had been cutting cane
when he heard the royal challenge.
He would take a shot, but it would
mean exile from a favorable rebirth.

His baby rice, his babies and wife,
his father, mother, brother, would all
disappear into diasporic mythology.

After this, he could not remain in
his hometown.

He would remember their names
and name his new children after
ghosts roaming the paddy fields.

baki ii raja eklauta raja na rahe. okar
ande angrej raja dwara chural gail.

okar sona mahel pinjara bhail. uu
aapan pankh kinchke nikalis.

din mein raja khali das-das minit
khatir so sakal aur sapna mein hamesa
hawa mein urat rahe.

aur oise uu rahe tabtak kokila ke
awaaj sunai na del.

But the king wasn't the only king.
His balls had already been stolen by
the British.

His golden mahal was a cage. He
began plucking his own feathers.

In the daylight the king slept in
ten-minute intervals and always in his
brief dreams he flew through the air.

And always he was flying until the
biting cry of the koyal.

raja ii sapana dekhela:

jangal mein akela hoike uu nadiya
ke dikhai del uu jab nadiya ke uupar
urdela. koi baat se darela baki na
janile ke, uu mani jaise hai hawa jab
oke le jaila—nadiya ke pani jaise koi
nauwa ke le jaila laheriya par. okar
pankha lakdri jaise bhail aur raja
kuch dekhela: ekgo pahar jaun par
himalaya chitaan aur barf se banayal
mandir hai.

uu surya mantra pardhat urdela.

uu aapan muh kholela aur aditya-
bhagwan ke namaskar karela.

The king dreams:

Alone in the forest and jungles he
sees the snaking rivers as he soars
and thinks the fear is in fact an
emerald as the gusts push his wings
along a ghostly current—urgently
ferreting his boatlike body of feathers away to see something grave and
important: a mountain covered in
temples—some hewn of the Hima-
layan rock and ice.

He flies among the mantras recited
at sunrise.

He parts his lips and bows to the
sun.

raja ii sapna dekhela:

jahaaj se uupar urdela aur goli cha-
layat dekhela banduk se. log jaun
jahaaj ke andar bandhe rahe okar
faane hawa mein phelat hai. okar
sange uu raja urdela. uu urdela.

uu gaana bhagwan se puchela, *ham
logan ka karis ke ham oise bandhe
hai?*

The king dreams:

He flies above wooden ships with
dark hulls like dusk and sees the
puffs of cannon fire. He flies with
the wailing songs of people trapped
in the ship's bellies.

Songs that ask the gods *what have
we done in this life to be trapped so?*

> koi nahin kokila ke hatya kare
> mangela.
> dwijah ke mare sabse barka paap
> mane jaila.
>
> aur dwijah ke matlab: dui—second
> jah—born.
>
> aur dwijah ke matlab: uu jaun ke
> janeu bhail.
>
> aur dwijah ke matlab: pesaab kare
> khatir janeo kaan me bandhela.
>
> aur bhala kaun oise daag aapan ke
> lage mange hai.

No one wanted to kill the songbird.

Killing a bird that is twice born is
the most heinous of sins.

And dwijah means: one who wears
the cotton thread.

And dwijah means: one who ties it
around his ear as he squats to piss.

And nobody wants such a stain.

> raja ii sapna dekhela:
> pital ke dabbe mein uu badariya
> mein kudela aur oke niche raat aur
> saheriya chamkela. andhera mein
> lagela ke koi pachhi ke mul, je
> kukariya jaise jamin par lagela.

The king dreams:

In a metal box he jumps to the
clouds and below, the night and
sparkle of cities, or towns spattered
like bird shit or blood on the earth,
which crusts over in cement scabs.

> uutar ke oriya urdela, barf ke dwip
> tak.

He flies north to the frozen island.

> purab ke oriya urdela jehar okar
> santan aapan haddiya jamin mein
> rakhi hai.

He flies west to the country where
his kin will bury his bones in the
ground.

dakshin ke oriya urdela oise dwip
tak jehar uu oise sapanwa dekhila
je khali angreji ganna aur creolese
bhasa ho. sach mein jehar bhi kahin
hosakela.

He flies south to the island he
dreams in English only of cane and
Creole—he could be anywhere, it's
true.

uu purab urdela, aur samay bhi bitela.
baki samay paachhe bhi urdela ii
dekhe khatir: ke agar mahades ke
tukarde ekgo hi tukarde jord sake
dubara, aur agar okar simiya ke kabi-
tiya angreji mein hoijai.

He flies east, forward in time but
backward to see if he will fit back—
the continental stone cleft in two,
tumbles in the sea, edges no longer
retroflexed and cerebral, and his
poetry alveolar.

chalal gayal jamana se ohe oke vapsi
kare nai na sakela.

He is gone so long that his return is
not a return.

daftar ke khirdkiya ke baahar, saher
ke roshni je niche hoi, badariya
chamkela, uu gaaye lagela.

Outside the window in his regulation-
size space, the dark clouds glow from
the city lights beneath.

dhanurdhari aapan baan iikwa
par tej karela. hawa mein se urdela
aur ekgo gayak ke marela. ekgo hi
tir se kokila ke hirday tardakela.
ekgo hi tir se dhanurdari ke yahso
chorde ke hai aur kabhi nahin
laut sakihai. ekgo hi tir aur anguri
chhap uu kantrak manjur karela.
so girmitiya bhail.

The archer sharpens his arrow on a
sun-dried brick. It sails through the
air and strikes a song. With one arrow
lined in feathers the koyal's heart
ruptures. With one arrow shot the
archer must leave the kingdom and
never return. With one arrow and a
fingerprint he signs his terms of indenture. So come so done: he becomes a
Girmitiya.

dhanurdhari pachhi ke panka
nochela, aur chamri nikaalela.
aante nikaalke uu dhard ke
pakayela tej aag se taaki okar
mans mein nami rahe jai. jeera,
mirch, dahi, saunph, aur kali
mirch ke chaunk. uu aag mein
rakhe tab tak laal na hoye.

The archer plucks the bird, skins it.
The disemboweled carcass he stabs
with a spit and roasts at high heat to
keep the tenderness that he let die
for money. Rubbed in cumin, chil-
ies, and yogurt, encrusted in anise
and black peppercorns. He roasts it
until it's golden brown.

jhola mein saman rakhela baki okar
kapra, murtiya, aur masala aapan
saath na la sake. angrej wale oke station mein bandhela aur chini ke
deswa tak le jaihai kaheki uu anguri
chhap lagal dhanus uthaiye ke samay.
angrej oke batiawela ke chinta na
kare, raja tohar sange jaihai.

He packs his rucksack but is
stripped of his clothing and sup-
plies, his pictures of the gods and
all his spices. The English guards
at the docks chain him onto a ship
bound for the sugar country, for he
signed this contract when he raised
the arrow to his eyeline. They tell
him not to worry, the king would
surely follow.

chandi ke thaariya par rakhal gayal,
raja pahile tukarda khaye ke ii koy-
aliya ke raat-git khayela. uu kokila
ke gaana nigalela.

The king, served a silver thali, raises
the first morsel to his lips, bites and
chews up the koyal's dusk and dawn
music. With the raising of his royal
tongue to his soft palate he swallows
the birdsong whole.

hawa leila etna pura khusi se. ehi
samay oke sab ke sab yaad okar
khopariya se urd chordela, pachhiya
jaise dussar ghosalwa ke khoj mein.

He gasps for air in sheer delight
for such delicious opulence. At this
moment, his memories all fly from
him, free birds of flight and wind,
seeking a new home across the sea.

uu na janela ke kaun hai aur kehar
jaila. darpanwa mein naak aur
aakhiya dikhayal deila baki uu
khali ekgo chehera dekhela, koi
aapan ke pehechan, koi katha, koi
gaana nahin rahe gayal.

He no longer knows who he is or
where he is going. He looks in the
mirror at his brown nose and dark
eyes, but all he sees is a face, there is
no I, no stories or songs of his own.

# My Veil's Stain

**March 3rd Prolepsis: At the Kitchen Table with Zeke**

"My grandfather died in a fire and his body was found charred." Zeke's face was expressionless as he said this. He'd come to spend the week with me when Zane threw his dresses in a plastic trash bag and clopped out of our apartment. It was still cold outside and the pipes began their kicking to warm the prewar building. Our friendship was able to bloom again after I asked Zeke, like I asked Sef, to forgive my lapse in judgement that caused us to not speak for the duration of my relationship with Zane.

Zeke rubbed his shaved head, took a sip of tea, and placed the mug on the round kitchen table. "Yeah, I can only imagine the pain he must have felt." We were only recently lovers, despite being attracted to each other for years. He came over that weekend and stayed for four days.

"Did your mother's family sue?" I asked and looked out the window and into the courtyard where the cement lions guarded the entrance. I got up to bring more cookies to the table. Our chai long since done and cold. We were used to talking about our families—especially in the kitchen.

"Who cares if Natives die?" he laughed. Zeke was from the Southwest and recently moved to New York for the same reason that I did—to be a fag of color in a big city. I was a settler and he was an indigenous person, though we were both called Indians by people who "discovered" us—named after the river Indus by idiots from the outside. Because of Indian indenture my family had our land erased from under our feet and became settlers on indigenous lands in Guyana. Because of American expansionism and settler colonization the US government and history books tried to erase Zeke's family from their lands. We shared our stories like long lost kin.

"Were you close?" I asked.

"Yes, he taught me what I know about our family tree."

I thought of what it would be like to lose someone. Zane left but was still alive. Sef left also but he was alive, too. I'd never really lost anyone I was close to. I had uncles who'd died when I was younger, but the pain never echoed inside me. No one I had ever loved had been taken from me.

Zeke continued, the desert full of life: night-blooming cacti and Gila monsters springing from his mouth. "But he came back to say goodbye."

I believed it. Ghost stories were the lifeblood of family get-togethers, long after the food was eaten and the drinks drunk—all of us well liquored and all the doors open to spirits. I opened my door to spirits with Zeke.

The wind stirred the leaves in the courtyard beneath us. I felt chicken skin tickle the nape of my neck and creep down my spine. I would want to meet my beloved elders on their journeys into their next lives.

## Sleep Paralysis

The corner of my bedroom was dark after Zane left. Learning to sleep alone was the most difficult part. I had grown accustomed to a heavy leg over my own. I tried my best to fill my bed with as many men as would stay. They filled the empty space in the bed and distracted me in my spiral into depression that would claim my last years spent in New York City.

My apartment was creepy when I was alone. At night the closet opened its mouth and yawned. The mirror on the closet door was probably as old as the building. It was tarnished in the corners and warped with spots of brown and black. I saw eyes and teeth shining back at me as I lay in bed, head turned to the room's entrance.

In the night the closet door creaked open. The mirror swung toward the wall and out of the closet's dark throat stepped a shadow with the figure of a man. It was seven feet tall and walked over to the side of the bed where I lay.

I could not move. My heart beat wildly and all I could hear was the thumping in my chest, in my head, in my mouth. Cold sweat dripped from my forehead.

The figure walked to me and loomed over my body. I couldn't see its face though I knew it was smiling a toothy grin at me.

*You will die come morning.* It whispered to me without moving its mouth or making a sound, its words projected directly into my mind.

After rolling around under the comforter for what felt like ages, I tried to scream, to move, but couldn't.

I thought, *If I could just move, it would go away.* I tried to scream, *Zane, help!*

The shadow dissipated, and so did my need for Zane.

### March 3rd Prolepsis: At the Kitchen Table with Zeke

We had just watched "Night of the Living Dead" during our horror movie binge. I wanted so badly to make a joke, but this was sacred territory: time to speak of our ancestors, not to make flippant references to American pop culture. The spirits were listening, after all.

"What do you mean? Your grandfather visited you?" I shifted my weight in my chair. I imagined that this was the beginning of a ghost story. I had my own. It was called sleep paralysis.

In the morning my friends would laugh at me when I admitted to believing in ghosts. But now I sat across the table from Zeke as we drank our afternoon chai and ate cookies. I took crumbs and made constellations on the table's veneer.

Zeke spoke finally. "My grandfather came to me three days later in a dream to tell me that he was okay. The entire next day I could smell burning mesquite."

## March 16th: In the Bedroom Alone

I couldn't move. The comforter was lead. I looked to my left. Zane had left almost three weeks before and I was here alone in my one-bedroom flat. Dread crept into the room like a thief. I was on my back and could see that the closet door was shut. Down the hall the front door's lock latch snapped. Heavy footsteps creaked across the floorboards down the hall. I could see my bedroom door slowly open.

Something sat at the foot of my bed. It was like a shadow in the darkness—a dense fog in the shape of a person. Like a person's shadow on a partly cloudy day, outline blurred. I felt the mattress depress. A palm on my chest pressed me into the pillow.

My forehead dripped. I could not move or turn over, my body still thick in the sleep of the gamma-aminobutyric acid and glycine that keeps the sleeping body still. If I could just wiggle my fingers, and turn my body over, this terror would end. Someone was there with me. Sleep paralysis be damned.

With a start I gasped and shot straight up. I was raining like a monsoon cloud; my sheets were soaked with fear. The clock glared red—6:37 a.m. I didn't have to get up for another twenty-three minutes, but I was wide awake and desperate to leave the apartment.

I got up and dressed for the day's work and had more time to drink all of the coffee's mud that I French-pressed in the morning.

## March 16th: Death Plays Chess

The hallway at the foyer level of the building was grand—or once grand. The lavish, former fireplaces were all filled in with bricks and plywood. Paintings were muraled onto the wall complete with frames, painted to look marginally three-dimensional. The floor was a checkerboard of white and black linoleum squares, a veritable David Lynch fantasyscape. Simulated and hollow. An old body falling into decay, covered in lead-based paint that was chipping away.

In the morning I moved about the chessboard floor as a knight. I always thought the horse pieces were the prettiest, the most realistic. I mused, this is what life is—a series of steps in the right or wrong direction. The right direction taken, I could be a successful teacher, a good lover and partner.

If I took wrong or rushed steps I would be taken down, killed, murdered, or worse—I would squander my life. Every decision was a compact with death. Crossing the street was a chess game with death. So was straining on the toilet. Or having unprotected sex with four different men in one week. Any move with Zane would have been one into destruction.

My cell phone vibrated against my thigh. *Pap*, it read, his picture grayed at the temples. I hadn't spoken to him in a while. Last time we talked he said that I was abominable. I think he meant *abomination*. I preferred being a snowman even if it had a seasonal shelf life.

"Hello, my son." My father's voice was a bird that was trapped and couldn't migrate south in December. It was March. I was his "son" again. His throat's feathers must have been ragged. I shuddered.

## Times My Father Said, Don't Call Me Pap

When I took a pushpin when I was eight and stabbed every picture of my brother that I could see through his nose.

When I didn't want to massage his legs anymore, but I had to because he bought me the hot-pink sunglasses from Pizza Hut. When he gave them to me I said, *I love you*.

When I came home from New York I told him that Pua thought that I was using her house as a gay brothel. He called up all of his sisters and told them that Clarice had lied about it all, making up the story because she was still angry about some time my father scolded her when she was a child.

When he found out that I was seeing a man.

## March 16th: Death Plays Phone Tag

"Yes, hi, Pap," I cleared my throat.

"I've been trying to call you. . . ." he trailed off. I checked my phone: five missed calls. Something was wrong. He would never just call me. Especially not in the morning.

"I'm just calling to tell you that your Aji passed away in Toronto this morning." The nurses said that she tripped and fell in the bathtub. They found her maybe an hour after it happened. I felt like my feet were made of cement. I couldn't move. I was stunned, for the second time this morning.

"They said she died instantly."

It couldn't be. I'd just talked to Aji on the phone. My stomach lurched and I felt lightheaded. I looked at my phone again. It was 8:15 a.m.

"What time did they say she died?" I didn't have to ask. I already knew.

"Between six and seven."

That was when I'd woken up, pressed into the mattress.

## Smear the Queer

One of my father's sisters lived in Forest Hills.

She didn't invite me to her home when I moved to the city.

She didn't invite me to eat when I was hungry, living on a small summer stipend.

E train from Roosevelt Ave to 71st Street.

One stop on the express train.

The night of March 16, I heard, she held a wake in her million-dollar home.

She didn't invite me into her house even when my grandmother died.

*You are nothing.*
*No one will ever love you.*
*You are fat and hairy.*
*You are good-for-nothing.*

## Christian or Hindu Burial

Three years before her death, Aji was hospitalized for an aneurism—not cerebral but aortic, brought on by aging. While she was unconscious Aji saw a line of women from her Guyanese village of Crabwood Creek— the pandit Hardowar's wife, Beti; Rupa; and Premwati—all women whom she had known when she was younger.

"Utho, Betiya," the pandit's wife called to her in Bhojpuri. "Get up, Betiya, you have to join us now."

"Ham na uth sake hai, didi, me na hable git up from hiya." She replied. "An' kaise ham jaibo, chunari mein lagal daag—how will I go with this stained veil?"

The women all standing in line looked at her, sucked their teeth and gradually began to fade away. Aji remembered hearing manjira and dholak playing faintly as they were waiting. No bright lights. No Aja— this time. The stained veil, how could she wear it to meet her love? It was a metaphor for the human body as worn by the jiva—that small part of the universe that lived inside her. The flesh could corrupt, but not the jiva. How would she go with a human body to the home of her beloved?

When she woke up, she narrated this story to my father. He quickly called all his sisters to ensure that Aji would have a Christian burial. He was horrified that all the people who Aji saw queuing up for the hereafter were Hindu women whom he believed were certainly burning in hell— his thinking a kind of postcolonial Stockholm syndrome.

When we were alone, Aji whispered to me in her gritty voice, "You must make sure they bury me in Hindu rites, beta." She wanted her body reduced to ashes and taken to Ganga ghat, which meant the ocean.

She wanted to merge with the divine through connection of all waters—the Ganga River flowing into the sea purified the brine, transforming it into the mystical waters, despite the truth and punishment of Kalapani.

But her children who'd become Christian wanted something else for their mother.

She had no recourse; Aji was a pawn in their game of class ascendancy. She was never educated by missionaries.

There were only a handful of people to whom Aji expressed that she did not want a Christian burial. But in my family, the people who speak loudest are the ones who are heard. To most, Aji couldn't even speak. She wanted to create as much peace in whatever situation she was in. She told her Christian children to bury her in a Lutheran service.

No one listened to me as I spoke what I knew to be the truth—that Aji wanted to be cremated. She wanted to pacify the insistence of her children. She wanted merger. She wanted to go home, not to be buried in frozen soil.

I thought back on all that my Aji had given to me. She entrusted her songs and stories to me. She expressed her final desires to me. I now had a problem: how could I give my Aji what she wanted, what she deserved? I wanted to send her soul off with love. It was poetry, in the end, that connected us profoundly, and I sent her off with a poem in which I set her ashes adrift in the flow of the Ganga ghat—the Ganga River, the river that I bathed in, the river she was named for.

# ANTIMAN

## Kashi, City of Light

*for Aji, named Ganga*

A silver moon bass clefs a still river;
clay lamps lick golden the water,

ink swirls with stars. Marigold petals
drift before dawn, constellations.

Ganga sings, brushing her silver hair:

*ham kaise jabo sasural,*
*chunari mein lagal daag,*

*how will I go to my in-laws,*
*my veil is stained.*

Toward her lover's humid voice,
her cheeks studded with diamonds,

she descends into the holiest of cities.

## Toronto

My family made arrangements to go to Toronto first thing. I would meet my father at the Toronto Pearson International Airport. He picked me up in a rental car and we went straight to Auntie Nisha's house. She was his first cousin and Leila's mother—the only aunt I felt safe with in Pap's extended family. Auntie Nisha never said anything bad against me, never tried to cut us down with her words. We whispered to each other. Mom would be delayed, as would be Emily and Emile.

The next morning, we went to the funeral home in Brampton. It was cold. Spring had not yet decided whether to commit to its carpeting of crocuses. I looked around the gray suburban sprawl. What flower would want to spring here in this desolation of grief and concrete?

The hallway was carpeted in checkered purple and yellow, fresh lilies perfumed the foyer. The funeral director asked us who we were there for. I held onto my father's coat. I didn't want to take it in.

He led us into a well-lit room with the casket propped up like an altar. She should have been wrapped in a white cloth. This all felt so wrong. The top half of the casket was opened, on the bottom half, a lace spread. It was the shape of horses crocheted into a large doily.

Soon Auntie Baby arrived from New Mexico and began to speak to Aji's cold body. "We heard the owl and we should have known. And we heard the shoveling outside—the dog barked three times. Now you've gone to Pa." The halogens hummed above us.

Aji told her Christian children what they wanted to hear, not what she wanted to say. She knew how to play a game where she vanished completely for the good of her family. I couldn't do that myself. I had to speak. The family ostracized me anyway—what difference would it make if I were vocal about what I knew to be true?

My aunts had assembled in the viewing room. Each one tear-smeared, grief-stricken. Auntie Sonia held Pua whose lip trembled. She held her weeping sister in all of the tenderness that she had.

"Don't cry," Auntie Sonia said to Pua as she patted her hair down. Auntie Rani stood behind and fished out a tissue from her pocket. Pua wiped her eyes. I went up to the casket and touched my Aji's feet. Her body was cold. Her lipstick was the wrong color. Aji never wore lipstick. I sang quietly to Aji's body.

I felt a hand on my shoulder. It was Auntie Sonia. She pulled me in for a hug and said, "I'm so sorry, Raimie." I held her and she cried.

"They gave her the wrong lipstick," I said. We both laughed with wet cheeks.

I looked at my father. His lip quivered. I wasn't the only one who loved this woman. She had so many people who respected her and admired her for who she was—no matter how she said the word *car*.

## A Poem for Aji

My mother and siblings were held up because of snow on the day of the funeral. They were not there when it came time to make speeches. Uncle after aunt spoke about Aji and how they loved her. She was their best friend. After the main eulogies had been delivered the pastor asked if there was anyone else who wanted to speak to the crowd.

I lined up with Aji's thirty grandchildren who were able to come to the funeral to say something on behalf of my brother and sister. I was alone before my father's entire family, the entire family who whispered about me behind my back. The church was long and made of dark wood. Dark wood paneled the ceilings and made the white marble altar gleam.

I walked up to the microphone and began with a Hindu mantra that I knew, one that accompanied both daily meditations and Hindu death rites from *Brihadaranyaka Upanishad*. I chanted while the Hindu elders joined me.

*om asato ma sadgamaya*
*tamaso ma jyotirgamaya*

*mrityor ma amritam gamaya*
*om shanti shanti shanti*

*Lead me from untruth to Truth*
*Lead me from dark to light*
*Lead me from death to immortality*
*Let there be peace, peace, peace*

My father looked away from me, from his mother.

I continued, "I speak on behalf of my brother and sister who are not here. This is a poem that I wrote for Aji that I've entitled "Ajiya." In Bhojpuri the 'ya' at the end means that my Aji was very dear to me. In the poem are words to a song that Aji used to sing that you all must have heard. We are lost without her." I unfolded the poem and read.

## Ajiya

I want to sing a dirge whose words
you will ride into forever.

I know you are singing too. You have taught
us all the sounds a heart can bear.

When they cover your body—
I will wrap you in your own song:

> *aawan yaawan kahe gaye*
> *ke dole barhomas*

> *patta tute daar se ke*
> *legaye pavan urdai*

*aise chhute yaar se*
*ki man kahan na jai*

*kaise kaise zabana*
*badal gaye re*

Eighty-nine years is a long song to sing, unhurriedly,
even when the heart stops, love does not.

*dil roke ta piyar kabhi nahi ruki hai.*

It endures states of matter, span of continents,
time between grand and pickni.

Ajiya,
I sing you to love in its native language.


## Disavowal

Three months after Aji's death I received word from Finishing Line Press. They had accepted a collection of songs I translated from Aji's Bhojpuri into Creole and English. These were only some of the songs she taught me when I asked her to sing.

My father's brothers and sisters and their children refused to buy it except for one uncle—the other one whom Aji had told that she wanted to be cremated, Uncle Naresh. I wrote to Jake to tell him that Aji's words would soon be in print. We used to talk about her songs and stories when we were children and I thought he would share my excitement. I thought my family would think better of Aji's knowledge, that it was vast and nuanced.

Jake replied to my email and told me to stop selling our grandmother's words. They are not mine. No one should have to pay for them. He said that he wouldn't stop me from publishing or try to stop anyone from buying the chapbook but that I should be ashamed to profit off our grandmother's death. That all the aunts thought so, too.

I was confounded. I wouldn't make any money off a chapbook that translated my Aji's Guyanese Bhojpuri folk songs—how could they not see that? This was never about money for me, it couldn't ever have been about money. I wanted people to be able to understand my Aji as I understood her. I thought that I was doing something for the family, preserving an inheritance.

I called my mother.

"If any other cousin had written anything about your Aji, your father's family would have all praised them," Mom said. "They are embarrassed that their mother was a Hindu. You're holding a mirror up to them and showing them what they refused to see when Ma was alive."

Did they really not want to hear these songs and stories because an antiman collected them? Or was it because it made them confront the truth of their Hindu pasts? My veil's stain was this: I was an antiman unworthy of support. They wanted me to believe that what I thought and knew was wrong. That I was wrong. That Aji didn't know what was best for herself. That I should try to wash off the stain, for it would forever bear the marking of the sinful, the bullah, the antiman who doesn't belong in the family.

"There's something else," my mother continued. "Before she died, Ma gave me her engagement ring—you know the one?"

"Yeah, the ring with SM engraved on it? She give you that ring? All of her daughters will be pissed if they find out." My words stuck in my throat.

"She said, 'Aw beti me na get nut'in' to gi' a you. Tek dis,' and she pulled it off of her finger and pressed it into my hand," Mom said.

"Do you think it was because she knew that Pap was so mean to you and tried to keep you from your family?" I asked.

"No. I mean, she was aware of that—but the real reason is because I think she really wanted you to have it," she said.

I felt dizzy. "What makes you say that."

"Well, you know she thought of you as someone who wanted to know all her history and stories. I think she wanted you to have it so that you would always know that you belonged—that you belonged with her," Mom said. "When you come home next time I will give it to you."

As I hung up the phone I was shaking.

The next time I saw my mother she gave me Aji's ring on a gold chain so that I could wear it around my neck, grazing my heart.

### Pieces of Aji's Songs

Kabir says, "Listen my brothers," and does not mention any women. We used to sing this song to plant rice.

I will not go to my in-laws—a veiled attempt to articulate women's trauma of leaving the father's house, a piece in a patriarchal game.

The veil is the body. We will leave it when we go home.

*India mein, langtime people been mad like a hell.*

How the world has changed.

### Leaving Toronto

The night after the funeral I went back to Auntie Nisha's house and turned down the comforter. I remembered how one of Aji's nephews— her sister's son—had come up to me, his gold rings shining in the spotlight that illuminated the casket.

"Your Aji was really proud of you, you know. She used to talk about how she had one grandson who spoke Hindi and was learning all of our traditions." People milled about after the ceremony and before we put her in the ground. It was raining outside and cold. "She said that you knew her like none other of her grandchildren, that you took time to learn her songs."

I hadn't realized that Aji talked about me, or that anyone was proud of what I was doing. People only told me I was wasting my time—Aji had nothing important to teach. But there on that purple-and-yellow checkerboard carpet, an unexpected play. Aji trusted me. She could see me, too. *I am something. I will love myself. I am beautiful. I am worthy.*

I lay at night and stared at the ceiling fan, my brother snoring beside me. I drifted off into sleep and was in Aji's Scarborough tenement in the early nineties long before she was moved to Brampton. It didn't feel like a dream. I poked my finger into my palm to see if I was awake. I was awake.

The apartment smelled like curry. Barah was frying in the kitchen. Aji was in the bedroom, her long hair tied back in a bun. She was ill. The lead paint had not yet begun to peel—it was her one-bedroom apartment that she'd had when I was a child. She wore a pink floral nightgown and sat up in bed. A faint buzzing whined in the background; the sound was said to keep cockroaches at bay.

"Aji, me gone." *Aji, I'm leaving,* I said, folding my hands in pranam.

"You gone?" She turned her head to face me. Her glasses were on—large cataract lenses that made her eyes look like two bright celestial bodies.

I approached her to touch her feet and to kiss her cheek. She grabbed my face and kissed my forehead and each cheek.

"Me love you, Aji." I said, choking on the words as they pricked my throat.

"Me know. You me loving son. Jug jug jiye, beta. You must care you self, you hear?"

❀

The next morning, I didn't tell anyone about my dream. They wouldn't be able to hear me anyway. I had my final goodbye. Aji came to me again like Zeke said she would. I could smell the curry of her Scarborough flat. Aji no longer lived only in Toronto. Now she was everywhere.

# Barsi: One Year Work

I.

I dream I am a humpback
    afraid of where
light does not penetrate

        past layers of ocean,
        thick with living.

How swimming is like flying:
    pectorals like wings,
the water ripples

        bending for miles—

*dhire dhire aaja nindiya*
*more piya jaibe bidesiya.*

*Sleep come slowly, slowly*
*at dawn my love departs.*

II.

A child traces the body of a pilot whale
   who swam too far inland.

The first day we see it, I hold my nephew.

   Over the deep, a cloud twists
   until it spins into nothing,

the last breath
expelled into a fifteen-foot cloud.

   Drops again become sea.

     We return the next day
to the carcass in saline outline,

   a fallen palm frays. My nephew says,

*Look. Feathers.*

III.

I woke one night
    to my canaries trembling,
a red-shouldered hawk perched

outside the window.

When they died
    I wrapped their bodies in plastic,

harrowed dual graves
    beneath the oak sapling
with my bare hands.

    I could not bear the quiet—

after six months
I dug them up
    to hold their fragile bones.

    So little was left.
Emily ran to mom—
    I couldn't hide
the dirt under my fingernails.

She said, *I will never forget their colors—*

    I did not tell her
    I found only one.

IV.

I sing back to you,
bird- or whale-song,

>  *chunari pahen ke*
>  *piya se milenge.*

>  *Tying my veil,*
>  *I will meet my beloved.*

You tell me,

>  *Ke ekgo din pinjare se*
>  *hamar pran urdijai,*

>  *One day my breath*
>  *will fly from this cage*

a sparrow released
   to the wild.

V.

That night you die
I dream you as a shadow,

open palm pressed to my chest.

One year after—
at dawn a sparrow's shell
    on the fire escape

withering flight feathers
laced as fingers,

    as praying hands.

# Reincarnate

A book, dusty pages or pages in slow burn to dust: *From dust you come*

When water evaporates: salt

*of the earth:* It falls back in English

How many monsoons has it been since I've returned

I once moved to India to find a trace of my jaw in an Uttar Pradesh
village but found only a random hand job on the train to Kanpur

I did not come back unburned by the fields of mustard or the
parched winter smell of scorched rubbish to keep hands warm

The Hindi word baras, year, sounds like barish, rain

How I looked for home in a man's chest but found only dust, but
that's a story I tuck under river silt

How many years has it been since the river dried up

When rain falls, what becomes of this body, this dust?

# Open the Door
# Reprise

I SAT AT her feet on the tiles. "One more, na?" I begged. Aji's eyes were shielded by her cataract glasses, thick as bulletproof Plexiglas. Heavy on her nose's bridge, the indentations were perfect reservoirs for her tears. She had been singing all day and night. There was a Bhojpuri song for birth, one for grinding grain, one for looking left before you cross the street, and one for looking right. There were Bhojpuri songs for being plucked out of your village in Guyana and placed in a Scarborough tenement.

She sang a song of never being able to go back to where she was born after the last of her children left for Canada to forget their brown. It was my brother's wedding and we sat in the Florida room. For her language that was dying—a language that she sang her children into. For Aji, this was a time when she missed the greens and reds of the wedding festivities in Guyana. The green-green bamboo that makes the marro—or the mandap where the dulha and dulhin sit before a pandit. The red vermillion that the dulha streaks in the part of the dulhin's hair.

She must have thought back to her own marriage—how everything changed for her when she entered a man's house. No more was she allowed to freely walk down the dirt road past the cows and donkeys. All this slipping away to be written in someone else's work of fiction. Some of it for the better. Some of it causing her to languish in silence. What did her grandchildren know of this life that unfolded its lotus petals far, far away in *back home*?

How far she was from this scene—where women gathered to sing and cook and teach the dulhin the ways of marriage, around a karahi with frying rice to puff for the fire sacrifices and the frying puri in the next fireside. And now, this: she lived in a place where the idea of a fireside—a chulha made up of mud with a section at the bottom to feed wood into the flames and an opening at the top to place the pot or karahi—was considered foreign or illegal, a fire hazard. So many customs that she brought with her were deemed hazardous to white bodies.

The acoustics were better in the Florida room than the living room— they carried Aji's verses into the place where lamentations float like dandelion seeds and plant themselves into fields of memory. These songs were the food that we ate. These songs forged our bodies from their longing.

"Me cyan't sing mo'," she said, her voice faltering. It was okay. I had recorded about three hours of her stories and songs. "But me go talk one story now."

❁

ultan sultan howe dono bhai ho
ultan sultan tare ho

pajire se kara kara bhaile dupahariya
kholo bahini baja rakhe ho

tohare dolar bahanoi janghiya par sowe ho
kaise ke kholo bhaiya, baja rakhe ho

lewo bahini lewo more sir ke pagri ho
kholo bahini baja rakhe ho

pajire se kara kara bhaile dupahariya
kholo bahini baja rakhe ho

kaise ke kholo bhaiya hamare lugariya
gaile dhobi ghatwa paas ho

lewo bahini lewo mor kandha ke kanawar
kholo bahini baja rakhe ho

kaise ke kholo bhaiya baja rakhewariya
gorwa mein lagal mehendi ho

pajire se kara kara bhaile dupahariya
kholo bahini baja rakhe ho

tohare bhaujiya toke pahur petaile ho
kholo bahini baja rakhe ho

kaise ke kholo bhaiya baja rakhewariya ho
bhaujiya hamar orahan petai ho

pajire se kara kara bhaile dupahariya
kholo bahini baja rakhe ho

ultan sultan howe dono bhai ho
ultan sultan tare ho

❁

'E seh, "How me mus' hopem de door, me foot got mehendi? How me
go hopem a door."

'E buddy tell 'am seh, "Hopem de door. F'om mahning me stan' up, you bhauji sen' pahur—some chawr—fe you. Hopem a door an' tek 'am."

You know, longtime India people been a too much kine people. So 'e seh, "'e sen' some rice fe you."

"Me cyan't git up fe opem de door, me husban' sleep pan me lap."

"Tek me head ke pagri an' put 'am pan you husban' head an' hopem de door."

"Me cyan't hopem de door. How me can hopem de door, how me can put 'e head pan da t'ing? Me bhauji go sen' complain' an' tell me zat, 'O, you been love you bruddah like you husban' everyt'ing you bruddah seh you do 'am.' So me na go do da. 'E go sen' orahan, 'e go insult me."

"Hopem de door an' tek de pahur. From mahning me stan' up til twelve now at night an' you na hopem your door."

"Me cyan't hopem de door because me clothes na deh, de gan a dhobi ghat, 'e gan a laundry. Me deh naked. When 'e go come how me go hopem de door? Me cyan't hopem de door an' me a naked an' me buddy go come in. Me cyan't do da."

'E tek out 'e kanhawar, de t'ing 'e get pan 'e shouldah an' seh, "Tek dis an' wrap youself an' hopem de door."

"Me cyan't do da. If I do da me bhauji go beat meh an' orahan 'e go sen'."

"Arright, if you na hopem de door abi go deh right yah an' drop doung dead an' you go see. You na go see abi.

An' so seh so 'e done. Sistah na hopem de door atall an' 'e stan' up-stan' up hungry, cole, an' rain a fall pan dem, you know? An' dem two buddy fall doung an' dead.

Me lahn dis song when me mumma dem does plant rice an' 'e does sing da song. So me been know da song good-good, man; right t'rough me been know 'am but right now me a fo'get, beta, too much t'ing. Me baice done now, mirt lok mein chala gayal.

Gaye jawani phir na ayehai
chahe mor mar mar ja

gaye samaya phir na ayehai
chahe dudh ham ek liter kha

Da day gone na ca'e wha' you do da day na go come back no mo'.
Young days cyan't come. You strengt' gan—you cyan't get no mo'.

I turned off the tape recorder, opened up my journal, and transcribed
the song to translate later.

❋

Upturned, a brother and sister's bond.
Go and see who is at the door, sister.

*Early morning, midday, the sky blackens.*
*Open the door, sister.*

> *Your spoiled brother-in-law sleeps on my lap,*
> *how can I come open the door?*

*Take this, sister, take this turban from my head.*
*Open the door, sister.*

*Early morning, midday, the sky blackens.*
*Open the door, sister.*

> *How can I open the door when my clothes*
> *have all gone to the washer's by the river?*

*Take this, sister, take this my shoulder cloth.*
*Open the door, sister.*

   *How can I open the door wide, brother,*
   *fresh mehndi dries on my feet?*

*Take these, sister, take these, my sandals.*
*Open the door, sister.*

*Early morning, midday, the sky blackens.*
*Open the door, sister.*

*Your sister-in-law has sent rice and daal.*
*Open the door, sister.*

   *How can I open wide the door, brother,*
   *my sister-in-law will send a complaint.*

*Early morning, midday, the sky blackens.*
*Open the door, sister.*

A brother and sister's bond is backward,
even the stars are broken.

# ACKNOWLEDGMENTS

This book was written on Kānaka maoli land in the occupied nation of Hawai'i Nei, where The People fight to protect their sacred land from the United States' genocidal machine, especially Mauna a Wākea, where the University of Hawai'i and the local government are forcing the installation of the Thirty Meter Telescope. The protectors of the mountain are winning, galvanizing, and preventing this desecration.

Parts were also written on stolen Mvskoke and Hitachi lands in Opelika, Alabama where the People were forced to march to reservations at the end of the Trail of Tears, displacing more than 60,000 Tsalagi, Mvskoke, Seminole, Chickasaw, and Chahta people.

Still more sections of this memoir were written and edited on land belonging to Wabanaki Confederacy, the Piguaket (Pawtucket) on the border of Revere and Malden on the banks of the Rumney Marsh Reservation, outside of Boston, Massachusetts. This land is called Wabanahkik, which means "Dawnland."

Hamar purakh logan ke aapan anant dhanyavaad.

Pranam Bhagwati Gangadai, Sewdass, Mahabir, Lachchiman, Phulkumari, Janghbahadur, Anupiya, Lakpat Singh, Tukrayan, Jakti Singh, Nandrani ke; Hari Prashad, Emma Louisa Vera, Sant Ram Mahraj, Etwariya, Arthur Vera, Maude (Janaki?) Watson ke; Kisnasamy ke; aur baki logan ke jekar nam ham na jani.

Jahaji logan, tu logan hamar pran ke adhar hai saat samandar par kare khatir anant dhanyavad.

✳

Thank you to Terry Hong, Héctor Tobar, and Ilan Stavans for selecting this manuscript for the Prize for New Immigrant Writing and to the folks at Restless Books and especially to Nathan Rostron for believing in this strange project and for helping me with making it the strongest that it could be.

Special magical shukriya to Anjoli Roy (Dr. Roy), who showed me that nonfiction was transformative and how to transform into a cat, who believed in this project and me even before I did myself, who read and gave me so many helpful comments, and who still gives me strength to endure. Thanks also to Devi Laskar, who broke open my thoughts on genre and who read versions of this memoir and gave me such insightful guidance. Still more thanks to Joseph Han for his prose devotion, the countless hours of listening to me, the thoughtful conversations, his reading this work, and for all his time and thoughts on genre, creative nonfiction, and the best ramen to be had in Honolulu. Thanks also to Shawna Yang Ryan, whose comments on "Antiman" moved me into narrative thinking. Thank you all for your eyes on my work and for your guidance during the stages of this book. Thanks also to Rigoberto González, who told me *some stories are too big for poems*. Thank you also to Shikha Saklani Malaviya for your poems and for the madad with the Hindi.

Thank you to my family, including Anjani Prashad, Emile Mohabir, Emily and Kalem Jones, Taylor, Devin, Lily, Nathan (Rajiv) Mohabir, and Silas Saiya-Baba Jones. To Jodi Miles, Sarah and Justin McIver, to Will, Rosie.

Thank you to Dr. Corinne Hyde—who I have known since I was eleven, who saved my life countless times but appears nowhere in this book.

To Robindra Deb, Suzanne Wulach, Jessica "Jegga" Bartolini, Mae and Atin Mehra, Gollu Mehra, Ryan Artes, Nicole Cooley, Kimiko Hahn, Roger Sedarat, Craig Santos Perez, Allison Hedge Coke, Akta Kaushal, Lyz Soto, Amalia Bueno, Sarah Stetson, Katie Williams, Andil Gosine, Rushi Vyas, Will Depoo, Kazim Ali, Mohamed Q. Amin, Caitlin Rae Taylor, No'u Revilla, Will Nu'utupu Giles, Lee Kava, Caribbean Equality Project, Zaman Amin, Blue Flower Arts, and to everyone else who has been in my writing life.

Thank you my colleagues and students at Emerson College and to Kundiman for the community of writers that I have found here.

Thank you, Jordan Andrew Miles, for supporting me as I wrote through in these dark stories. Thank you, Enkidu and Kajal, for bringing me the joy you do.

❁

And to you, dear Reader, thank you.
*Jug jug jiye.*

# ABOUT THE AUTHOR

**RAJIV MOHABIR** is the author of *Cutlish* (2021, Four Way Books), *The Cowherd's Son* (2017, winner of the 2015 Kundiman Prize) and *The Taxidermist's Cut* (2016, winner of the Four Way Books Intro to Poetry Prize and finalist for the Lambda Literary Award for Gay Poetry in 2017), and translator of *I Even Regret Night: Holi Songs of Demerara* (1916) (2019), which received a PEN/Heim Translation Fund Grant Award and the Harold Morton Landon Translation Award from the Academy of American Poets. His essays can be found in places like the Asian American Writers Workshop's *The Margins, Bamboo Ridge Journal, Moko Magazine, Cherry Tree, Kweli,* and others, and he has a "Notable Essay" in *Best American Essays 2018.* Currently he is an assistant professor of poetry in the MFA program at Emerson College.